Singers and Storytellers

Edited by

Mody C. Boatright
Wilson M. Hudson, Associate Editor
Allen Maxwell, Associate Editor

Publications of The Texas Folklore Society Number XXX

University of North Texas Press
Denton, Texas

Copyright © 2000 by The Texas Folklore Society

All rights Reserved

Copyright © 1961 by The Texas Folklore Society
Southern Methodist University Press

Printed in the United States of America
All rights reserved

Permissions:
University of North Texas Press
P. O. Box 311336
Denton, Texas 76203
(940) 565-2142 FAX (940) 565-4590

ISBN 1-57441-107-1

Contents

Storytellers I Have Known J. Frank Dobie	3
The Singer or the Song Mac Edward Leach	30
Some Forms of the Mexican *Canción* Vicente T. Mendoza Translated by Américo Paredes	46
Folklore and History Américo Paredes	56
Don't Look Back George D. Hendricks	69
The Oil Promoter as Trickster Mody C. Boatright	76
Folksay of Lawyers Hermes Nye	92
Feathered Duelists Haldeen Braddy	98
Old Thurber C. Richard King	107
Ghost Stories From a Texas Ghost Town Tucker Sutherland	115
Old Days at Cold Springs William Henry Hardin	123
Prayer Meeting at Persimmon College Joseph T. McCuller, Jr.	132
The Frontier Hero: Refinement and Definition Robert H. Byington	140
Belle Starr and the Biscuit Dough John Q. Anderson	156

CONTENTS

Legend of the Lad ELEANOR MITCHELL BOND	166
Stories of Ranch People STANLEY W. HARRIS	173
Tall Timber Tales EDWIN W. GASTON, JR.	178
Anecdotes of Two Frontier Preachers ALVA RAY STEPHENS	185
Wolves, Foxes, Hound Dogs, and Men A. L. MILES	194
The Magic Art of Removing Warts GRACE PLEASANT WELLBORN	205
Owl-Bewitchment in the Lower Rio Grande Valley HUMBERTO GARZA	218
Tales of the Paisanos MIRIAM W. HIESTER	226
Folklore of the German-Wends in Texas GEORGE R. NIELSON	244
Tales the German Texans Tell CAROLYN MANKIN	260
Tales of the Lost Nigger Mine GAYLE L. COE	266
Family Stories and Sayings KIM S. GARRETT	273
The Origin of the Word *Gringo* ROBERT H. FUSON	282
On *Gringo, Greaser,* and Other Neighborly Names AMÉRICO PAREDES	285
Contributors	291
Index	295

Singers and Storytellers

Storytellers I Have Known

J. FRANK DOBIE

THE FIRST TALETELLER I recall was a man who got down off a tired *canelo* horse at our ranch in Live Oak County about sundown one fall evening. He was from up, away up, the Nueces River. In the darkness out on the front gallery after supper he got strung out on panthers. One about which he wove a tale would have eaten up a turkey-hunter if the man had not had enough turkeys to feed the screaming, hungry brute, dropping them one by one at intervals on the ground while hastening through the brush to his horse tied at a "bob-wire" fence. This panther man, whose name I never did learn, shivered my timbers in a way from which I have never recovered or wished to recover. Many nights out on the front gallery with Papa—Mama inside with the endless work—we listened to an owl in the live oaks saying, "I cook for myself. Who cooks for you-all?" We listened to the crickets and to the coyotes and to the wind from the Gulf galloping in the treetops and to other components of silence; but on this night only the panther man spoke—to my ears at least.

The next storyteller to enter my life came about twenty-five years later, after World War I. I was bossing Los Olmos Ranch on the Nueces River, in LaSalle County, for my uncle Jim Dobie. Most of the nights—the only time I kept under a roof—I stayed by myself in a cottage near the big house, which was seldom occupied. One of the ranch hands named Santos Cortez had killed a man in Mexico and didn't want to cross back to the other side (*al otro lado,* of the river—the Rio Grande). He was a *pastor,* a goat-herder, and also a hunter. Great numbers of deer existed in that country at that time and still exist; more than once in a half-day's ride out in a big pasture I counted over a hundred. It was customary among larger ranches of the region to detail one man in an outfit to keep it in meat, especially during the cooler seasons. Santos Cortez kept the fencing and tank-building crew well provided with venison and javelina meat.

Once in a while after supper, when the crew had come into headquarters, he would appear in my room, where a bed, some books, a kerosene light on a table, three or four rawhide-bottomed chairs, and a fine fireplace furnished comfort. Santos would explain that he was bored with talk about cow tracks, bogged-down cows, some vaquero's horse that had got a thorn in his knee, and things like that. He wanted conversation; conversation generally consisted of his encounters with deer, men, and ghosts. I have said something about him in an introduction to my book *Tongues of the Monte.* Santos was a kind of liberated mind; he was not religious. He would observe of any priest, "El tiene huevos como yo." But he believed in ghosts. That's where the intellect of a sophisticate comes in. I accept without reservation the ghost in *Hamlet* but reject the Holy Ghost as a metaphysical superstition.

One night after Santos had told what was to me a gripping story about his experience with a *bulto,* a ghostly bulk, that held him flat on his back at a goat camp, I thought of how John A. Lomax had collected cowboy songs and ballads, and decided that I would collect traditional tales of Texas. Texas soon got too small for me, and other coherences came to supersede man-made geographical lines, and life inherent in tales extended itself. I have been listening for and to tales ever since, though I learned to have little truck with the literalists designated as scientific folklorists. The first collection of the tales for which I was responsible was published by the Texas

Folklore Society in 1924, under the title *Legends of Texas*. Bertha McKee Dobie helped edit and write it.

It was in 1923 that I left Beeville with a small rancher for Duval County on the trail of a legend pertaining to San Caja Mountain—just a long hill. At that time Archie Parr, in the Texas Senate, was known as "The Duke of Duval." His son George has been notorious for years as the inheritor of the Duke's ways. The little rancher I went with was not a good storyteller at all. He was too much of a literalist. Not far from his squat we passed a one-teacher frame schoolhouse inside about a half-acre of black brush and catclaw enclosed by three strands of barbed wire. "You might be surprised to know that that fence cost the county a thousand dollars," the little rancher said. I wasn't surprised. That's all he said on the subject.

I remember this helper in my search for stories mainly on account of his bed furnishings. There were not any sheets in the house, and the quilt I slept on had more *animalitos* in it than any other quilt I ever encountered. Really, though, it was not as bad as a bed I slept on in Karnes County while I was on the trail of a story about ghost riders, a story well told by Henry Yelvington in his *Ghost Lore*. This Karnes County bed didn't have any more sheets than the Duval County bed, but it had the seven-year's itch—"just waiting," like the boll weevil, "for a home."

In the summer of 1933, I went down to Saltillo with Henry Nash Smith, of *Virgin Land* fame, now at the University of California. From Saltillo we rode on a short train over a jerkwater railroad to the end of it and got burros to take us to a hacienda in Zacatecas called Los Cedros—the only time I ever rode a burro on a pack trip. The *administrador* of the hacienda was a good storyteller. He helped a person soak up life. When the Madero Revolution began in 1910, Los Cedros had an extensive vineyard, but every time the Carranzistas came they sacked the wine cellar, and every time the Villistas came they sacked it again, and finally the owner ordered all the grapevines uprooted so he wouldn't have any wine, and that's the way it was when we were there.

We left this hacienda on good horses, with a good *mozo*, and took nearly a day to travel to an outpost to which the *administrador* had sent word that hospitality be extended to us—as it certainly was. The *caporal* of the outpost insisted on our sleeping inside. The house was beautifully whitewashed, but at that time over great parts of the outlands of Mexico any traveler took his bedding. I've been to *posadas* (inns) where I was expected to use my own bedding. Henry Smith and I each had a bedstead on which to spread our bedrolls. Our *mozo* lay on the floor with his head just inside the door, to guard us. No sooner was our candle blown out than I began to feel something, something conducting itself in a vulgarly familiar manner. The familiars were not the fleas in one of Roy Bedichek's stories. A cowboy said he didn't mind what the fleas ate so much as what they tromped out. These weren't fleas.

"Henry," I asked, "do you feel anything?"

"I certainly do," he replied. "It bites, and I don't know what it is."

"Well," I said, "I do." I lit a match and saw bedbugs by the hundreds scurrying up the whitewashed walls and over my tarpaulin.

I said to the *mozo*, "We're going to get out of here."

The moon was full and we took our beds off about a hundred yards from the house and spread them down on the ground, where we got rid of what we could see on the sheets and tarpaulins.

You're not going to get tales that linger in the imagination except from people who have time to linger, time to stare at cows or anything else that comes along. In my experience, the best taletellers did not spend hours a day in a bathroom scrubbing themselves. The first time that Bertha Dobie and I were in Saltillo at the old Saenz Hotel there were no tourists in the town, and the cook served *frijoles fritos* for breakfast, plain *frijoles* for dinner, and *nacionales* for supper. Our waiter had time to tell a story about a coyote and a cricket—a story that years later I put into my coyote book. Imagine a waiter in a wholesale eating place having enough time to tell you a long *cuento* and to pass the time of day besides that. The diners were so sparse in this hotel of repose that two of them, entire strangers, upon finishing their meal and passing near our table on the way out, murmured politely, "Buen provecho!" (May it, the food, benefit you!) Tales belong with such courtesy and leisure.

The last time we were in Saltillo, which was in 1954 during the big drouth, we stayed again at the Saenz Hotel, all rebuilt, modernized, with lots of business. In front of it the afternoon we arrived, I was accosted by a young man who said he was a guide, and would I accept his services? "No," I said, "I don't want a guide. I want a story. I've been guided too much already."

"What do you want a story about?" he asked.

"It doesn't make any difference what — about a rattlesnake, a coyote, a woman without any head who keeps crying, a bear—whatever you wish."

"Oh," he said, "my grandfather has a story that's true about a bear."

"Well," I said, "guide me to your grandfather."

He said, "*Mañana.*"

"You'll find me here at this hotel *mañana*," I said.

Late the next day we met on a street and I asked, "Why did you not come to take me to your grandfather?"

"My grandfather's sick and can't see you," he replied.

"How am I going to learn that story about a bear?"

"I know it. I'll tell it to you."

"When?"

"I've got some people to guide now. *Mañana.*"

The next day when we met I gave him five pesos and said, "I want to hear that story about the bear."

He said, "Con mucho gusto." We went into a *cantina* where there were chairs at an empty table, peace, and beer. There he told me a fine story about a bear that kidnaped a bride and took her off and made her his own mate.

That reminds me of one of the best stories I ever heard anywhere, and of a philosophy about stories. Luck is being ready for the chance. I've had lots of chances, have missed lots of them, but not all. In hearing stories much depends on chance—as in falling in love and in getting married.

In the fall of 1932 I was with pack mules and *mozo* twisting around, through, and across the mountains of northern Mexico to the west—always to the west—just looking, listening, and living the most independent form of life I have known. Except for a few fences and *ranchos,* the country was all open and unrestricted by man—a country immense, immense. It seemed to belong to me as much as to anybody else. In the high Sierra Madre itself there were no fences at all excepting poles around little corn patches, no ranches, only *rancherías* (settlements) of poor—but always generous—squatters. Some of these squatters instead of fencing corn patches guarded them in season against bears.

One morning I saw a small bear running up the side of a mountain. I was not ready for the chance to shoot, despite the fact that I always carried my .30-.30 in a scabbard attached to my saddle. My saddle mule was bent on going the opposite direction. That afternoon we came to a perfect place to camp: wood, water, grass, scenery, all outdoors to hunt in if one wanted to hunt. I had a strong impulse to linger, but had set out to reach the Colorado Ranch that night. I was making for high country and left next morning for the Piedra Blanca Ranch at the foot of the Del Carmen Mountains. This was in Coahuila. It was the time of the year for cold nights and hot days. I rode ahead across a plain of greasewood, breathing the dust raised by my mule. Late in the day I came to the first watering—well, windmill, troughs—at a place called Los Huérfanos (The Orphans) on account of two sharply defined hills, the Del Carmen range looming over them. The shack at Los Huérfanos was deserted. Three or four horses with scarred backs were near the troughs. My mule was absolutely played out. I drove the horses into the pen, roped the freshest looking, saddled him, and led my mule on for the Piedra Blanca. I knew I was in the Piedra Blanca range. After *mozo* and pack mules arrived two hours later, we made camp but ate with the Piedra Blanca vaqueros.

A superannuated American who had been with Frederic Remington in Mexico was very hospitable, locating me in a room with two beds. The house was small. After supper he disappeared, and I went out to the kitchen, with thatched roof and walls of tightly-wattled poles, apart from the house. A good fire was burning on a platform of clay and rocks in the center of the kitchen (or roofed corral) and against the walls pine logs that had been dragged down from the mountain served as benches. Four or five vaqueros sat on them.

The cook, a powerful man named Ismael, was washing dishes. He was *puro indio*, pure quill, as black as Othello. I guessed that instead of shaving he just pulled now and then a few stray hairs out of his face. Tonight he had a fresh audience, and from something I had said or from the way I looked he knew he had an eager listener. Almost at once he launched into a long story, a true epic, of Juan Oso (John Bear), the son of a he-bear and a Christian woman. The story split off into and incorporated several fairy tales and parts of other hero tales. I later put the Juan Oso part into *Tongues of the Monte*. It was midnight when we went to bed.

I had hardly more than gone to sleep when a voice very far from gentle roused me. The owner of the Piedra Blanca Ranch, from Del Rio, was standing over me. He had brought a beef-buyer from Kansas; both had their wives and had to sleep in the house. I got up, got out with all my personal belongings, unrolled my bedroll in my own camp, and was perfectly contented. When you become at home with pack mule and camp you find yourself gloriously liberated from things—things—things.

The next morning when I got up, the beef men were gone, but the wives were there. They seemed to expect me to entertain them, and when I told them the story of the half-breed bear-man, thus fixing it better in my memory and learning how it could be improved in spots, they were manifestly shocked.

A thousand times I have reflected on swart Ismael there in the corral kitchen at Piedra Blanca as about the most picturesque, abounding, plenteous storyteller I have encountered, a kind of Alexandre Dumas in energy of creation, anything but "mute," however illiterate, and glorying in his own output. Many times also I have reflected: What if I had stayed at that fine camping place a day and a half back and had arrived at the Piedra Blanca after the money-hungry owners and their respectable wives were already established there? I should have eaten with them, been obliged to share their domestic dulness, never have heard Ismael at all, never learned about Juan Oso. Of course, after I heard this bear-man story, I went to hearing kindred variants, just as after acquiring a new word one begins noticing its use in all sorts of places.

> I tell you a tale tonight which a seaman told to me
> With eyes that gleamed in the lanthorn light and
> a voice as low as the sea.

Maybe I never heard but one taleteller who had a voice in which was the sound of the sea. Late in 1940, before the United States had joined against Hitler and his Germans, I was in Montana hunting bear stories. I headquartered on the ranch of my old friend Marcus Snyder, who wasn't a Texan but a Texian. He and all his people were out of the old rock. He wasn't much of a storyteller, but he was *muy amigo* with Chief Yellow Tail of the Crow Indians. Chief Yellow Tail wasn't much of a storyteller either, but he knew well the leading storyteller of his tribe. In fact, he knew several storytellers. Yellow Tail got me an able and understanding interpreter named Shiveley, a half-breed, and for several days I listened to ancient Crows tell stories about bears.

One of them I remember more vividly than I remember even his best tale. He was tall, spare, maybe six-feet-two, dark, saturnine in countenance, decayed in frame, but majestical in representing the mighty past of his people. We were sitting where we could look out at approaching winter, getting colder every day, snow coming down. Some days I would ride out on Marcus Snyder's ranch and watch the rabbits turn white. Every day they'd be a little whiter, and after a while what looked like jack rabbits to begin with were snow rabbits. This ancient Crow sat where he and I could both contemplate with our eyes the Big Horn Mountains. Sometimes we sat there for whiles without breaking the silence. I told him that I did not want just a bear story. I wanted a story of a bear hero, as there are men heroes. He told about a bear named Looks Both Ways. This bear had killed a woman, and the warriors had gathered to go against him. He rose up in a thicket of wild chokecherries to meet them, and he made signs, taking the bravery away from each enemy heart and putting it into his own heart. They could not defeat him, although they were mighty warriors. I shall never forget the mountain-and-sea-combined sounds of that old Crow's voice, or his dignity as he told on in harmony with the vastness and the silences of the Big Horn Mountains.

On this fruitful expedition to Montana I went from the Crow Indians to the Lame Deer Cheyenne reservation, where I was taken for an importer of peyote but got another good bear story. Then I went to Great Falls. As soon as I had parked my car, I made a beeline for the Mint Saloon to see the Charles M. Russell pictures. Almost at once I became *muy amigo* with Sid Willis, owner of the Mint, and, according to him, at one time a boon companion with Charlie Russell. He told me some

Russell stories that belong in another place. One slash of realism may never get printed. Sid advised me not to pay out good money on a hotel but to go upstairs in a house across the street and I could find a room at a very reasonable rate.

Staying at the same place was an old cowpuncher named Bob Kennon who had known Charlie Russell and whom Sid Willis designated as my guide and guardian. We drove up to the Canadian line, where it was cold enough to freeze the horns off a brass billy goat and where, because the system craved it, plain meat tasted like something the gods had ordered. I found another interpreter and learned two or three more bear tales from the Blackfeet Indians. While Bob Kennon and I were holed up in a little hotel in the town of Browning he told me the story of a noted lobo wolf named Snowdrift. When we got back to Great Falls, he came into my room and retold the story slowly while I took it down in longhand. Eight or ten years went by before I referred to it. Then, upon request of an outdoor magazine, I wrote it out and got a check for $500 for it. I'll die feeling mean because I did not at once make a search for Bob Kennon and share with him. I regard the Snowdrift story as one of the best I've written on any subject. How casual the chances for good stories seem!

To approach Nat Straw logically I must go away back in time. When *Coronado's Children* came out in 1931 as a Literary Guild book, the promoters held something of a blowout in New York. At one function an editor of *Vanity Fair* commissioned me to write two pieces. I wrote one entitling it "Golden Liars of the Golden West"—mostly a concatenation of yarns. One of them I had heard told by a hunter of mountain lions on the Double Circle Ranch in Arizona. He credited it to Nat Straw. It's a bear story. As I know now but didn't know then, it is a folktale that has traveled from one host to another.

Nat Straw had tamed a grizzly to ride and one day rode him up the mountain just for exercise, or maybe to enjoy the scenery. He didn't take a gun with him, and so couldn't shoot when he came upon another bear away up in the tall timber. This second bear wasn't a bit shy and the saddlebear wasn't either, and so Nat Straw dismounted and let them fight. He rode without saddle or bridle. The two bears fought and they fit, and Nat got scared that his bear was getting the worst of it. Easing up to the bears, he grabbed one by the ear, straddled him, and headed him down the mountain. About halfway down he became unable to guide the animal and in pulling its ears noticed that one of them was gotched—not his bear at all.

At the time that *Vanity Fair* published "Golden Liars of the Golden West," with Nat Straw leading all the rest, a friend of mine named Clarence Insall was covering lots of country gathering walnut roots to ship to France so they could be made into briar pipes and shipped back to the United States for us smokers. He knew Nat Straw and, expecting to see him on the Gila River, took him a copy of the magazine making vain use of his name. After reading the piece, Nat Straw told the walnut root hunter to tell me that he certainly was not the only liar in the West.

Maybe seven years later, I was in New Mexico trailing down the Lost Adams Diggings, one of the happiest trails I was ever on. After having received, high up in the Mogollones, among the mountaintops, authentic tidings of things both visible and invisible, I went to Santa Fe on the road to Texas. Here I ran into two old friends, Stokely Ligon, naturalist, and Dub Evans, rancher and lion-hunter. When I told them what I'd been doing, they said, "The idea of being on the trail of the Lost Adams Diggings and not seeing Nat Straw! Why, Nat Straw took up with a Navajo squaw so he could learn the tribal secrets of the Adams gold. You've simply got to see him before you leave New Mexico. He's got more lore on the Adams Diggings than any other man in the country."

I found Nat Straw on the Gila River above Silver City,

living with a young couple. Out a short distance from their house I camped under the biggest cottonwood tree I've ever seen. Nat had quit yarning, he said, and had lost all interest in the Adams Diggings. He said that at the time he lost interest he wrote high up on an aspen: "The Adams Diggings is a shadowy naught that lies in the valley of fanciful thought." Yet he had experienced some fine stories before he came to that poetical conclusion. While he was telling all he knew and a little that he didn't know about the Adams Diggings, he kept bringing in bears, bears, bears. Frequently I had to pull him off bears back to gold.

After I had pumped him dry on the main subject I encouraged him to head out on bears. When he got wound up on Old Susie, the last famous grizzly killed in New Mexico, I said, "Mr. Straw, I can sell your bear stories to the *Saturday Evening Post*. I'll give you 20 per cent of the check."

I spent another day with him getting bear stories and on the road to Austin composed the piece in my mind; it was rising like yeast and composed itself. Within two or three weeks Wesley Stout of the *Post* had written as warm a reception as anything of mine sent to an editor ever aroused. Maybe this was the happiest experience I have had with a storyteller that I hadn't been looking for. If you are ready, you'll meet them when you're looking for them, and you'll meet them when you're not looking for them. They show up as deer show up to a deer-hunter.

On the way to England in 1945 to teach in the GI University at Shrivenham I was delayed a few days in New York. About sundown one evening while I was walking from 42nd Street up a short block to the Biltmore Hotel on 43rd Street next to the Grand Central Station and only a block from the Air Terminal, the street not crowded at all, I saw a Negro man looking mighty happy. Maybe thirty-eight years old, slenderish, wearing a smile and a little hat, he came tripping my way.

Under one arm was a bottle-shaped package. There could

be no doubt that he had been keeping company with a bottle. His smiling face shone with joy. Every now and then his feet were flashing cuts of the Pigeon Wing, or maybe it was the Double Shuffle. Then he would let out a very low and not at all peace-disturbing shout of joy.

I stopped, fascinated. Other pedestrians paused, then passed. I moved toward the corner, and the joyful one capered my way. A young Negro passed him, turned his head slightly and without coming to a halt gave him a warning. The celebrator raised his voice, his spirits rising with it. "He's back from France, and thinks he'll tell us folks how to act."

He came to me talking. "Yes, I've danced in high places. Boss Man said he wanted me to dance. I said I'd dance if he paid me top money. Boss Man said he'd pay me top money if I could tell a bigger lie than anybody in Europe. This is what I told him:

"One time there was a planter had 2,800 acres black bottom land, and he planted it all in corn, every acre of it. The rains came right, and the crop turned out fine. He gathered it and next year planted another crop, and it was fine. He went on that way for eight years, and gathered all that corn off them 2,800 acres, and he never sold a sack of it, just kept it. He was laying it all up.

"He built what we call a crib. It was two miles and eight square feet this way and two miles and eight square feet that way, then two miles and eight square feet over yonder way, and two miles and eight square feet the other way. It had a cement floor so weevils couldn't come up. It had a concrete wall all around 100 feet high, and it had a roof all over it. And when this planter got all that corn for eight years off his 2,800 acres in the crib, it was chock full. He locked it up and said he didn't need no more corn.

"There was just one hole in that wall, and it was a little hole to let air in. And then along came the seven-year locusts. One of them spied the hole and he flew in. Locusts like corn, you know. This seven-year locust, he stayed there seven years, and then he flew out with a grain of corn. Another locust was waiting to take his place, and he flew in and he stayed seven years, and then he took out another grain.

" 'It wasn't the same locust?' Boss Man asked me.

"No, 'twan't same locust. It was 'nother one. Then No. 3 locust, he flew in and stayed seven years and took out his grain of corn. No. 4, he was ready, and he sizzled in and he stayed seven years.

" 'Looky here,' Boss Man says, 'you going to keep them locusts flying in there one at a time and staying seven years till they get every grain carried out this big crib?'

"That's jest what them locusts have to do, Boss Man," I says.

" 'Well,' he says, 'you done told a bigger lie than any of them people from Europe can tell.' "

Here a man who had paused a minute or so to listen to this New York sidewalk variation of one of the *Arabian Nights* tales warned the entertainer that his package was about to slip from under his arm.

"It don't make no difference if it does break," the shining one said. "I got plenty of money, just plenty."

And he skipped away and out of sight.

"The best adventures are not those we go to seek."

Some of the most memorable storytellers I have encountered were, like this dancing Negro on a New York street at the end of the day, but ships that pass in the night. Two I'm thinking of gave me only a single sample each of their powers.

Away back in the 1930's when I used to go panther and wildcat hunting with Bob Snow, game warden of the Texas Game and Fish Department and exponent of the border country, he spoke frequently of the storytelling abilities of his friend Saturnino Cantú away down in the lower Rio Grande Valley. One fall day my wife Bertha and I were in the vicinity of Raymondville, where Bob Snow's brother Luther reigned as sheriff and where Bob was lingering a little while. They had us for a fine supper of white-winged doves. I'd been prodding Bob on the storyteller. It must have been more than an hour after dark when we finished eating. "Now we'll go hear Saturnino," Bob said.

"He's asleep by now," I countered.

"We'll wake him up."

Then Bob drove us a few miles over a dirt road to a jacal with a field in front of it and with thickets of mesquite and other brush surrounding the other three sides. The cabin was in darkness, but Bob, with his cheery and loud voice, soon aroused Saturnino. He came out in the starlight buttoning his shirt.

After a swift introduction in Spanish, Bob said to Saturnino Cantú, "This gentleman likes stories. I have been telling him what a fine storyteller you are. Please do us the favor to tell a story."

"With pleasure," Saturnino responded, "but what shall I tell a story about?"

"About anything you please," Bob instructed.

By now Saturnino was wide awake. He didn't hesitate for a minute. He was a professional troubadour in his way. He did not have to be reminded by something of something else. He struck out at once into an ancient story, probably brought by the Moors to Spain and then taken by the Spaniards from Spain to Mexico, of "the two companions." He told on like an accordion, giving out notes while both inhaling and exhaling. His voice was musical, rising and falling in the manner of many old-time Mexicans. We sat in the car while he stood there in the starlight and told on and on the picaresque traditional tale of two rascals exceedingly fertile in their creative lying. I put the story in the yearbook published by the Texas Folklore Society in 1944, *From Hell to Breakfast*. As I look back, the ebullient liars of the tale do not seem nearly so interesting to me now as the storyteller named Saturnino.

During World War II while the patriots of what is now

West Germany and also East Germany bombed London almost nightly, I was living with the dons in Emmanuel College, Cambridge, as visiting professor of American history. There's nothing in America like the colleges of the old English universities. Every night, almost, some man from far away who had been at Emmanuel came to High Table for dinner. After dinner we always repaired to the Common Room for talk with wine and then with coffee and tobacco. A man might linger there a good while or he might rush away to work or to some other pleasure.

On the night I'm thinking of, I lingered. The guest was a taut, slender man somewhat short of forty, back from India or Afghanistan or Egypt or some other country that I cannot be sure of. He wasn't saying much, but everything he said went home to me, and before long only we were left in front of the grate in which coal burned cheerfully. There was a little wine left in the decanter, for Page, the butler, had not taken it away. I've forgotten this man's name. Worst of all, I've forgotten the details of the story he told. It was a kind of fable with biting irony on life, something akin to the seven ages of man in Shakespeare or the three ages of man in the folktale that does not get into respectable print. After I was alone, I wrote the story down. I sent it back to Texas for printing in a few newspapers for which I've written a Sunday column for many years. I've been unable to find it either in my files or in any newspaper. I guess it never got across the Atlantic.

Many, many times I've remembered that Englishman sitting there by the coal fire telling this ancient tale of withering irony. I imagine he had many other such tales, for a person who loves stories learns many, and if he can tell one, he's bound to tell others.

I remember a few storytellers, not the very best, because they entered into my life in a way to change it. *Legends of Texas* was in the past, and I was gathering, gathering tales of lost mines and buried treasures to be woven into *Coronado's*

Children. A bright student in a very bright class of mine at the University of Texas was named Leeper Gay, brother to a successful and respectable lawyer—but Leeper never intended to be either successful or respectable. A theme he wrote me was about a man looking for the Lost San Saba Mine. Then he introduced me to Wes Burton.

Wes must have been toward fifty years old at the time and lived with his parents in South Austin, across the Colorado River from the main areas of culture and self-righteousness. His father, who had been a Confederate soldier and a trail driver, had a bully story on the origin of that sad ballad, "When the Work's All Done This Fall." His sister Pinkie, corpulent and blind, played an organ and sang ballads going back to the eighteenth century and beyond. What with singing and with taletelling, sometimes it would be two o'clock in the morning before I got home from a visit to the Burtons.

They had a ghost in the yard, had seen him on several occasions. He belonged to a man who had been killed in the kitchen, and Mrs. Burton said they couldn't scrub his blood out of the floor. They tried to show "the damned spots" to me, but I couldn't see them.

Wes was a blacksmith turned mechanic; he would work a few months and get money enough to stake himself and some fellow-dreamer for a long hunt for what he called Los Almagres Mine—another name for the Lost San Saba, or Lost Bowie. One time he brought in some kind of ore that he was melting in an iron pot over a wood fire out in the yard when I got to the Burton house. He had extracted about a tablespoonful of it and didn't know what it was. He knew very well it wasn't silver.

"Wes," I said, "I'll just take it over to the University and get the Geology Department to analyze it. It won't cost you anything."

"That's fine," he agreed.

After staying and enjoying myself for maybe two hours, I said, "Well, I'll take that ore now."

"No," Wes said, "I don't believe I'll let you take it." Then he added, "Them fellers over there would just bumfuzzle me with their assaying business."

To quote Henry Ford, "I don't like to read books. They mess up my mind."

The first word I had from Bill Cole of Valentine, Texas, was in 1924. Newspapers over the state had been generous in helping me stir up interest in legendary tales. After reading a sample I had sent to an El Paso paper, Bill Cole wrote me to ask how much he would have to pay the United States government when he lifted out twenty-five mule-loads of Monterrey loot buried at El Muerto Springs in Jeff Davis County. He knew that the stuff was there and that he was going to lift it out before the coming summer rains set in—if they came. His sole uncertainty was on how much he would have to fork over to Uncle Sam.

One of his early letters—slightly trimmed, with a few punctuation marks and capital letters applied for the sake of clarity—will say more about the man's mind than I can say.

Kind Sir. In 1917 the state stoped my business, pool hall and siegar stand. I went after 3 different bunches of burried stuff, an I will say without braging that I am the chieff finder of texas up to date. [This simply means that he had found lots of places to dig.] You nodout have heard of the 2 sets of crosses and 2 springs near Davis peak at location of old stage stand where there is 25 mules loads under a big flat rock sealed up with concreet made up with Blood. I thought that was to many mules but it is all true. They made up the concreet with granite gravel an a white lime formation an stuck it to gather with antelope Blood. The stuff had to be blowed with dinimite.

I want to know when an who got a patton on 320 acr in Block 360, sec 21, Jeffdavis Co. If you get a chance to get that information for me you will get paid for your trouble. Capt Fox knowes me. I think he is on the poliece force at Brownesvill. When ever a man dont think them oldtimers did not bring gold an silver a cross [the Rio Grande] by mule train he is badly mistaken, there is 105 mule loads in pinto canion, precidio Co. there is a bunch in marves [Maravillas] canion in Brewster Co.

I have a map to the pinto canion stuff if you will come out here about next may or June wee will try them both a whirl. I will be done with my Jeffdavis Co stuff an I will furnish all the expence money we will need. I know that sounds like B S but its a fact. The old time mexicans know it but there priest tells them not to work after burried treasure. I had to do all my work myself—could not hire them at $4.00 per day.

         hoping to hear from you
         W. E. Cole
         Valentine, Tex

There is no occasion for retelling here the story of the Monterrey loot. I dwell on Bill Cole's satisfaction with the evidence. "While I was digging through the concreet made out of antelope Blood and granite gravel," he wrote, "flies would blow my clothes whenever I came to the surface. When I told this to anybody in Valentine they would look at me as if they thought I was crazy. They've had a chance to help raise money to dig on down but they don't take it. They don't know what the evidence is."

In the summer of 1926 while on a ranch out from Sierra Blanca, I sent Bill Cole a telegram saying that if he was to be in town on the following Saturday, I'd see him. He telegraphed, "I'll be here." Perhaps he was looking for me to come by car. I took the Southern Pacific train and got off at Valentine late in the afternoon. While the train was pulling out, I spotted the combination telegraph operator and passenger and freight agent. He wore those funereal black covers over shirt sleeves from wrist to above elbow that telegraph operators used to wear. His complexion was sallow and his eyes were dim; he was chewing tobacco.

"Could you tell me where to find Bill Cole?" I asked him.

He grunted, made a motion, and walked up the platform maybe forty feet, I following. Then he stopped and spat on the ground and said, "You see them whittlin's?" I saw them. "Jest follow them whittlin's," he said, "and you'll come to Bill Cole's house." Valentine was and is a small village. It wasn't hard for me to find the house.

Bill Cole, about fifty-five years old, was there reposing

behind his black handlebar mustache. His hair was as black as his mustache, his black eyes flashing whenever he spoke with any feeling. He had deliberate ways but was emphatic in his views, and he was very hospitable. His mother kept a rooming house for railroad men, feeding them at times. She had a room for me. I appreciated her cooking. I stayed two days and nights getting the story of the Monterrey loot and going out to El Muerto location where Bill had been digging for years and was to keep on digging—at his leisure—for the remaining thirty years of his life.

He was always bothered by water seeping into the shaft. He couldn't raise enough money to get strong enough pumps to pump it out. His crowbar got stuck in silver two or three times, he claimed, but he never could pry any silver out. To use the words of a Bill Cole letter, "I can make afidivid that I seen refined gold an silver in that hole in two different places. The last time in the botum it showed on my crowbar plain."

The book with the story of the Monterrey loot was published in 1931. After that I heard from Bill only occasionally. One time while driving through Valentine, distinguished by extra ample shipping pens, I saw a charcoal sign on a vacant building beside the road: "Bill Cole Champion Burried Treasure Hunter." He felt, I think, that I had not taken him seriously enough in the book I sent him. As in the song of Frankie and Johnnie, "I meant no harm."

After ten or eleven years had gone by I was on the Southern Pacific going to El Paso. As usual, the train stopped at Valentine for the engine to drink water. I thought Bill might be down to see the train pass and walked forward to where some baggage trucks stood on the platform. Bill was sitting on one of them, slumped over, whittling.

"Hello, Bill," I said.

He looked up and said, "I'm in water now."

"Why you were in water when I saw you fifteen years ago," I said.

He looked as wise as a treeful of hoot owls, and commented, "There are wimmin and wimmin, and there are waters and waters."

"You mean you're in the right water now?" I asked.

He looked at me as if to say, "You are a damned fool for asking a question with such an obvious answer." The conductor called all aboard, and that was the last I heard Bill say on the Monterrey loot.

In 1948 a man working for the State Department in Washington wrote me that he and his son George had been to California and had returned east through Valentine, Texas, in order to visit Bill Cole. That was George's idea, attracted by Bill Cole's hunt for the Monterrey loot as told in *Coronado's Children*. Sixteen years old, George did not want to go to school any more; his parents hoped he would be led into the respectable path of either geologist or mining engineer. The State Department man wanted to know whether I thought Bill Cole would be a proper mentor for George. Before I could make up my mind on what to say, George's mother wrote me in great concern also. I inferred that she did not know her husband had written. She said Bill Cole had offered to board George and pay him $2.00 a day to dig. What did I think of Bill Cole as a beginning teacher in mining?

I never have felt as sufficient as Dorothy Dix, or a father confessor, or Dear Abby in advising people how to conduct their private lives. On the other hand, I never have felt so insufficient that I wanted to turn my life over to some myth, some Billy Graham form of sensationalist, some ecclesiastical corporation. The Department of State man had seen Bill Cole and talked with him; he had a better chance than I at knowing his son George. I left it to the pair to make up their own minds. So far as I know, George did not enrol in Bill Cole's school of mining. Of course, he could have done a lot worse. He could have enrolled in some School of Education.

The last letter I had from Bill Cole, written in March, 1947, concludes thus, most of the punctuation marks being added:

> Since I seen you, instead of one location out where I was at work, there is 5. I have done work on all 5—enough to satisfy me that I am right, but have not finished any one place. If you come out this way this summer stop an see me, if you get here at night and I am gone get a kee from Conring and take my room—the east front room, there will be a bed in there, then next morning come on out to the mountains—you know the way.

In the summer of 1958 an intelligent and able young man of Austin named Ed Wallace, who had prospected in the Chinati Mountains and elsewhere out from Valentine, came to see me. He had been with Bill Cole a good deal before Cole died in 1957 at the age of eighty-six. Bill, he said, had maintained a wholesome unconcern for his soul until he died, had carried himself erect as of old, and always had money enough to drink good whiskey and eat good meat regularly. He enjoyed sharing both with somebody he liked. He evidently liked Ed Wallace, who had come across him first in the mountains.

Bill had not confined his digging to the mountains. He dug two big holes in his own front yard and tore down the gallery—some call it porch—to the house in order to dig under it. This was after his mother, old, old, had died. He was following "sure leads." His crowbar had got hung in what Bill pronounced "bullion" in one of the holes in the yard. It took a block and tackle to pull the crowbar loose.

Of all the storytellers who imparted something out of themselves to me, Railroad Smith alone revealed a plan for stringing together stories that he either told or left half-told, besides a lot untold altogether. Back in the days when the University of Texas campus consisted of forty acres and no skyscraper, R. R. Smith used to "come home," as he put it, once in a while to talk. He could talk through the day and talk through the night. He was long beyond the longest of art. His figure was as elongated as that of Abraham Lincoln and his countenance was as tristful as that of Don Quixote, though he had a strong laugh in his belly. He had a long-drawn-out voice that was lingeringly pleasant to hear; his eyes could see a long way into space and also into people. He belonged to the live oaks, mesquites, prickly pear, ranch manners, dry weather, homemade ethics, and take-your-time psychology of Atascosa County, which is down in the brush country.

He was a lawyer—mainly a criminal lawyer—belonging to times antedating the corporation practice of retaining most of the good lawyers of the country. He was proficient in selecting juries and also in swaying them with voice and words; he studied humanity more perhaps than he studied law books. He lived on a few acres including a calf pasture out from Jourdanton. He called his place Goat Hill and his friends called him the Philosopher of Goat Hill. A few people knew that his first name was Ralph, but everybody called him Railroad. He had read a good deal of history and poetry. He admired Jim Hogg—the one statesman, a liberal, that Texas has had for governor since Sam Houston—and he had a genius for letting things soak into him while he rested in the shade.

The bent of some of his ideas may be deduced from a pamphlet that he published in 1925. The title-page reads: "A Little Preachment and a Short Epistle to the Bigots of Texas, by Brother Railroad Smith. For sale to Students of the University of Inquiring Minds and to Ex-Students of the University of Texas at 25 Cents the Copy, Prepaid." The time could come when this will be as much a "collector's item"—often a term for something nobody wants to read—as a pamphlet written by some ignoramus on some criminal of six-shooter notoriety. However, I myself do not expect to see the cult of violence surrender to cultivation of the civilized.

One of my long talks with, or, more accurately, listenings to, Railroad Smith was about the time "A Little Preachment" came out. I don't remember where we started, but midnight and then two o'clock found us sitting on the sidewalk at the corner of 23rd and Guadalupe streets in front of the University of Texas. One of Railroad's ideas was to write down a collection of old-time Texas stories. They were to be told in a blacksmith shop by a blacksmith sharpening an ax on a grindstone. This blacksmith would pour water on the grindstone to keep it from making the steel too hot and taking away its temper. While he talked on, holding the ax in his hand, the water would evaporate. Meantime, telling on, he would be running his thumb over the ax-blade, testing its sharpness, or dulness. He would spend the whole day watering the grindstone and testing the ax without grinding it at all, but in the end he would have told enough stories to fill the hopper of a corn-grinder waiting to be repaired.

Among the stories that Railroad Smith told me that night and on other occasions was one of two oxen that, after being driven to South Texas by an early settler, got loose and made their way back east of the Mississippi River. I put those oxen into *The Longhorns*. He told me the stories of John Booth's ride of vengeance and of Gregorio Cortez on his little brown mare, both of which I put into a long piece first called "The Saga of the Saddle" and then "Riders of the Stars." After appearing in several places, these rides were finally lodged in *The Mustangs*. I am not sure, but I think Railroad Smith had defended Gregorio Cortez. Anyhow, he visited Gregorio in the penitentiary in Huntsville, where the convict gave him the details of his ride. It takes details and details to make a story, and Railroad Smith's memory held details as securely as the vise in the blacksmith's shop held the handle of a branding iron. Even better than his memory was his ability as creator to supply details. "Disremembering" may at times contribute more to art than remembering.

Storytellers, storytellers. They string out in my memory like a long, long *recua* of pack mules, each of a different brand, different color, and different disposition, twisting through the mountains, going down in the canyons, climbing up over the *cumbres,* trailing across plains of fine grass to an unreachable beyond. Compared with the ideals of slickness, noise, and religiosity, they seem almost mythological characters but they were more real than facts, all of them belonging to times when folks had to amuse themselves, before machines to furnish amusement had been invented. There was John Rigby of Beeville, who had bossed herds of longhorns up the trail to Wyoming, and who for years was brand inspector for the Texas and Southwestern Cattle Raisers Association. I judge that he made up a good deal of the story of Old Sancho, the steer that came back to Esperanza Creek in Frio County, Texas, after being trailed clear to Wyoming. I myself did some constructive work on the story. My publishing it and other stories from John Rigby made him an object of derision among certain masculine vulgarians of the town. He did not end life with the joy deserved by a wonderful storyteller. He did not belong among ignorant literalists.

One afternoon I started from Albuquerque to Santa Fe, expecting to spend an hour with my old friend Jack (N. Howard) Thorp at Alameda, a few miles out on the road. When night came Jack was still telling, and I was still hearing on. We had supper and he kept telling. I was welcomed to stay all night, but there wasn't an extra bed. In those days I always carried a bedroll. Jack made coffee before daylight, and kept on talking. I put a very fine mustang story of his in my mustang book. Some of his superb stories are in the posthumous book *Pardner of the Wind,* but some of his best stories never got into any book. It takes the right chemical mixture to bring any talker, any storyteller, alive. Jack and I were finely suited to each other and each knew it.

If I ever write a book of rattlesnake lore, on which I've been gathering for a third of a century, I shall reveal Dr. Syfert of the Cusihuiriachic Mine of Chihuahua in all his abundance. He had seen with his own eyes, heard with his own ears. I never knew Captain Frank Hamer of the Texas Rangers so well as I wanted to know him. One night in the latter part of his life at a dinner out on a ranch, before we had eaten but not before we had drunken, he unloosed his word hoard on the creatures of the Southwest as he had observed them while riding for years on a horse and sleeping on the ground. That night he made me realize what a delightful, although not historically or biologically accurate, observer he could be in narration. Any good talker, no matter how many non-facts he employs, is better than the encyclopedia.

I never heard a really good talker who could not narrate. I suppose Roy Bedichek was the most excellent civilized narrator I've known. He seldom told folktales. He excelled in sketches of people and in narratives of incidents out of his own life, weaving in enrichments from the classics and also from barbers, cedar-cutters, farmers, freighters, cowboys, and other men of the earth who had never read a classic and very little of anything else, infusing humor and humanity into the whole.

John Lomax could not be surpassed in stories of human beings connected with his own wide experiences. Many of Carl Sandburg's best stories do not grow out of his own experiences but out of what he's heard and read; perhaps Abraham Lincoln gave him something in the art of applying a story. Will Burges, lawyer of El Paso, is gone now. In his gusto for life he was one of the best eaters I've ever seen eat and one of the best talkers I've ever heard talk. He never let his eating interfere with his talking or his talking interfere with his eating. All he needed to turn a feast of beef into a flow of soul was a good listener. I tried more than once to get him to put down some of his stories. He would merely laugh and say, "O that mine enemy had written a book." His lack of ambition to make literary use of what he knew made his talk better, I suppose. Dr. Samuel Johnson became the great talker after he had ceased to write much.

Walter Webb, the thinker, does not weave narratives into

his histories nearly to the extent that he weaves them into his talk. He has lived, observed, and remembered. Now the wells of narrative and characterization are in artesian flow with him. I can truly say that I've enjoyed reading Herodotus more than any other historian. Herodotus never allows fact to get in the way of narration—or truth—or rhetorical laws of coherence to dam the flow. He is one of the great storytellers of all ages. When Evetts Haley cuts loose from documented facts, he's the same kind of storyteller that Herodotus was, perhaps now with more irony.

What's the use of going on? It's pictures and stories that count—not allusions.

I do not believe that any young man of parts could today set out to find storytellers and meet them on every hand as I met them between the World Wars. Instead of entertaining each other with tribal lays now, tribesmen listen to radio and look at television. I suspect that the percentage of good storytellers among the sophisticated who spurn sponsored amusements along with canned advertisements is higher than among the unsophisticated who can afford television and radio. Slick stuff may promote sterile wisecracks but will never engender characters and stories.

When Chaucer comes with his tales and John Aubrey with his character anecdotes, ideas and causes fade away. All of Samuel Taylor Coleridge's metaphysical theories, spun out of philosophy-befogged intellect, are forgotten; his sure passport to immortality is that tale called "The Rime of the Ancient Mariner." I have an enormous respect for thought. I surrender all to a storyteller—if he's good enough. It's the despair of a writing man who has known the best of storytellers that he cannot translate their oral savor into print.

The Singer or the Song

MAC EDWARD LEACH

IT WOULD BE something of a major catastrophe in literary scholarship, I suppose, if we should find the answers to all the great problems. Would we want to settle definitively such questions as: Was there a romantic story of Arthur before Geoffrey of Monmouth? To whom were the sonnets of Shakespeare dedicated? Was the Holy Grail story originally pagan ritual? Was Robin Hood a real person? How did the ballad actually come about? It might work hardship on students looking for dissertation topics or scholars looking for material for articles to fatten bibliographies, but I think many scholars might give a deep sigh of relief if we could bring ourselves to agree to accept even a negotiated answer. The old arguments periodically presented and not always in new garb become wearisome. It was a great moment for Chaucer scholarship when a member arose in the Chaucer section of the Modern Language Association meeting some years ago and offered the resolution that the Chaucer group of MLA recognize Chaucer's birth date as 1340. With a feeling of great accomplishment we voted unanimous approval. Here was one problem we could tick off and no longer bother about. But alas, evidently either the present generation of scholars are lacking in a sense of humor or they court difficulty, for an article is soon to appear with the title, "Was the Chaucer Group of MLA Justified in Considering Chaucer's Birth Date as 1340?" At any rate, a new element has been injected into the controversy. I am certain that, no matter what others may do, ballad scholars would never settle ballad problems by popular vote—however difficult they become.

The bibliography of the ballad, recently completed for the revised edition of Wells's *Manual of Middle English Literature*, contains some 2,500 entries, each representing an article or a book. Assuming the average length to be twenty-five pages, we arrive at the astonishing figure of 62,500 pages written about the ballad from c. 1750 to 1955. Surely in those 62,500 pages we should find the answers. But even so we do not, and largely, it seems to me, because the early ballad scholars did not ask the right questions or did not ask their questions at the right time. They asked questions, for example, about the origin of the ballad long before the ballad as a genre of literature was established, and they asked questions about the date of the ballad before they asked questions about the history of individual ballads. And even today one finds scholars referring with evident approval to Kittredge's theory of origins; and, today, many anthologists still put "Barbara Allan" and Percy's "Edward" in the fifteenth century.

Nevertheless, the present generation of scholars have thrown much light where it is needed first: namely, on the texts of the ballads themselves. Many such studies of individual ballads handled expertly by the historical-geographical method have been made: Erich Pohl's study of "The Hangsman"; Archer Taylor's study of "Edward"; Brewster's "The Two Sisters"; Chappell's "John Henry" and Johnson's "John Henry"; Gilchrist's "Lamkin"; Christophersen's "Sir Aldingar." And now Bernard Bronson's great book on *Tunes and Texts of Child Ballads*. Out of such concrete data valid generalizations should come.

But there is evidence that ballad scholarship may be developing tangentially instead of hewing to the center. I refer specifically to the influence of cultural anthropology on folksong scholarship. Books like Lloyd's *The Singing English-*

man, Miss Clarke's *Study of Jamaica*, Reginald Nettel's *Sing a Song of England*, Anderson's study of Australia, seem to be based on the assumption that folksongs are largely valuable as socio-historical documents and of little importance otherwise; that they should be studied solely for the light they throw on the culture of the time. A paper at a recent meeting of the American Folklore Society took scholars to task for using intrinsic worth rather than social value as a criterion for ballad selection. One wonders if such a point of view may not be based on the unexpressed or even unrecognized feeling still lingering on that the ballad is a folk communal product and therefore to be considered as autobiographical of a particular folk group. Of course, no one would deny that a poem or song is a part of its creator's society and that it may owe much to that society and may even give information about that society; yet this is, I think, of minor importance, and oftentimes may be misleading. A work of art—and the ballad is primarily a work of art—is a product of selection and of creative imagination; it is a synthesis of old and new in subject, thought, and emotion.

Ballads especially are untrustworthy as indexes of culture and consequently must be used with caution for the reason, first of all, that the ballad has no basic text. Consider, for example, the Corpus Christi carol-ballad. We have two versions of this song: one collected in Staffordshire in 1865, and the other from Wessex in a manuscript of the fifteenth century.

> Over yonder's a park which is newly begun
>   All the bells in Paradise I hear them ring
> Which is silver on the outside and gold within
>   And I love sweet Jesus above a thing
> And in that park there stands a hall
>   Which is covered over with purple and pall
> And in that hall there stands a bed
>   Which is hung all around with silk curtains red.
> And in that bed there lies a knight
>   Whose wounds they do bleed by day and by night
> At that bedside there lies a stone
>   Which is our blessed Virgin Mary then kneeling on

> At that bed's foot there lies a hound
>   Which is licking the blood as it daily runs down
> At that bed's head there grows a thorn
>   All the bells in Paradise I hear them ring
> Which has never so blossomed since Christ was born
>   And I love sweet Jesus above a thing.

Is this the expression of the religious beliefs and attitudes of Staffordshire of the nineteenth century or of Wessex of the fifteenth century? And if we did not happen to have the fifteenth-century version, what would the socio-historians make of such a song found in nineteenth-century rural, Protestant England?

In the second place, ballads, rather more than other poems, are untrustworthy purely as records of events or as indexes of social attitudes, because of the multiplicity of hands that manipulated them as they made their journey down in time. Certainly Lord Darnley was never involved in an affair with one of the Queen's Marys, nor was one of them named Hamilton, though some of the ballads would have it so; "Chevy Chase" gives a very different account of the Battle of Otterburne from that found in the ballad by that name, and both differ from Froissart's *Chronicle* in detail and in attitude. The murder ballads rarely report accurately the spirit in which murderers meet death. The ballad generally makes them repentant with some such last stanza as:

> It's drinking and bad company
> That's made a wretch of me
> Come all you men a warning take
> Bid a curse to the pirate sea.

Ballads may preserve beliefs and practices simply because those beliefs and practices are interesting in themselves, even though they may not be understood. Such elements are certainly no index to contemporary culture, either directly or indirectly. Nineteenth-century ballads of fairies do not prove a nineteenth-century belief in fairies. Certainly the fallow doe in the ballad of the "Three Ravens" has meant little to the folk in the last two hundred years:

> Down there comes a fallow doe
> As great with young as she might go
> She lift up his bloody head
> And kist his wounds that were so red

There is a world of difference, too, in how the folk and the folksinger interpret a ballad and what a socio-historian may read into it. Mr. Nettel thinks that "The Foggy, Foggy Dew" reflects the sad plight of the weavers in nineteenth-century England. "John Henry" is frequently presented as a song of social, racial, and economic protest, though there is no evidence for this in the earliest folk texts of "John Henry."

The ballad of "Johny Cock" illustrates most of these points: it is a nineteenth-century ballad, yet it contains bespelled dogs, second sight, poaching in the king's forest, medieval terms of venery, reference to putting off the king's scarlet garb for the Lincoln green of the outlaw, eating raw liver and tongue of the slain deer and drinking its blood, boots of American leather, the hero fighting on his stumps, the epic formula address to the weapons, the sister's son as messenger or a talking bird as messenger, reference to the innate chivalry of animals like wolves. Here in one ballad is a mixture of the very ancient and the modern, all cunningly articulated into a stirring song story. It illustrates perfectly the nature of ballad story that knows no place nor time, but is like a traveler from long ago and from far-off places with luggage full of mementoes.

Theories like the socio-historical fail too, I think, because they neglect to take into account the basic nature of the ballad, its primary meaning to the folk who made it and sing it. The very indefiniteness and many-sided nature of the ballad has brought about this proliferation of theories about it. It has survived among others antiquarianism, primitivism, sentimentality—all imposed on the ballad from without. And the socio-historical is another such extrinsic theory. Is it not time to make an intrinsic study of the ballad? Should we not study the ballad objectively for its own sake and as a work of art?

Oddly enough the first collectors and anthologists concentrated on the song rather than the singer and his culture; yet they never carried this point of view to their critical works. The ballad has always been praised; yet the praise has always been uncritical and subjective. Writers all the way from Sidney, Addison, and Goldsmith to Hardy and Yeats have voiced extravagant appreciation of the ballad. Johnson would rather have written "Chevy Chase," he said, than all of his work; yet none tell why.

This essay then is a plea for an intrinsic study[1] not only of the aesthetics of the ballad and folksong but of traditional literary narrative in general—tale, myth, drama—for we have, I think, been led astray in these categories as well. Here I can do no more than sketch the form such a study might take, with concentration on the ballad.

Let us begin by taking as our fundamental premise the observation of Cecil Sharp that the ballad differs in quality from literature of record, that literature of record is one kind of art, folk literature another kind of art, and that we must disabuse ourselves of the persisting idea that literature of record is art while folk literature like the ballad is artless, naïve, accidental. We must realize that we do not have an antithesis between art and no art, but that rather we have art of two qualities, and that consequently the same techniques and aesthetic criteria do not obtain for both.

The first consideration in presenting a ballad for the appreciation of a sophisticated audience is its frame of reference, as it is, for example, with medieval romance, though for different reasons. The sophisticate approaching folksong is inclined to place it in *his* frame of reference and as a result he finds it crude, or childish, or amusing, or quaint, or incomprehensible. Sensing this attitude the editor and the singer tend to try to give the piece a modern frame of reference, tend to prepare it for such an audience, by changing it toward sophisticated song. The text is regularized in grammar, dialect, and meter. Crudities are smoothed out: Lord Randall is sick at his heart rather than at the stomach.

> They took out his bowels and stretched
>   out his feet
> And garnished him over with lilies
>   so sweet

becomes

> They lowered him down in the grave
>   so deep
> And there he takes his sleep.

Then disregarding the fact that the ballad is a story, they give it an instrumental accompaniment: guitar, banjo, autoharp, even a piano, and finally the singer tries to make it his personal song by singing it in a highly stylized manner.

And so the ballad has not remained in the high hills and lonely mountains; it has come to the radio, to the night club, the juke box, Carnegie Hall. The result is that a whole generation is growing up with confused and downright wrong ideas about the ballad and folksong in general. The whole problem may be one of semantics. We confuse the utilization of folksong by sophisticated artists with folksong. We call Richard Dyer Bennett, Cynthia Gooding, Harry Belafonte folksingers just because they use folksongs and folk melodies as the basis for the songs they sing. Let me illustrate: A few months ago I found myself in a night club in New York. The place was so dark that we should have been equipped with miners' head lights to make our way around. A cacophonous din was being created by a group of musicians, some of whom were twisting their bodies into the most grotesque positions as if they were experiencing exquisite agony. There was the odor of tobacco smoke, mixed with the sweetish odor of alcohol. The musicians finished their piece, or at any rate they stopped. The lights came up briefly, then they were turned completely off. Half a minute later a spot picked out a girl sitting on the raised platform, with a large harp standing before her. She was dressed in green; her hair cascaded down. Her white arm rested lightly against the strings of the harp. It made a lovely picture. For a moment the place quieted down. Her fingers ran lightly over the strings; she began to sing the "Ballad of Lord Randall." "Where have you been, Lord Randall my son?" It was dramatic singing; she sang the mother's questions with sternness and the son's replies with hesitation. Then on the testament the tempo increased almost to a bolero effect with the answer to "What do you leave to your sweetheart?" being a great defiant shouted "A ROPE FROM HELL TO HANG HER!" (and then a sob), "Make my bed soon for I'm sick to the heart and fain would lie down." The audience appreciated the performance; they did not at all appreciate the ballad. It is interesting to contrast this performance with that of a real folksinger.

John Snead, a great singer of ballads, who lived in the Smokies in from Bryson City, North Carolina, used to sing "Randall." Everybody around about would gather in his kitchen near the fireplace where John's wife would be busy preparing food. He'd sit in the chair, head back and eyes closed as he sang. Like all folksingers he let the song speak: it was all deadpan—no histrionics, no acting. The story came through uninterrupted by singer or background accompaniment. Ballad understatement, ballad simplicity, and ballad starkness could build up their effect unobstructed. The knowing and feeling audience was all a part of it. But rarely does anyone from the outside share a complete ballad experience such as this.

Attempts to bring folksong to the non-folk are being made constantly on radio, on record, and in music books. The radio song "Irene," the more or less current ballad "Tom Dooley," Harry Belafonte's "Banana Song" are examples of what I mean.

Consider the last. This is a lively song with pronounced calypso beat, accentuated by the drums. There is the suggestion of dance. The jacket blurb identifies this as a Jamaican folksong, a work song sung by the laborers as they load the banana boats. The words are meaningless; some lines merely count 1, 2, 3, 4, 5; there is however, a note of social and race protest.

The original folksong is much more effective, and honest. It has a slow measured rhythm—there is no calypso in Jamaica except as it is imported from Trinidad to the brassy hotels on the north shore to serve the tourists. The original song *is* a banana loading song, but let me give you the frame of reference. You are on a banana scow in the harbor of Orcabessa, Jamaica, watching the tedious business of loading the United Fruit freighter, *Belize*, with sixty thousand stems of bananas. The long procession of bearers, each with a stem of bananas on his head, moves slowly up the gangplank past the tallyman. It is like a giant centipede without head or tail. In the early part of the night there is much laughter, much calling back and forth from the bearers to the crowd gathered around; toward two o'clock weariness sets in and you hear only the shuffle of bare feet on the rough boards and the soft lapping of water alongside, but punctured regularly by the tallyman's count as the bearers pass before him: six hands, eight hands, bunch (that is, nine hands or more), seven hands, six hands, bunch. As the night wears on, the line grows slower; shoulders begin to sag; hands go up more often to steady the heavy loads on the heads. Then with the dramatic suddenness with which nature operates in the tropics, daylight comes with a quickly widening streak of light over the sea and with it the first puff of the trade wind. Then somewhere along the line of bearers a slow and somewhat mournful song starts. It passes along the line, reiterated over and over, a work song helping them get through the last hours:

> Day oh, Day oh
> Deh de light an' me wan'a go home
> Deh de light an' me wan'a go home

> Me no ask no harse 'n bridle
> Me don wan no house an' lan
>
> Day oh, Day oh
> Deh de light an' me wan'a go home
> Six han's, seven han's, eight han's—bunch
>
> Day oh, Day oh
> Deh de light an' me wan'a go home
> Deh de light an' me wan'a go home
> Me no ask no silver pitcher
> Me no ask no crown wi' jewel
>
> Day oh, Day oh
> Me back jus' bruk
> Wi' pure exhaust'n
> Deh de light an' me wan'a go home
> Deh de light an' me wan'a go home.
> Six han's, seven han's, eight han's—bunch.

They are very tired; the night is over; with the coming of day they should go home to food and rest, but the impelling refrain made of the never-ending and compulsive words of the tallyman drives them on: *six han's, seven han's, eight han's—bunch*. The rhythm is slow, monotonous, regular—far removed from calypso as the folksong itself is far removed from the art song. Ballad critics and theorists have tried repeatedly to see in such songs as this just naïve or undeveloped examples of song in general. It has never occurred to them that such a song might be an example of absolute art of its kind, and that only with difficulty can you make it grow into something else.[2]

If it is true that a different kind of art exists between folksong and song of record, just what is the difference and what form should a critical theory take? I can do little more than suggest some of the answers to these questions, for the subject needs extensive discussion and illustration. Let us recognize in the beginning that tradition endows all types of folk culture with common qualities; language, tale, song, drama, all would show this close kinship. An analysis of this common basic quality would, I think, reveal the following five primary components: (1) understatement, (2) use of formula, (3) presentation of the material through concreteness and specifics, (4) translation of idea and emotion into action, and (5) conservatism, the key to selection. Let us briefly examine these five elements.

Understatement: the ballad tells its story always with a supreme understatement, lack of emphasis, level reporting, matter-of-factness:

> She's taen her by the milk-white hand
> And led her down to youn sea stran
> The youngest stood upon a stane
> The eldest came and threw her in.

And again:

> It's whether ye will be a rank robber's wife
> Or will ye die by my wee pen knife
> It's not I'll be a rank robber's wife
> But I'd rather die by your wee pen knife
> He's stabbed that may and he's laid her by
> For to bear the red rose company.

Note that understatement is a common characteristic of folk language and folktale as well as folksong. You may ask a Newfoundland fisherman, "Will you have some more fish and potatoes?" and get the answer, "Just a sign." By that he means, "Yes, another plateful." And should you ask him, "Could you use a pull of screech [rum]?" you would certainly get the answer, "Just a nibble." And the nibble, of course, is a good half-pint, swallowed without taking the bottle from his lips.

Similar parallels can be shown for the second element: formula. Folk experience and observation fossilize into formula, not only into proverb but into phrases, figures, and customary combinations of words. The ballad builds with these formulas. We thrill to the beauty and the inevitable phrasing of the stanza from "Sir Patrick Spens":

> Late, late yestereen I saw the new moon
> With the old moon in her arm
> And I feir, I feir, my dear master
> That we shall come to harm.

But the old moon with the new moon in her arms belongs to "Sir Patrick Spens" only through the skill of integration, for it is widely used in folk speech, and this is true likewise of ballad formulas like "turn to clay," "as brave as ever sailed the sea," "before cock crow," "a little bird told me," "pale and wan," "white as milk," "brown as mead," "between the long ribs and the short," "he swore by the moon and the stars," "lie there till the meat drips off your bones."[3]

No quality is more characteristic of folk expression than the concrete, whether in tale, in drama, in song, or in everyday speech. Seldom is a generic word for seal used in Newfoundland, but twenty-six words naming concrete aspects of seals are found: a *beater* is a three-year-old seal swimming north; a *quinter* is a young migrating seal; and a little fat seal is a *jar*. Ballad diction is equally concrete: "tirled at the pin," "whey-white face." And so concrete are ballad episodes that they are immediately transferable to pictorial art:

> The red that is in my love's cheek
> Is like blood spilt among the snow
> The white that is on her breast bone
> Is like the down on the white sea mew.

Or—

> Ye'll sit on his white hause bane
> And I'll pike out his bonny blue een
> Wi ae lock of his gowden hair
> We'll theek our next when it grows bare.

Moreover, the ballad as it develops in time moves ever toward concreteness. Consider, for example, the evolution of those ballads that are derived from tales, such as "The Hangsman." This ballad is based on a detailed and circumstantial story of a girl captured by pirates and held for ransom and of her unsuccessful appeal to her family until she summons her husband. This story is built through description, explanation, and motivation, but the ballad that is the end product is nothing but the concrete climax:

> Hangman, hangman, slack your rope
> Slack it for a while
> I think I see my father coming, coming
>   many a mile...

Two years ago in Jamaica I collected a charming song:

> Seven steep hills I have climbed for thee
> Climbed for thee, climbed for thee
> Seven steep hills I have climbed for thee
> Turn to me King Henry, Turn to me
>
> Seven drops of blood I've shed for thee
> Shed for thee, shed for thee
> Seven drops of blood I've shed for thee
> Turn to me King Henry, Turn to me
>
> Seven sweet babes I've born to thee
> Born to thee, born to thee
> Seven sweet babes I've born to thee
> Turn to me King Henry, Turn to me.

The singer could give no information about the song other than that her grandfather had sung it and that she liked it. Even the socio-historian would be hard put to it to fit this into a pattern. But this is a part of an old tale which tells a detailed story of a man (incidentally not a king) who, tired of his wife though she had borne him seven sons, discarded her for a younger woman; how he later was overcome by his enemy and told by this person that he would be spared only if he could answer certain riddles; how the man offered to give anything in his power to one who could help him; how his ex-wife came, answered the riddles, and then asked to sleep with him for one night as her reward. He had to agree, but he turned his back on her. Then she said, "Seven steep hills..." and of course they were reunited.

This song, then, is the only bit that has survived in Jamaica. All of the exposition, panorama, preparation, is sloughed off and the last concrete scene is made into concentrated drama and the quality of mystery that ballad evokes.

Allied to concreteness of detail and of diction is the folk practice of translating all aspects of story into action. Used in the ballad, this gives a fluidity of movement that is one of the ballad's most distinguishing characteristics. It is, again, a quality of all traditional material. In parts of Newfoundland today they still measure distance by gunshots ("He lives three gunshots down the road"), or by bird flight ("It was two puffin flights away"). The ballad uses this device extensively. In "Sir Patrick Spens," instead of telling the reader the succession of feelings that Sir Patrick had, the ballad translates it into the resulting action:

> The first line that Sir Patrick read
> A loud laugh laughed he;
> The next line that Sir Patrick read
> The tear blinded his ee.

And again, Lady Margaret, as she was combing her hair at the window, saw her rival going to the church with William, Lady Margaret's own true love. Characteristically, the ballad tells the story through the action—not, as the self-conscious storyteller of today would, through the motivating emotion:

> Down she cast her ivory comb
> And up she tossed her hair
> She went out from her bower above
> But never no more came there.

Narrative on the conscious level presents material by alternation of panorama and scene. The panorama is the connective tissue, building up to the scene which falls away to another panorama. Ballad and folk narrative in general give the scenes only, without the connective tissue, but this does not mean that the ballad lacks the fluidity all narrative must have; it gets this running quality by the skilful use of repetition, and especially incremental repetition. Note in the following the concrete pictures, with the running action suggested by the repetition:

> They had not been a week from her
> A week but barely ane
> When word came to the carlin wife
> That her three sons were gane
>
> They had not been a week from her
> A week but barely three
> When word came to the carlin wife
> That her sons she'd never see.

Finally, the ballad, like all traditional narrative, carries the quality of archaism, cultural lag, a looking back. This shows itself in subject matter, in attitude, in character relation, and in style. So an eighteenth- or nineteenth-century ballad may have carried down elements, such as blood brotherhood, matriarchy, fairies, magic gardens, seal folk, palmers. Often in the same ballad widely disparate elements exist side by side— heaven, hell, and fairyland; pindars and palmers; animism and materialism. But two opposite tendencies work here; along with the tendency to preserve the past is also a tendency to adapt it or supplant it. Sometimes one wins out, sometimes the other, and the result is the patchwork we are so familiar with in balladry. And it is the same kind of patchwork that is found in other folk products.

My point then is: Now that ballad scholars have pretty well done the textual spade work, our next task is the consideration of the ballad from an aesthetic point of view, recognizing that the ballad is a work of art and that the art of the ballad is different in quality from that of the poetry of record. When that task is complete, then, and only then, can we profitably

THE SINGER OR THE SONG 45

undertake the extrinsic studies, like that of the ballad as an index of culture, and then only can the socio-historian properly *fit* ballad into the general context of culture.

    1. The studies of M. J. C. Hodgart, *The Ballads*, Ch. ii, and John Speirs, "The Scottish Ballads," *Scrutiny*, IV, 35, all too briefly consider the ballad as a work of art; but they employ the criteria of the literature of record.

    2. Of course, I am not making a wholesale condemnation of utilization of folk materials. A million examples could show that a finer product is often the fruit of the folk original: Goethe's *Faust*, Bartok's music, Anatole France's *Thaïs*. But Goethe was not writing a folktale, nor was France a hagiographic legend. In every case the material is worked into a new thing; utilization must be organic. Taking a ballad and simply dressing it up with the tinsel of sophisticated art is like making a cocktail table from a cobbler's bench or a living room lamp from an old sap bucket.

    3. Not a part of this is the literary or structural cliché that the ballad often presents: "lily white hand," "red roan steed," etc.

Some Forms of the Mexican *Canción*

VICENTE T. MENDOZA

Translated by AMÉRICO PAREDES

Address to the Texas Folklore Society, March 27, 1959

THE *Canción* is among the genuine lyrical manifestations of the Mexican people. It may be said that it no longer exists as a vital form, being a product of Mexico's cultural past. It is still widely sung, however, and is a part of Mexico's literary and musical heritage. One still hears the *Canción* over the radio and on television; recordings of it are still made; and it is used to give character and color to those Mexican movies which travel over the world, making known our idiosyncrasies. But the romantic *Canción,* in fact, is no longer composed, first because the age of romanticism is past, and second because room must be made for the appearance of new genres, which displace those that have become worn out by time. Now we have the commercial song, lacking the traditional elements of our culture.

The trajectory of the Mexican *Canción* may be traced from the closing years of the eighteenth century to the end of the nineteenth. This needs some explanation. So long a period, of almost a century and a half, cannot be maintained by any musical genre in the evolutionary life of a people. Generally, the vital periods of a genre are about half a century in length. This is precisely the vital period of our *Canción:* from 1850 to 1900.

Then, how are we to understand the century and a half of

existence? It is simply that, like all things biological, the genre with which we are dealing did not come into being—as some would like to think—by spontaneous generation. Or as a picturesque author says, "The Mexican *Canción* was born as is born the first flower of spring." No; it required a period of gestation, more or less long, another of development, a third and culminant period, and finally a period of decline. I shall attempt to define these stages.

Preliminary Period

The remote origins of the Mexican *Canción* go back to the traditional Spanish lyric, above all to those lyrics found in the literature of the Spanish Golden Age, as one can see from the use of the word *canción* in the writings of that period, for example in the titles of poems by Lope, Góngora, and Baltazar de Alcázar: "Canción to a lady, sending her some flowers," "Canción to a little bird, who bit the tongue of his mistress." Undoubtedly there were *Canciones* set to music in the court, accompanied by the lute, the harp, or the guitar. If not, why are the collections of songs or poems of the fourteenth and fifteenth centuries called "Cancioneros"?

In Mexico during the seventeenth and eighteenth centuries, the lyrical impulse had become established only in the salons of the viceroy. The people of New Spain sang to guitar accompaniment native *coplas* such as the "Verses to Don Antonio de Benavides, the Masked One" and "To the Prostitutes Banished to Pensacola," along with traditional Spanish *romances* like "Gerineldo," "Las Señas del Marido," and "Bernal Francés" and broadside ballads like "Rosaura la de Trujillo," "Pedro de Frías y Antonio Moreno," "La Ciudad de Jauja," and "Sansón."

Nevertheless, it is known that in the last days of the Spanish rule there were already in Mexico couplets and songs which alluded to King Charles IV and to the Viceroy Apodaca. It is also known that in 1810, upon the arrival in Mexico of the Viceroy Venegas, some *zorzicos* were sung in his honor. These newly arrived forms owed their existence to the theatrical *tonadilla*, a form very closely connected with the theater of peninsular Spain. It was undoubtedly in the Coliseo of Mexico City, and in the provincial theaters of Veracruz, Puebla, and Guadalajara, for example, that the first Mexican *Canciones* began to appear, saturated with the rhythms of the Spanish dance, patterned along the lines of the *seguidilla*, the *boleras*, and the *tirana*, an example of which is "Cielito Lindo," which is still sung.

With the war for independence from Spain, the members of the folk who marched in the armies of the rebel chieftains, and their sympathizers back home as well, used fragments of the *tonadilla* as the basis for revolutionary songs. We still have extant the "Song to Morelos," with its picturesque refrain:

Rema, nanita, rema	Row, Nanny, row,
y rema y vamos remando.	Row and let us keep rowing.
Por un cabo doy dos reales,	I'll give two bits for a corporal,
por un sargento un doblón,	For a sergeant a doubloon,
por mi General Morelos	For my General Morelos
la vida y el corazón.	I give my life and my heart.

It is, then, the patriotic song which appears at this time. A song about the execution of Morelos is still sung, with the rhythm of a march and in verses which stress the antepenult:[1]

Oíd, hijos de México,	Hear, oh sons of Mexico,
la historia triste y mísera,	The sad and mournful history
de aquel Generalísimo,	Of that Generalissimo,
Mártir de Ecatepec.	Martyr of Ecatepec.

True *Canciones* were detached from the theatrical spectacles which accompanied the *tonadilla* and lived on the lips of the people, but still betrayed quite clearly their Spanish origin in the octosyllabic line. An example is "La Morenita":

| ¿Te acuerdas cuando pusiste | Remember the day you placed |
| tus manos sobre las mías | Your two hands within my own, |

SOME FORMS OF THE MEXICAN CANCIÓN 49

y llorando me dijiste	And weeping you said to me
que jamás me olvidarías?	That you would never forget me?
Adiós, Adiós, morenita,	Farewell, farewell, dark girl,
Adiós.	farewell.

Another song derived from the *tonadilla* is "Los Baños," which shows in its decasyllabic line that it has departed to some extent from the Spanish influence. The song is still Spanish, however, and the scene it describes is that of Madrid, where in the summer the ladies of high degree would go down to the margins of the Manzanares, accompanied by their corteges (after the French fashion), to take mud baths, since the river held too little water for baths of any other kind. García Cubas publishes the song, which was current in Mexico around 1850:

Madre mía, lléveme usté al baño,	Mother of mine, please take me to the baths;
Madre mía, lléveme usté allá;	Mother of mine, oh, you must take me there;
los calores a mí me consumen ¡Ay!	This terrible heat is consuming me, ¡Ay!
Madre mía ¡Qué fuerte es mi mal!	Mother of mine, this ailment is intense!

It can be seen that during this period the *Canción* was strongly influenced by the Hispanic culture in theme, versification, rhythm, and melody. During the first third of the nineteenth century our people, given more to imitation than to creation, parodied the songs of the time.

Period of Development

In truth, the real traditional ingredient in the making of the Mexican *Canción* was Italian opera, which in the first decades of the nineteenth century appeared in the programs of the Coliseo Theater in Mexico, alternating at times with the *tonadillas* most popular at the moment. In such a manner did the audiences of the capital hear Paesiello's *The Barber of*

Seville, the best works of Rossini, and later those of Bellini and Donizetti. These works were what developed in our ancestors the liking for the *bel canto.* Soon the taste for it descended to the rural classes, who made up the gallery in both the old Coliseo and the new. To such an extent was the taste for Italian opera propagated that in 1840 the Marchioness Calderón was present at a performance of Rossini's *Barber* at Izúcar, done in the open air at a peseta per person.

By royal order of Charles IV, Italian opera had been sung in Mexico translated into Spanish since December 28, 1799. It was not until 1827, when the celebrated Manuel García visited Mexico, that opera was first sung in its original tongue. During the period from 1831 to 1842 the frequent visits of operatic companies to Mexico confirmed an opera-derived tradition that influenced our musical destinies, leading to the rise of the Mexican *Canción.* The formal elements assimilated were those of idiom, versification, orchestration, singers, style—in short, the whole technique.

To this there was added the influence of Spanish literary romanticism through two representative writers: Fernando Calderón and Ignacio Rodríguez Galván, authors of romantic texts which were adapted to Italianized melodies. The second third of the nineteenth century begins with this phenomenon of literary and musical assimilation, which was to last twenty years, that is to say until mid-century. This is the period in which the romantic influence of Espronceda triumphs in Mexico —especially with his poem "El Pirata," which is sung among us as a *romanza*—an influence which could not be escaped by either Fernando Calderón or Rodríguez Galván or Guillermo Prieto, or even Aguilar y Marocho in his "Batalla del Jueves Santo" (Battle of Holy Thursday). Furthermore, it is the hendecasyllabic verse of Tuscan origin which dominates literature and music.

There were during this period some true *Canciones,* what one might call examples of the "primitive type." Don Guillermo

Prieto in his *Memoirs* mentions them as vital manifestations of Mexican music of the time. Writing about the Paseo de la Retama he says, "In the upper part there was performed the *zorzico* and the 'English dance,' and there were sung 'La posesora,' 'El ámbar,' 'El susurro del viento,' songs made especially for romantic souls at bargain prices, as a tradesman of the period put it."[2]

Culminant Period

By mid-century the poets, and the musicians who followed in their footsteps, had fixed the definitive form of the Mexican *Canción*. This must have taken place in the Bajío region of Mexico,[3] because a popular songster, Antonio Zúñiga of Silao, Guanajuato, appears about this time as the author of a great number of songs fitted to a definite pattern. This pattern consists of a quatrain—sometimes in the redondilla or *abba* form, most often composed of hendecasyllables—followed by another quatrain in the same meter, in which the second line is a repetition of the first, while the third and fourth repeat the third and fourth lines of the first quatrain, thus forming a ritornello. Since the musicians faithfully fitted their musical pattern to that of the texts, the music of the *Canción* repeats the characteristics found in the verses: that is to say, the repetition of the first phrase of the second stanza, and the ritornello.

Though this pattern is a tyrannically demanding one, it was followed by all the composers of *Canciones* during the second half of the nineteenth century, and it is followed today by those who would revive this genre. Here is a typical case:

Se fué y abandonó la muy ingrata,	Ungrateful one, she went away and left me,
burlaba de mi amor cual hoja al viento,	She mocked my love, a leaf caught in the wind,
se fué y me abandonó sin sentimiento	Without regret she went away and left me,
y yo lloraba la desgracia de los dos.	And I wept the misfortune of us both.

Ella me dijo que mi amor burlaba,	She told me that she laughed at my affection,
ella me dijo que mi amor reía;	She told me that she mocked my adoration,
se fué y me abandonó la vida mía	Love of my life, she went away and left me,
y yo lloraba la desgracia de los dos.	And I wept the misfortune of us both.

Since this pattern served as the basis for all other *Canciones* written during the century, and since it was so strictly observed by both professional musicians and rural troubadours, preserving fixed norms in regard to keys and modes, it may be considered as the classic type; and because from a literary point of view it contains the elements of the romanticism of its age, we should by all means call it the Mexican Romantic *Canción*.

The themes of the *Canción* fully substantiate its romantic origins. Almost every one of the themes of literary romanticism found expression in Mexican *Canciones:* religion, solitude, skepticism, sentiment, parted lovers, idealization of woman, patriotism, nature, evocation of the past, fatalism, death, the grave, and the churchyard. In all cases, the songs which exemplify these themes are in hendecasyllabic verse.

Decline and Passing of the Canción

It seems probable that, just as romanticism in literature had its day and then was supplanted by the movement initiated by the poets of the *Revista Azul* and *Revista Moderna*,[5] so the romantic *Canción* was replaced by other types. The rise and fall of the romantic movement in Mexican poetry, which can be traced from Fernando Calderón to Luis G. Urbina, culminating in Manuel Acuña, was also seen in music. The difference is that, since the *Canción* began as a folk rather than a literary form, it has its beginnings with the folk musician Antonio Zúñiga, culminates with "Toma Esta Flor" by Melesio Morales, and disappears fitly with "La Cajita," sung to a poem of Luis G. Urbina, but reworked by thousands of anonymous authors.

The *Canción* fulfilled its destiny and gave way to other musical forms. So it is that by 1914, in spite of the Revolution, the aristocracy of the Porfirio Díaz era could be scandalized at the harmonization of popular *Canciones* by Manuel M. Ponce, calling them "songs of the straw hat, the *huarache* and the *pulque* shop." Some would probably say that the *Canción* continued its existence in the songs of the Revolution; I say that it did not. The revolutionary soldier merely made use of a genre that had already disappeared. It is true that in 1918 there was a movement to revive the *Canción* by means of composers' contests, but this was an attempt to inject life into a corpse. Nevertheless, the Mexican *Canción*, romantic and sentimental, has a glorious past. Mexicans can be proud of *Canciones* like "La Golondrina," "La Pajarera," "Marchita El Alma," "Paloma Blanca," and many others too numerous to mention.

The classification of the lyrical songs of a people is an arduous and complicated task. Don Manuel M. Ponce classified the *Canción* according to tempo: slow, moderate, and quick. This seems to us rather childish. Some suggested methods of classification are the following:

According to chronological order: beginning with those of Spanish origin, down to the present.

According to musical structure: beginning with the simple type, consisting of one musical period; the *ranchera*, with two periods and containing irregularities; the semi-erudite, with three or more musical periods.

According to literary form: the length of the line; the influence, classic or romantic, of the verse.

According to the subject treated: love, nostalgia, hatred, solitude, vengeance, constancy.

According to the character of the text: patriotic, historical, satirical, political.

According to geography: mountain, island, coastal, plains, sea; north or south.

According to the region of Mexico: Michoacán, Yucatán, the Bajío region.

According to the occasion: aubades, serenades, weddings, farewells.

According to the calling of the singer: student, soldier, sailor, muleteer, drunkard.

According to the country of origin: Italy, Spain, Cuba, Colombia, Argentina, Central Europe.

According to the rhythm of the European dance from which it derives: polka, mazurka, waltz, habanera, bolero, march.

According to its musical evolution, or because it has a known author: derived from art song, originally pseudo-folk; known author, such as Guty Cárdenas.

According to the style used in singing: with refrains, with echoes, antitheses, and contrasts; with endings stressing the antepenult *(esdrújulos);* characterized by interrupted breathing.

Miscellaneous: mythical subjects, work songs, etc.

The interruption or break in the singer's breathing in the *Canción de aliento entrecortado* is worth noting. One may say that the effect is to reverse the order of the lines. The break comes in the middle of the line; thus the last part of one line is run over into the first half of the succeeding one, making the last half of the line come first in actual singing. These types originated in the Spanish province of Navarra and have spread throughout Spanish America.

Ando en busca
de una blanca palomita // de señas traigo
un dolor dentro del alma // dolor ingrato;
si me dieras tu retrato // ya nunca, nunca
yo me olvidaría de ti.

    I am in search
    Of a little white dove // I'll recognize her
    By the ache within my soul // Oh cruel ache;

If you gave me your picture // Then never, never,
Would I forget you.

It is almost certain that the romantic *Canción*, with a capital C, has strong ties with the Bajío region, that part of Mexico which has set the pace for much of Mexican life. In the evenings, after work is done, man and wife sit at the door of their jacal, their heads close together, cupping their hands over their mouths for resonance, and sing these morbid songs full of sentiment and nostalgia, in harmony, the husband carrying the tenor and the woman the alto, filling the air with melancholic vibrations that seem to stretch the horizon into the infinite.

Or else, lovers go through the streets at night, carrying to the loved one the serenade or *gallo* to the sound of the harp, the guitar, and the fiddle. The *Canción* is also heard at the fairs, the weddings and birthday parties, the dances and the cockfights, in which musician, singer, and dancer participate. In sum, though the *Canción* is no longer composed, it still is an essential part of the emotional life of the Mexican people.

1. The *esdrújulo* or verse ending with stressed antepenult is relatively rare in Spanish, being used for special effects.—A.P.

2. Guillermo Prieto (1818-1897), Mexico's most popular poet for some fifty years and a Liberal politician and pamphleteer. He was in Juarez' cabinet. His *Memoirs* are a rich source of information about Mexican life during the mid-nineteenth century.—A.P.

3. The Bajío or Lowlands area of Mexico comprises parts of the states of Jalisco, Michoacán, and Querétaro and all of Aguascalientes and Guanajuato. It is a fertile, well-watered region in central Mexico, early colonized by Spanish settlers.—A.P.

4. The poets of the "modernist" movement, beginning about 1898 under the leadership of Rubén Darío, revolted against decadent romanticism and led the way toward a revitalization of Spanish American poetry.—A.P.

Folklore and History

AMÉRICO PAREDES

*Address to the American Folklore Society
And the Sociedad Folklórica de México,
Mexico City, December 28, 1959.*

"PAST EVENTS, it is argued, have no objective existence, but survive only in written records and in human memories." Thus did Winston Smith read in the forbidden book of Oceania, in George Orwell's novel *1984*. It was Winston Smith's job to change documents according to Oceanic policy, so that history became the fiction demanded by the needs of the moment. This was accomplished by tampering with documents. The memories of men were of small concern because, unsupported by recorded evidence, men's memories change.

Many a folklorist would agree in principle with the Inner Party rulers of Oceania. The mention of folklore and history in the same breath is an anomaly. The human mind preserves the memory of rituals, of psychological states and dreams, of responses to the environment. But it forgets events. Folklore is the last place one should go in search for anything that resembles history.

It is not my purpose here to enter into the sorely argued question about the birth of folklore. I wish to approach folklore as something already alive and kicking. For the purposes of this paper I would like to define it as oral tradition in periodic contact with a more complex, literate society. The British border ballad, the Spanish *romance fronterizo*, the Mexican *corrido*, the North American legendary anecdote and hero tale—these shall furnish most of my examples.

We are all familiar with what folklore can do to history, how it changes dates, places, and names to suit the pattern of the moment—the moment the singer is most concerned with. In an article entitled "Shakespeare, Abélard, and 'The Unquiet Grave' "[1] the North American folklorist Herbert Halpert gives us two typical instances of the way in which folklore sometimes uses history. "The Unquiet Grave," a British ballad (No. 78 in the collection of Francis James Child), has as its theme the universal subject of the lover who mourns excessively for his beloved, until the dead one comes to reprove his exaggerated grief. One American singer from whom Halpert collected this ballad identified the hero with the poet Shakespeare, and added to the narrative elements from the story of Abélard and Héloïse. Shakespeare, the source declared, had been castrated by a jealous rival; his love had entered a nunnery.

In this instance the poet Shakespeare, a historical character by general if not unanimous agreement, is seen in the process of becoming a folk hero. His name came to be attached to the Abélard story and to a ballad, obviously because people who knew nothing about his works did know his fame. A like fortune has been the lot of the Spanish poet Quevedo, to whom anecdotes of a universal character are attached, many of them obscene. Among the stories attributed to Quevedo are some that were associated with the Latin poet Virgil during the Middle Ages, such as the one about the poet's entering his mistress' room by means of a basket.

Halpert's other example is concerned not with poets but with warriors. In Nova Scotia a ballad singer gave the following "historical" data about "The Battle of Alma," a song commemorating a British victory over the Russians in the Crimean War, 1854: The British were led by King William, who prayed to God that the sun be prevented from setting until his troops had defeated the Russians. The sun stopped in the heavens until the British victory was assured. Aside from the reference to the Hebrew champion Joshua, it may be noted that in 1854 the British ruler was Queen Victoria.

Tradition, Halpert concludes (quoting Robin Flower's *The Western Island*), "remembers but not as history remembers . . . building its own timeless world out of the wreck of history." Grant for the moment that this is the only way we can find history in folklore—in a state of wreck. We may still ask, "May anything be done with the pieces?"

From the folklorist's point of view the value of studying the relationship between folklore's "wreck of history" and history itself is well recognized, not requiring great elaboration here. Such studies may throw light on the development of popular traditions. Where documents are available for comparison, one may actually trace the process—the reshaping of history to conform with the folk group's own world view, the embellishment of bare historical detail with universal folk motifs. And even when documents are not available, the presence of historical elements in folklore may mark out certain patterns. The development of literary figures such as Virgil, Shakespeare, and Quevedo into folk heroes is a case in point.

But the question I would like to dwell on especially is whether historians may derive any benefit from the study of folklore. First we may consider the importance of folklore in the writing of history books, though it is not always easy for us to admit that what we accept as historical fact may be nothing but the traditions which our particular culture approves. Everyone is aware that the medieval chronicles are more folklore than history. Herodotus, laughing at the Egyptians for their superstitions, has left us a mixture of Greek folklore and history, so that one could call him the father of folklore collectors as well as the father of history. The skeptical eighteenth century should be different; yet the historian Gibbon in some respects is not quite as enlightened as Herodotus. Where the Greek is skeptical, the Englishman is full of petty contempt toward that which does not fit his own particular scheme of things. Yet, when Gibbon is not dealing with churchly miracles or saints' legends, his skepticism is much less vigilant. Cruelly rewarded faithful servants, heroes with seven fathers, and warrior maidens march through his pages untouched by the merciless shafts of reason.

And what about more recent times? Let me mention one example, from my own native state of Texas, about the Mission of the Alamo in San Antonio. The defense to the death of the Alamo by a handful of Texas Federalists against Santa Anna's Centralist forces occupies much the same position in the emotions of Texans as the defense of the Castle of Chapultepec by the Niños Héroes in the feelings of Mexicans. Hundreds of books have been written about the Alamo, and they are still being turned out today. One thing they all have in common is their dependence on folklore for their color and detail. It is impossible really to know what the last moments of the defenders of the Alamo were like, since the defenders died to the last man, while the attackers were too occupied to note the drama of their last moments, nor did they know the identities of the men they finally overcame. Still, detailed accounts of the last moments of the Alamo are passed off as history.

One interesting detail concerns the Lone Star flag, which is mentioned as flying over the Alamo during the siege. I have met Texas college students, and college graduates, who were not aware to this day that the flag defended at the Alamo was the Mexican flag, with "1824" (for the Federalist constitution of that year) inscribed upon it. And this after the Walt Disney movie about David Crockett, which though it uses much folklore does stick to history in this instance. Apparently the history which these people imbibed in the public schools had some distinct elements of folklore, and its effects were lasting.

Perhaps it is true that in every new country folklore and history develop side by side, and that local pride, prejudice, and passions play their part in the "folklorization" of history. This certainly has been true in the American Southwest. The folklorists must also be regional historians; and the historians, it would seem, too often have been folklorists too.

But this sort of thing is not restricted to one place and to one time. The defense of Chapultepec, for example, has its legends too, which are accepted as history by some. A long list could be compiled from the Mexican histories about the United States. I will mention but one example, concerning the role of the United States in the murder of President Madero, and note how the more fiery Mexican historians have tended to show Madero's assassination as a plot of that modern Machiavelli, Woodrow Wilson.

But passions are really a subordinate factor. Dominant is the same instinct for drama, for universal themes, for the reshaping of an oft-told story nearer to the heart's desire that is found in true folklore. It is this impulse that makes Border Mexicans insist that it was not Carranzista troops but Pancho Villa himself who defeated Captain Boyd's American troopers at El Carrizal. Villa, after all, was the hero of the Pershing invasion; it is only fitting that he should be the hero of the only major action in which the expeditionary forces were engaged.

It is because of this human instinct for drama, for the most fitting description instead of the most factual one—it is because of this pertinacity of universal themes in most human narrative that an acquaintance with folklore may serve the historian who has to use oral report, or documents which are based on someone's verbal account. Gibbon could identify a story as folklore (or "superstition" as he called it) if it contained marvelous incidents. The early writers of the Southwest (and many contemporary ones) shared Gibbon's contempt for "superstition." But they tended to accept as fact any pleasing story which did not betray elements of the marvelous or the supernatural. The general who slays all his opponents except one, whose ears he cuts off and then sends to the enemy as a messenger of doom; the servant who saves his master's life and is rewarded with death; the beautiful maiden who takes her aged father's place in battle; the hero who knows only that his father is one of his mother's seven lovers—all of these are in the realm of human possibility.

Some knowledge of the frequency with which motifs of this kind occur in folk narrative would put the historian on his guard. In other words, Gibbon would have been aided by a motif or type index of folk narrative. It is too late for him to profit from such works, but on this continent there may be many historical writers, not all of them from the American Southwest, who could find a use for some knowledge of folklore.

One might say that this is looking at the relationship of folklore and history in a negative sense. Folklore, however, can serve a more positive function in the study of history; for not always does folk narrative make a complete wreck of historical facts. The British ballad "Johnie Armstrong" (No. 169 in the Child collection) is an example. Armstrong was put to death in 1530 by order of the Scottish king. According to the chronicles he was legally executed after being captured as a rebel and outlaw. The ballads tell a story of treachery on the king's part toward a semi-independent chieftain of the border. Modern historians feel that the ballads tell a truer story than do the chronicles.

In respect to a primitive culture David M. Pendergast and Clement W. Meighan have shown in "Folk Traditions as Historical Fact: A Paiute Example"[2] that traditions may have a basis in historical fact. The authors show how Paiute traditions describe pre-Pueblo peoples in a way substantiated by recent archeological evidence.

The Indiana University scholar Merle E. Simmons has

shown what can be done with one type of folklore in elucidating the historical attitudes of a people. His *The Mexican Corrido as a Source for Interpretive Study of Modern Mexico (1870-1950)*[3] considers a vital period in Mexican history from the point of view of the songs of the people. Some of the deepest feelings that moved Mexicans of this period appear much more vividly in the *corridos* than they do in the official documents of the time. The American historian wishing really to understand the Mexican point of view toward the United States would do well to begin with a study of the Mexican *corridos*.

For if history is the history of peoples as a whole, then folklore has something to contribute to it, even when there is enough documentary evidence about a period to make the investigator feel that he knows it well. There are attitudes and feelings, undercurrents of emotion in the masses of people, which are not recorded in official documents but which may have a profound effect upon events. The folklore of a particular period or region is at least as important to the historian as are the newspapers and other mass media of more urbanized societies. More so, perhaps, because a newspaper editorial may represent the opinions of one single man—the editor—while a ballad, if it truly enters oral tradition, will express the feelings of a great number.

The Treaty of Guadalupe Hidalgo resulted in the incorporation into the United States of the territory between the Nueces and Rio Grande rivers, where people of Mexican culture had lived for a hundred years. Almost immediately these people came into economic and cultural conflict with the English-speaking newcomers who moved into the territory after 1848. The pacification and final Americanization of this area is an important chapter in the history of the United States. But, with few exceptions, documents available for study of the region are in English, being for the most part reports made by officials who were, to put it mildly, prejudiced against the people they were trying to "pacify." Where it is possible to check their reports with other existing data, it can be seen that their bias often led them to exaggerate or even to falsify the facts. The Texas-Mexican version does not exist in documents. It can be found in *corridos* and in prose narratives passed from father to son. It is folklore, and as such unreliable. But no history of the Rio Grande border which ignores this folklore can be complete.

I would like now to submit for your consideration two songs from the Mexican border with Texas, collected at Laredo, Texas, on August 7, 1954, from Mercurio Martínez, a seventy-eight-year-old native of the region.[4] These two songs were first performed in 1867 in the town of San Ignacio, Zapata County, Texas, by Onofre Cárdenas, a local guitarrero. Mercurio Martínez learned them from his mother in the 1880's. The songs were current in oral tradition for at least two generations, though few people know them today.

One is to Ignacio Zaragoza, victor over the French at Puebla, the other to Ulysses S. Grant, conqueror of the Confederacy. Both songs are in Spanish, the first language of these bilingual people; they are much alike in both structure and melody. Professor Vicente T. Mendoza, your eminent folklorist and musicologist, has been kind enough to transcribe and analyze the melodies for this paper, noting their relationship to Mexican music of the mid-nineteenth century. His remarks, we may note in passing, shed considerable light on the way that the folksong maker combines materials from folk and art sources in fashioning new tunes.[5]

Musically, the first thing to be noted about these songs is the strong similarity of their opening bars to the Mexican national anthem, which had but recently been adopted after a competition in which Mexican and foreign musicians took part. In the closing bars of the song to Grant and in the middle of the one to Zaragoza, there are echoes of another, universally known patriotic song, the "Marseillaise." That much did the

Texas-Mexican songmaker borrow from the current art music of his day. For the rest he went to the Mexican folk forms with which he was familiar. The structure of the Song to Grant is that of the Mexican romantic *Canción*, which in 1867 had reached the height of its development. The same is true of most of the Song to Zaragoza, except the final part, which goes from a martial movement into allegro. Here the songmaker harked back to the folksong of Spanish type, which was current in Mexico before the rise of the *Canción*.[6]

A GRANT

Viva Grant, viva Grant ciudadanos
que cinco años la guerra sostuvo,

y un ejército enorme mantuvo
en defensa de la libertad.
Y después de sangrientos combates
do murieron valientes soldados

fueron libres aquellos estados
que jamás pretendían la igualdad.

Dios te salve, Caudillo del Norte,
yo saludo tu sacra bandera
que en el mundo flamea por doquiera
ofreciendo la paz y la unión.
También México ensalza tu nombre
porque fuiste con él indulgente,
fuiste siempre y serás el valiente

que defiende la Constitución.

Long live Grant, citizens long live Grant,
Who withstood the war for five years,
Who maintained an enormous army
In defense of liberty.
And after many bloody battles

In which courageous soldiers died,
Those states were free
That had never aspired for equality.

God save thee, Chieftain of the North,
I salute your holy flag
That flutters everywhere in the world,
Offering union and peace.
Mexico too exalts your name

Because you were kind toward it;
You have been and shall be the brave one,
The defender of the Constitution.

A ZARAGOZA

Dios te salve, valiente Zaragoza,
invicto general de la frontera,

yo con los libres saludo tu bandera
que en Puebla tremoló sin descansar.
Los hijos de la patria te saludan

solemnizando tu triunfo en este día,
los venideros también con alegría
bendecirán tu nombre sin cesar.

God save thee, brave Zaragoza,

Unconquered general of the Border;
I and all free men salute your flag
That waved unceasingly on Puebla's battlefield.
The sons of the Fatherland salute you,
Celebrating your triumph on this day;
Those to come also joyfully
Will bless your name until the end of time.

El pueblito y sus autoridades	This little town and its authorities
tu nombre ensalzan repetidas veces	Exalt your name on numberless occasions
porque fuiste el terror de los franceses	Because you were the terror of the French
en Guadalupe, Loreto y en San Juan.	At Guadalupe, Loreto and San Juan.
La mañana del cinco de mayo	The morning of the fifth of May
que con muy pocos soldados mexicanos	When with a handful of Mexican soldiers
un golpe rudo le diste a los tiranos	You dealt a rude blow to the tyrants
que se acercaban a Puebla con afán.	That were hurrying to Puebla eagerly.
No olviden mexicanos	Mexicans, don't forget
que en el cinco de mayo	That on the fifth of May
los zuavos como un rayo	The Zouaves with lightning speed
corrieron... para atrás.	Ran... towards the rear.
Tirando cuanto traían	Casting off all that they carried,
los que a Puebla venían,	They that to Puebla were coming,
apurados decían,	Exclaiming in their haste,
"Pelear es por demás."	"It is in vain to fight."

The particularist point of view of the Borderer is evident in these songs. Grant, then secretary of war and soon to be President, is shown as "Chieftain of the North," a title which later would belong to Francisco Villa. Chieftain Grant belongs to the North of the United States, but "El Norte" to the man of the northern Mexican border has private—and heroic— associations. Even more revealing is the view of Ignacio Zaragoza. He is not a Mexican general but "the general of the Border." Zaragoza was born in Texas and received his early education in Matamoros, Tamaulipas, on the border. The song to Zaragoza, then, is more than a commemoration of the Fifth of May. It celebrates the fame of a native son.

Here we have two songs, in the same general pattern and using similar tunes, presumably composed by the same person and sung by the same group of people: one of them might be classified as a Mexican, the other as an American patriotic song. Composed just nineteen years after the Nueces-Rio Grande area had ceased to be Tamaulipas, they show the strong ambivalence in the Texas-Mexican's attitude toward Mexico and the United States, a state of mind that is important in understanding the history of South Texas from the days of Juan N. Cortina to the present.

In the song to Zaragoza we hear American citizens called "sons of the Fatherland." Which one? Mexico or the United States? Zaragoza's flag is saluted, and so is Grant's. It is not easy to decide which Constitution the individual singer would have in mind when he praised Grant as "defender of the Constitution." Perhaps he thought of both: the American Constitution, challenged by the Confederacy, and the Mexican Constitution, threatened by the French.

Just what the Border Mexican's attitude was toward the political and ideological issues of those two conflicts is a debatable question. On the whole, northern Mexico was pro-Juárez. With a few exceptions, such as that of the notable Benavides family, Texas-Mexicans were not active supporters of the Confederacy. But Matamoros and its port of Bagdad served as an outlet for Confederate cotton; so that if the Border Mexican did not give active military support to the Confederacy, he did support it at times in an indirect way.

A view often expressed is that the average Border Mexican cared nothing about the issues that had brought civil war to both nations. But if these two songs have the long history in oral tradition that we are justified in believing they have, then the Border Mexican did have some knowledge of the more abstract issues of the two wars in which he became involved.

The very fact that the songs have come down to us as a pair indicates that the Border people were aware of a similarity between Grant and Zaragoza, that they were the chief military figures in defense of certain ideas. The more sophisticated mind, in personifying the ideals of the American Civil War and the

French invasion, would have chosen the figures of Lincoln and Juárez. These songs indicate that the average Border Mexican saw in Grant and Zaragoza personifications of certain concepts which he valued. They also illustrate the service that folklore may at times do for history, lighting up the dark corners of the past, serving in this instance as a commentary on the history of two countries.

    1. Herbert Halpert, "Shakespeare, Abélard, and 'The Unquiet Grave,'" *Journal of American Folklore*, LXIX, 74-75 and 98.
    2. David M. Pendergast and Clement W. Meighan, "Folk Traditions as Historical Fact: A Paiute Example," *Journal of American Folklore*, LXXII, 128-33.
    3. Merle E. Simmons, *The Mexican Corrido as a Source for Interpretive Study of Modern Mexico (1870-1950)* (Bloomington, Indiana, 1957).
    4. The two songs discussed here are part of the University of Texas Folklore Archive, where they may be found as items P43-3 and P43-5 in the taped folklore collections.
    5. I wish to express my thanks to Professor Mendoza for his valuable collaboration on the musical side of this paper, and to absolve him from responsibility for any errors committed by me in my version of his musical analysis.
    6. See Professor Mendoza's article on the Mexican *Canción*, elsewhere in this volume.

Don't Look Back

GEORGE D. HENDRICKS

A MULTITUDE of motifs in proverbs, folk sayings, folk beliefs, and folktales warn us against looking back. Some few tell us that we *should* look back. As expressions of the folk, these ideas involve basic psychological problems and indicate serious and usually valid philosophical outlooks upon life.

There are, of course, two ways to look back: one is in a physical or directional sense, involving space; the other is chronological, involving time. In both of these senses there are dangers to be avoided and values to be sought; these dangers and values may be internal or external.

Don't cry over spilled milk. Wipe the slate clean and start from scratch. Bury the hatchet. Let sleeping dogs lie. Let bygones be bygones. Don't give it a second thought. That's water under the bridge. Burn your bridges behind you. Such are the sayings everybody knows. Whoever follows the dictates of these sayings believes that somehow things will turn out all right in spite of what has gone before. He is, in this sense, essentially a man of faith.

Even nursery rhymes imply the same disregard for troubles of the past or present, the same confidence in the future:

> Little Bo Peep has lost her sheep
> And can't tell where to find them.
> Leave them alone and they'll come home
> Wagging their tails behind them.

> Mary had a little lamb.
> Its fleece was white as snow.
> And everywhere that Mary went,
> The lamb was sure to go.

Neither Bo Peep nor Mary need worry about what's behind them. If their animals are well trained, they will follow.

Some folk cures prohibit the backward look. For removing warts, take a penny you have earned from your mother. Give it to her and ask her to rub it three times with her thumb. Then take it to the back door and turn around and throw it over your shoulder into the back yard. If you don't look back at it, and if you never try to find it, your warts will go away. If you have no faith in this cure, it simply won't work.

Other superstitions practiced the world over, from ancient times to the present, also demand that a person have faith. If you see a load of hay, make a wish and look away (without confidence you cannot have your wish). If you put on underwear wrong side out, you must leave it that way. If you discover you have left something important at home, you must not go back after it. To do so is to bring on bad luck. If you decide to take the risk anyway, you must sit down, take a deep breath, say "damn it," take your hat off, turn it around three times, spit over your left shoulder, and replace your hat. It is doubtful, however, that this will remove your apprehension.

Both folk and literary proverbs warn us against looking back. Remorse is the echo of a lost virtue, according to one American proverb. Plutarch wrote, "Memory is to us the hearing of deaf actions, and the seeing of the blind." Longfellow wrote that we should let the dead Past bury its dead. Sandburg writes, "The Past is a bucket of ashes." And Shakespeare wrote, "What's past is prologue."

Certainly a man's attitude is conditioned by his emphasis upon a segment of time—whether it be past, present, or future. Professor A. L. Campa most succinctly delineates the corresponding philosophies:

In formulating our criterion of spiritual guidance, we have before us three periods in life that determine the order of our existence: the past, the present, and the future. Our philosophy of living will revolve around one of these three as a point of departure, depending upon what time of life we consider most essential. The present is a reality, the past a recollection of a reality that has ceased to exist, and the future a conjecture of what may come to pass. Hence, the last two form the basis of romanticism, since one is no longer here and the other has not yet arrived.[1]

Campa implies that the Latin American is more the realist who enjoys the present moment, whereas the Anglo American is the romantic who misses out on most of this life while contemplating the future. He is too busy counting his chickens before they hatch.

This latter expression has an interesting history. Among primitives the female knew better than to count the buns before putting them into her oven or to count the eggs and plan on the same number of chickens. Furthermore, as she began her household duties of a morning, she was careful not to break anything. However, if by some misfortune she did, she quickly put everything *back* exactly where it was before she started, and began all over again in earnest to ward off bad luck.

Just what the very best solution may be to this problem of emphasis upon a time segment has been dealt with extensively in folklore. A Chinese proverb says that the palest ink is better than the most retentive memory. Here we may look back *if* we are sure of the record. An English proverb says, "He that looks not *before* finds himself *behind*." The American says, "Look before you leap." A German proverb tells us what to do with all three segments: "Three things belong to a happy life—to sink the past, to guide the present, and to reflect on the future."

One aspect of primitivism is the desire to look back, or return to, one's youth when things were better. Anybody's grandfather is likely to say two things: "Now when *I* was a boy, we did it *this* way," and "The world is going to the dogs."

The best reply to this charge is the following poem, whose author I have been unable to find:

> My granddad, viewing earth's worn cogs,
>   Said, "Things are going to the dogs."
> And *his* granddad from his house of logs
>   Said, "Things are going to the dogs."
> And *his* granddad from the Irish bogs
>   Said, "Things are going to the dogs."
> And *his* granddad in his old skin togs
>   Said, "Things are going to the dogs."
> There's just this thing I have to state:
>   The dogs have had a good long wait!

The primitivist wants to go back and start all over again. "Had-I-Wist" was a common allegorical expression from the fifteenth to the seventeenth century. Authors like John Skelton and Gabriel Harvey warned their readers against the attitude it represented. The sentiment persists, however, as Stephen Leacock exemplifies it:

You know, many a man realises late in life that if when he was a boy he had known what he knows now, instead of being what he is he might be what he won't; but how few boys stop to think that if they knew what they don't know instead of being what they will be, they wouldn't be? These are awful thoughts.[2]

Aesop told of a fox watching a man trying to count the waves. The fox advised the man to count only those immediately before him and to pay no attention to those which had already passed. In another fable the wasp twits the butterfly with having come from an ugly chrysalis, but *now* the butterfly is much more beautiful than the ugly wasp. The moral of both tales is that the past is unimportant; it matters not what you were or where you came from.

From the *Gesta Romanorum*, we learn of the seven counsels Aristotle gave Alexander. The fifth of these was, "When you have once commenced a proper undertaking, never turn from it." And Davy Crockett's motto was, "Be sure you're right,

Then go ahead." The question is germane: How could Alexander *or* Crockett *know* they were on a proper undertaking unless they had previously considered the past? Kierkegaard said that life can be understood only backward, but it must be lived forward. Janus was a *two*-headed god; he reviewed the past before looking to the future.

To understand and face the pitfalls of the future, in view of those of the past, requires not only faith but also asceticism. Orpheus is the classic example of the man who could not resist looking back prematurely upon the wife he was retrieving from the abode of the shades, and thus lost her forever. Here is a legend that extends from Ovid in first-century Rome to Alabama Negroes in twentieth-century America, who tell their version of "Dicey and Jim Orpus." Lot's wife is the classic example of the woman who could not resist looking back. And here is a legend that extends from pre-Christian Israelites to modern native Peruvian Indians, who have ten different versions corresponding to the story of Lot's wife. This, incidentally, testifies to the universality of folklore in general and of the superstition against looking back in particular.

Among the ancient Hittites there was a myth about a dragon-slaying hero who practiced a folk taboo: he refused to look back upon his wife or child before setting out upon his adventures. He thus conformed to the ritual of sexual continence before battle and kept foremost in mind his mission. Modern U.S. Air Force pilots have a related custom; many will not allow their wives to see them take off, saying it is bad luck. The serious or vital pursuits of life require ascetic continence. To go without it may be fatal.

Zuñis practice rigid, stoical asceticism when they refuse to look back during certain of their rituals. Before a raid, aside from avoiding sexual incontinence, the warrior goes to a river seeking omens and performing these rites: Four times he takes four steps backward from the river and each time pauses for omens. Then without a backward glance, he proceeds to the

War Chief for an interpretation of these signs. Hopis believe that they must not look back at the lake where they have gathered salt lest they die soon and their souls be trapped in the lake.

The man of reasonable faith is an idealist. The extreme, unreasoning idealist, however, refuses to recognize dangers, either real or imaginary. He is like the ostrich with his head in the sand. They say it's bad luck to run and look out the window when you hear a siren. But you'd better; you may be personally concerned. They say, also, that if you look back at a funeral procession and count the vehicles, you will be the next to die. There is a common saying, "Don't look now, but somebody is following you." This seems a roundabout way of dealing with a possible troublemaker. Like the three monkeys, you must hear no evil, see no evil, speak no evil. Ignore it, and it doesn't exist.

The realist knows better. He will not stick his head in the sand when there is real, external danger. He will be even more wary if it comes from behind. Traditionally, whenever Wild Bill Hickok entered a saloon, he would always "side" around the room so that its walls were always to his back and its patrons to his front, where he could keep his eye on any potential enemy. Only once did he get careless—and that was when Jack McCall shot him in the back in a saloon in Deadwood, Dakota, in 1876.

Cadets in the Air Force at Randolph Field are taught caution by means of what appears to be an absurd practice. Whenever a cadet walks to a street corner or whenever else he must change direction in his walking, he must extend his arms (simulating wings), come to a stop, and perform a seemingly ridiculous ritual. He turns his face to the left and says, "All clear on the left." After repeating this procedure for all other directions, he finishes with what is considered particularly important. He bends over and looks backward between his legs and says, "All clear behind." Though many consider this ludicrous, no one questions the tactics it symbolizes: the tactics of reasonable caution.

The less cautious realist minimizes real, external danger from the rear. As General George Patton once said, "Never worry about your flank or rear. Just shoot one bullet, take three steps forward, shoot one more bullet, take three more steps, and keep on going straight ahead." Everybody knows Admiral Farragut's famous battle cry, "Damn the torpedoes! Full speed ahead!" The best defense is an offense. Everybody for himself and the devil take the hindmost.

Jesus Christ told the Devil, "Get thee behind me, Satan." But his danger was not external; he was wrestling with temptation. Christ was, in this respect, a well-balanced idealist, not the type to stick his head in the sand ostrich-like and ignore evil. He was, furthermore, a man of faith. Pandora lacked the faith to put her box behind her and walk away from it. Ichabod Crane lacked the faith to quell the fear he felt within himself; he looked back and saw something even worse than he had imagined. The fabulous turtle lacked faith in the eagle which was carrying him aloft. He looked down, against the eagle's advice, got dizzy, lost his grasp, and was smashed in the fall. His danger was more internal than external.

There is a western cowboy expression: "The man who wears his chin on his instep never sees the horizon." Were he a man of faith, he would look forward, not downward or backward. The direction in which one looks, in either a physical or chronological sense, indicates his attitudes. It has some bearing upon his cowardice or bravery, caution or lack of it, idealism or realism, primitivism or futurism, fatalism or its opposite, ambition or indifference, asceticism or lack of it, pragmatism or its opposite, and finally his faith or lack of it.

1. A. L. Campa, "Mañana Is Today," *New Mexico Quarterly*, IX (February, 1939), 3-11.
2. Stephen Leacock, *Literary Lapses* (New York, 1918), p. 37.

The Oil Promoter as Trickster

MODY C. BOATRIGHT

AMONG the archetypical characters in folklore none is more universally known than the trickster—the one who prevails, or sometimes fails to prevail, by his wits. Other archetypes may win by their prowess, by their use of magic, or by the aid of helpers, often animals who spy for them, often supernatural agencies like genii and fairy godmothers. But the trickster's only weapon is his wits, his cleverness, and his only technique is deceit.

He exists in the lore of all cultures, literate and preliterate. He may be the coyote of the North American Indians, the spider of North Africa, the Brer Rabbit of American Negro slaves. He may be a human being like Pedro Urdemales, known to the Spanish-speaking world; like Hans, the unpromising third son of the German peasants; he may be John the southern slave, who gains privileges and escapes punishment by outwitting his master. He may be the Yankee peddler with his wooden nutmegs and his eight-day clock, which runs eight days and then stops forever.

Under one name or another, he is known everywhere, and everywhere commands a mixture of admiration and condemnation. His universal appeal is not easy to account for. It may be assumed that he is in some sense a projection of a quality inherent in the human condition: perhaps of our consciousness of our insufficiencies in our universe;[1] of our intuitive knowledge, if not conscious awareness, of original sin, expressed in the adage that "there is a little larceny in us all"; or of revolt against necessary social restraint.

Sometimes the trickster will have our complete sympathy, sometimes our bitter contempt, and sometimes we rejoice to see the trickster tricked. Our attitude will depend partly upon the motivation of the trickster and partly upon our sympathy or lack of it for his victim. Lazarillo de Tormes resorted to trickery to live, Jack Wilton in order to live merrily, Brer Rabbit sometimes to live and sometimes to live merrily. But the most typical motivation of the trickster is greed.

While certain archetypes seem to survive all cultural changes, they are not themselves unchanged. The knight errant trades his armor and spear for a six-shooter. Cinderella learns a new technique. Her godmother has a big bank account, and may be an industrialist, an oilman, or a movie producer. When it's all three, Cinderella has it made. The trickster no longer sells money-bearing trees to simple country folk, not even gold bricks to country merchants. But the rise of industry, of finance capitalism, and more recently of mass communications has opened doors of opportunity that would have bewildered Pedro Urdemales or Sam Slick. By no means is the trickster disappearing from our culture and our lore. At mid-century, in his most sophisticated persona, he manipulates symbols of popular value from his Madison Avenue office. But for the first thirty-five years of this century he was most often and most conspicuously an oil promoter.

In a denotative sense, anybody who promotes an oil venture is an oil promoter, but among the oil folk he is one who promotes a venture from which he hopes to gain whether oil is found or not. Whether he sells interests in a well or stock in a company, he expects to be compensated for his trouble, oil or no oil. This is not to say that he always, or indeed in most instances, is a trickster. There were and are legitimate and ethical means of promotion. For a simplified example often used in the past, let us say a promoter secures a lease on a town lot in Breckenridge in 1918. He estimates that he can sink a well to the producing sand for $50,000. He sells seventy-five one-per-cent interests in the well for $1,000 each. He has $25,000 above the expected cost of the well, and if he finds oil, one-fourth of the seven-eighths remaining after the landowner's royalty has been deducted is his. He hasn't deceived anybody.

He becomes a trickster if he does what many promoters are reported to have done—that is, if he sells interests totaling more than 100 per cent. I have been told that two men operating under this plan had the misfortune to strike oil and that they plugged up their wells and left in a hurry.

There is no conclusive reason for assuming that these latter men are more typical of promoters than the first. Nevertheless, they and their kind have cast suspicion upon the whole fraternity. It is significant that Dad Joiner's friends have resented his being called a promoter. They want it understood that he was a bona fide wildcatter seriously looking for oil.

This suspicion dates from the first oil boom, when the gold excitement had somewhat abated and sharp practicers were turning to oil. A musical publisher, taking advantage of the excitement that Drake's well had started, brought out the *Oil on the Brain Songster* in 1865, in which several songs satirize oil promoters. One[2] lists the following companies or partnerships:

FAMOUS OIL FIRMS
By E. Pluribus Oilum

There's "Ketchum and Cheatum,"
And "Lure 'em and Beatum,"
And "Swindleum" all in a row;
Then "Coax 'em and Lead 'em,"
And "Leech 'em and Bleed 'em,"
And "Guzzle 'em, Sing 'em and Co."

There's "Gull 'em and Skinner,"
And "Gammon and Sinner,"

"R. Askal and Oil and Son,"
With "Spongeum and Fleeceum,"
And "Strip 'em and Grease 'em,"
  And the "Take 'em in Brothers and Run."

There's "Watch 'em and Nab 'em,"
And "Knock 'em and Grab 'em,"
  And "Lather and Shave 'em well," too;
There's "Force 'em and Tie 'em,"
And "Pump 'em and Dry 'em,"
  And "Wheedle and Soap 'em" in view.

There's "Pare 'em and Core 'em,"
And "Grind 'em and Bore 'em,"
  And "Pinchum good, Scrapeum and Friend,"
With "Done 'em and Brown 'em,"
And "Finish and Drown 'em,"
  And thus I might go to the end.

Similar ridicule appeared in newspapers and periodicals. The Boston *Commercial* published a burlesque prospectus of The Munchausen Philosopher's Stone and Gull Creek Grand Consolidated Oil Company, with a capital stock of four billion dollars, and working capital of $39.50. Dividends were to be paid semi-daily, except on Sunday. The directors were S. W. Indle, R. Ascal, D. Faulter (treasurer), S. Teal, Oily Gammon, and John Law. The *Typographical Advertiser* in the same year (1865) announced the organization of The Antipodal Petroleum Company, with a capital stock of one billion dollars, with a par value of $10,000 per share, but offered to the public at twenty-five cents. The company proposed to drill through the earth and thus obtain production in both the United States and China from a single well. The treasurer was Mr. Particular Phitts, and the president was The Hon. Goentoem Strong.[3]

Thirty-five or more years later Texas was to have its quota of D. Faulters, R. Ascals, and Particular Phitts. In referring to some of them I have used such terms as "it was said," "it was reported." Some of my informants have been reluctant to name names or to give clues to identification. Thus not all my information can be verified, nor does it need to be. I am concerned with the public image of the trickster-promoter. I shall not attempt to follow in detail the careers of any of the notorious tricksters exposed in court. It was their tricks that brought great crowds into the courtrooms, and that led to legendary embellishments of their exploits. It is the type, the persona, that commands our interest. There is, however, sufficient documentary evidence in the form of newspaper advertising, exposures in journals, and reports of court trials to suggest that the popular image has its objective correlative.

The trickster's greed is taken for granted, and a degree of cleverness—which, however, did not always see him through. How did he operate? What were his tricks?

The simplest of all was well-salting, a trick he might have learned from the gold and silver mine promoters who preceded him. The first salters of whom I have record were a couple of Vermont Yankees lured to Pennsylvania by the first oil boom. In 1864, when Alfred W. Smiley was working as a clerk, a report reached him that an abandoned well had been deepened and was good for twenty or thirty barrels. Smiley went to the well and saw oil flowing into a storage tank. The Vermonters sold the well to a Bostonian for $40,000 cash. The purchaser found that the pumps had been rigged so that oil from the tank flowed back into the well to be pumped back into the tank in an endless cycle. But before this discovery was made the gentlemen from Vermont who had made the sale were "extremely absent." Apparently they were never brought to trial.[4] Thus the country boys triumphed over the city slicker.

This trick, then, seems to have been a Yankee invention, but Texans have not been averse to making use of it. In 1921 John H. Wynne and his partner acquired six sections of land in Reeves County. They had not particularly wanted the land, but had taken it on a debt when money was not forthcoming. Six months later word came that oil had been found near by, and a lease hound offered them five dollars an acre. This was more than they had considered the land worth in fee simple. But instead of signing up, they decided to investigate. Wynne found the well. When the man on duty would open a valve, oil would flow from the casing head. It would be permitted to flow only a few minutes, for, the operator explained, he had no storage. But the driller gave the secret away. The oil flowed from a tank car on the railroad siding near by, and there was enough gas in the well to bring it to the surface. Leasing activity ceased abruptly and Wynne and his partner did not get their $19,200.[5]

This method of salting is rather crude. The more sophisticated salter leaves the evidence for others to discover or interpret. This is more convincing and less dangerous. He may sprinkle the derrick with crude oil, and if he means to sell stock, he will photograph it. He may pour oil in the slush pit, or bring oil sand from a producing well and leave it on the derrick floor for a scout to find. When Dad Joiner's driller hit the oil sand, he washed the bit in a bucket of water and left it on the derrick floor. The stories resulting from this are too many to recount here. One man told me of going to the derrick and finding it unattended, of examining the sand and finding all the evidence of salting. He joined the legion of East Texans who failed to grasp the forelock that Dad Joiner's discovery provided.

It was inevitable that some well salter would be hoist with his own petard, for wherever there are stories of tricksters, there are stories of the trickster tricked. My story comes from Burkburnett and the operator will be called A. D. Siever. He poured crude into his well and hauled it out with a bailer in the presence of prospective buyers, a couple of New York Jews. They bought, and Siever was happy in his success. To outwit a New Yorker was a considerable achievement, to outwit a Jew was a greater achievement, but to outwit two New Yorkers and two Jews at one and the same time was a superb achievement. But Siever's complacency was short-lived. The

New Yorkers deepened the well and brought in a producer worth many times what they had paid for it. And Sievers never knew whether his salting sold the well, or whether the buyers had geological information unknown to him.[6]

How extensively well salting was practiced can hardly be known, but both the legal record and the oral tradition would indicate that it played a relatively minor role in dishonest oil promotion. The trickster relied mainly upon the sale of corporate stocks, and his indispensable assets were imagination and verbal skill. Mr. Ecks furnishes an example of what was needed. Hauled into court on a charge of selling fraudulent oil stock, he somehow got access to the witnesses for the prosecution. He sold every one of them a share or more of stock, and agreed to take in payment their vouchers for mileage and witness fees. The judge declared a mistrial. Years later my informant saw Mr. Ecks, who told him that he had suffered his punishment, had repented of his sins and been converted to religion, and was now successfully using his talent in the service of the Lord. He was a revivalist.[7]

My informant was silent upon the name of Mr. Ecks's company, but I am sure it was well chosen. For the trickster knew that a rose by any other name would not smell so sweet to the people on his sucker list.

If the company was a modest one, with holdings limited to a single locality, the trickster often sought a name that would link his company with a producing well or field. For example, the discovery well at Desdemona was on the Duke farm. Eighteen companies used the word *Duke:* The Grand Duke Producing Company, Heart of Duke, Duke Extension, El Paso Duke, Italian Duke, Post Duke, Duke-Burk-Ranger (three fields represented), Duke Knowles Annex, Royal Duke, Duke Consolidated Royalty Syndicate, Erath Duke, Duke Dome, Alma-Duke, Tex-Duke, Giant Duke, Duke of Dublin, Comanche Duke, Iowa Duke.[8] Some of the Dukes were found to be fraudulent, as was also the Blue Bird Oil Company, one of several making use of symbols of luck. Others were Lucky Boy, Lucky Seven, and Rainbow. Uncle Sam suggests patriotism, but the company so named was a notorious swindle. The great supercorporation through which Dr. Frederick A. Cook and Seymour E. J. Cox swindled thousands bore the innocent and co-operative-sounding title of The Petroleum Producers Association.

Another device was to choose a name suggesting an affiliation between your company and a well-known successful one. Two such companies offering stock for sale during the Beaumont boom were the Rockefeller Oil Company of Beaumont and the Stephenville Standard Oil Company of Beaumont. The only connection they had with John D. Rockefeller or any of his Standard companies was in the names.[9]

The General Lee Development Interests would seem at first sight an inspiration for a corporation seeking to sell stock in Dixie. But the organizers were not content to rely upon the magic of the name. They found a janitor named Robert A. Lee, conferred a military title upon him, declared him a descendant of Robert E. Lee, paid him $12.50 a day for the use of his name, and described him as a famous geologist. Their literature proclaimed that just as "Robert E. Lee gave his life to the South, so is now General Robert A. Lee giving his life to the oil industry and the cause of humanity." But a federal court found that he was no kin to Marse Robert, and that he was not a geologist. Nor was the jury convinced that he was giving his life to the cause of humanity. He and sponsors paid fines and went to a federal prison.[10]

During the heyday of the oil trickster, from 1918 to 1924, radio and television were not available, but he had other means of getting his message to the public. One was to get his propaganda published in reputable papers as news. A notorious example is a story that appeared in the New York *Sun* in 1903 (May 10). Whether payola was involved, my sources do not reveal.

Under the 200 square miles of rolling prairie land controlled by Mr. King and his associates, there is a vast sea of petroleum. While its length and breadth have been pretty well established, no plummet has ever yet sounded its depths.

It lies in its subterranean bed, where it will sleep until the suction pumps of the big King-Crowther Corporation begin to thud and clank in the oil-filled caves. As yet, the surface has been barely scratched, as it were, and seven oil wells have been found. By a fair process of reason, it may be assumed that in the entire 200 square miles of territory, when fully developed, there should be at least 8000 oil wells.

The general idea is to pay the investor not less than 20% a year so that in five years he will receive his original investment, leaving a profit of from three to five times the original amount.

These estimates are based on Mr. King's knowledge and experience. As a matter of fact, investments may pay anywhere from three to five times in excess of the figures quoted.[11]

A few days after this story appeared, the attorney general of Texas filed a petition alleging that the King-Crowther Corporation had obtained its charter through false information. The court estimated that shareholders had been fleeced out of two million dollars.

As newspapers grew more wary of publishing free advertising, the trickster, knowing the advantage of the seemingly impartial news story, began acquiring control of oil journals by founding, by purchase, or by lending them money. The *World's Work,* in an article exposing fraud in the oil industry (1923),[12] listed eleven periodicals as owned or controlled by oil promoters: *Pat Morris Oil News (Fearless and Truthful Oil News), Independent Oil and Financial Reporter (Fair, Faithful and Fearless), International Investors Bulletin, Independent Oil News, Texas Oil World, Texas Oil Ledger, National Oil Journal, Arkansas Oil and Mineral News,* the *Banker, Merchant, and Manufacturer, Mining and the Industrial Age,* and *Commercial and Financial World.* It was charged that one of these was for a time hostile to Dr. Cook, but was brought to see the light by a substantial loan.

But not all tricksters could afford an independent oil

journal. They relied chiefly on newspaper advertising and direct mailing. In spite of the better business bureaus and the Vigilance Committee of the Associated Advertising Clubs of the World,[13] which in 1921 declared that 95 per cent of oil stock offered through newspapers was unworthy, it was still possible to get wide coverage. Because security laws were more lax than now and because both the post office and attorney general's department were grossly understaffed, fear of legal action was not a wholly effective deterrent, a fact which gave vigor and scope to the imagination.

The *New York Times* (March 9, 1924), commenting particularly on conditions in Texas and more specifically in Fort Worth, known as the capital of fraudulent oil promotion, observed that the oil stock promoter "has contributed some of the glibbest, most convincing writing of our era. Some of this writing is so broad and highly colored that the secret story should be plain to see. But the public is greedy for this sort of fiction, and the oil stock frauds flourish in the fertile soil of the public imagination."

A sampling of this writing tends to support the judgment of the *Times* editorialist. There were a number of approaches, each with its appropriate style and tone. One might be called the unqualified promise, delivered in bold, simple, and direct English:

> Oil will always be in demand, it will always yield its fixed, profitable price, and it will make dividends to the holders of shares in the Bonnabel Refining Company as sure and steady as the progression of time.... The company can guarantee at least 20% per annum.[14]
>
> I absolutely guarantee $200 returned for every $100 loaned me for oil development, with a full 100% profit remaining as a permanent investment.[15]

"Conservative estimate of profits... 350%." On the inside cover of the prospectus was the following unacknowledged quotation:

> Our doubts are traitors,
> They make us lose the good
> We might win by fearing to attempt.[16]

One syndicate "aimed at" 10,000 per cent profit in from four to six months.[17]

Such statements as these are what the *Times* writer had in mind as so broad and highly colored as to give the secret away. One could sound more convincing by promising big profits and then adding qualifications that would leave the profits still big. One promoter had a tract of a hundred acres upon which he said there was room for fifty wells.

> Even if these fifty wells should make *only* 100 barrels apiece, the oil, being Pennsylvania grade, commands a price of $4 per barrel at the well, and will net us a nice profit ... 50 times 100 will be 50,000 barrels a day, which at $4 per barrel, will equal $200,000 a day. This multiplied by 300 [perhaps the wells were not to produce on Sundays and holidays] will make a total income of $60,000,000 a year from this 100 acres alone.

But he goes on to say that 10 wells would be sufficient to develop the property, and, even if the production were only 25 barrels per well, the income would still be $300,000 a year.[18]

Another theme is: others have got rich, why not you? Often there was the warning that you had better hurry, for the stock is going up!

> ARKANSAS GIRL MAKES $300,000 ON OIL ACREAGE.
> BUYS LAND FOR $500; REALIZES $900,000; BIG PROFIT, EH, WHAT?
> THREE MEN POOLED THEIR ALL, $25. AND SOLD FOR $250,000.[19]

Others preferred a tone of frankness. There is risk in the oil business:

> If you ask my advice about investing, I don't give any. I have acted on my own judgment, and have invested in the Company with which I am identified. I don't advise anybody either one way or the other. If we strike oil our stock will be worth ten to one, or more. If we don't strike a well there will be no difficulty in selling our holdings at a greatly advanced price, as values are doubling, quadrupling and quintupling there from

day to day. I determined, however, that I would give nobody advice in the matter. If I should give the advice and our stockholders made a thousand per cent on the investment, they would think I was a great man; but if I gave the advice, and there was nothing made out of the investment, they would lay the failure in the realization of their fast profits, to my account. I shall accumulate no such liabilities as these. I have unbounded faith in the oil fields there, and I believe they are going to supply the fuel and the illumination for the world; but I don't advise anybody either one way or the other. I can only say this: If any readers ... are going to buy oil stock, our oil stock is as good as any oil stock in the market and far better than ninety per cent that is being sold.[20]

If you cannot afford to take a chance to lose $10 to $25, do not go into this scheme because oil investments are uncertain. Admittedly it is a "long shot." The backers of the company have such a firm belief in it, based on the best geological information obtainable, that they have put their own money into it.[21]

In our exaltation of the hero we have sometimes without the warrant of fact made every discovery somebody's folly. There was Columbus' folly, Fulton's folly, Morse's folly, and in oil Drake's folly and Higgins' folly, and if we may trust a newspaper advertisement, Carruth's folly. One of his ads ran:

Hog Creek Carruth: The name that will live throughout the ages as the name of the man who toiled singlehanded for seven long years to prove up his belief and attain his goal—who traced an oil structure 20 miles across the ranges from Strawn to Desdemona—who conceived and organized the famous Hog Creek Oil Co.—who drilled the discovery well of the great Desdemona field at one time called the richest spot on earth—who transformed a desert into a fountain of liquid gold—who built a city of 30,000 souls from a village of 200 people and who paid every person who held shares of stock in his renowned Hog Creek Co. $10,133 for every $100 invested.[22]

Thus were the doubting Thomases confounded.

One very successful copy writer found the folksy style effective:

Now, folks, I'm going to tell you a lot of things in this ad that will be good for your souls. I'm not a promoter and I'm not an ad writer—I'm just plain old Harry Bleam. All I can do is just sit down and tell you this stuff the way I know it to be. Most everybody knows about Harry

Bleam. I'm just a common guy. I'm not in politics, but I'm a square shooter from who laid the chunk, and I put my cards down on the table face up. I'm not a promoter. You will know that anyway in just a minute, because I'm going to tell you something no promoter ever told you. If the well I'm getting ready to drill on my big little 4-acre tract down there don't come in a gusher, then there ain't no such thing as a bellyache....

Why, if I didn't believe I was going to get oil here—and I don't mean just a dinky little 1,000 barrel well—I mean a 10,000 or 15,000 barrel well—I'd never try to sell anybody an interest in it.....[23]

Boyce House tells of a promoter whose literature showed a picture of a cell block at the Leavenworth Prison underneath which was the statement, "The doors of this prison will open to receive _____ _____ if he fails to make good every statement made to the public."[24] This statement is no mean achievement. But Dr. Cook could visualize a worse fate. Here he describes his thoughts while watching an oil-well fire:

I stood on a hill about a half a mile away watching this shaft of light and heat as its wicked tongues of flame leaped and roared while the men rushed around in their feverish haste to extinguish this great torch of the oil fields. I was standing there with the black of the night behind me and the clear white light of this burning well in front of me, wondering if possibly all this roaring fire wasn't in reality sent as a kind of warning to the fake promoters—the meanest rodents that ever breathed God's pure air.

I don't believe that a man who would wilfully defraud the public and take from the investors who are willing to help develop nature's resources the money which they have so carefully saved, without giving them a fair return, deserves much better an end than might be typified by this flaming gas well.

The preachers tell me that the day of fire and brimstone in the church is past but we have plenty of it left in the oil fields and I wonder after all if his Satanic Majesty isn't retaining just a little supply of the old fashioned hell-fire torment for the reception of a few phony promoters.[25]

Whatever the ultimate fate of Dr. Cook, a cell block at Leavenworth did open to receive him.

What the promoter trickster's take was can only be hinted at.

Within eight months after the Spindletop discovery, the capitalization of Texas oil companies had reached $231,000,000, although actual investment in the Beaumont field was estimated at only $11,000,000.[26] Within a year there were five hundred Texas oil companies doing business in Beaumont, not to mention hundreds more chartered in other states.[27] Not wholly untypical were four companies capitalized at one million each. Their assets were a jointly held lease on a block of land forty-five feet square.[28] It is little wonder that Spindletop became known as Swindletop.

Carl Coke Rister says that out of 1,050 new stock companies formed in 1918-19, only seven paid dividends. The Oklahoma Commission of Corporations estimated that only one dollar was returned out of every $550 invested in stock companies. In Kansas it was estimated that in 1916-17 only 12 of 1,500 new companies showed profits. An Oklahoma writer estimated that there had been a $555 capitalization for every barrel of oil produced.[29] In 1924 the *Financial World* estimated that the capital of defunct oil companies had aggregated $500,000,000.[30] Rister estimates a total accumulated investment of $102,000,000,000 up to 1947, against a return of $61,000,000,000.[31]

It is not to be assumed that all, or even a majority, of the unsuccessful companies were fraudulent. But there are indications that the aggregate sum that went into the pockets of the tricksters was considerable. The *World's Work* in 1918 said that one promoter (he was jailed) had fleeced 25,000 people out of $2,500,000.[32] In February, 1924, there were in federal courts sixty-three cases pending against persons representing or claiming to represent Texas oil companies, who, the Department of Justice claimed, had taken in $140,000,000. A year earlier the solicitor general of the Post Office Department estimated that during the preceding five years $100,000,000 had been lost to fraudulent promoters in Texas alone:

No doubt some of these companies were started by men who hoped to strike oil and make money from the production, but in practically every case the promoters had laid their plans to profit from stock selling, regardless of the result of field operations. Seldom was it that a promoter invested his own money.[33]

The great crackdown came in 1923. The Securities and Exchange laws of the 1930's made it considerably more difficult for the trickster to operate. I would not be so bold as to say that he has left the oil industry altogether, but his heyday in this industry is over.

A convicted bank robber once made this defense of his trade: When he robbed a bank, nobody lost a dollar but the insurance company, and it obviously gained in the long run; for if the bank robbing ceased, the sale of robbery insurance would cease soon afterward.

I know of no such ingenious defense having been made of the oil trickster. When he was brought to trial, he typically pled guilty. When he pled not guilty, he was an honest man who had exposed himself to the great hazards of the business in a sincere effort to help his fellow-man. If, in imitation of the bank robber, he had attempted to rationalize his conduct, he might have said that his social role was to alleviate the disastrous economic effects of oversaving. But Keynesian economics was not in fashion in the days of Harding and Coolidge and Hoover.

1. See "Trickster," *Standard Dictionary of Folklore, Mythology and Legend* (New York, 1950).
2. *Oil on the Brain Songster* (Cincinnati, 1865), p. 19.
3. Both quoted in *The Derrick Handbook of Petroleum* (Oil City, Pennsylvania, 1898), I, 1047-49.
4. Alfred Wildon Smiley, *A Few Scraps (Oily and Otherwise)* (Oil City, 1907), pp. 72-74.
5. John Wynne, tape-recorded interview, January 26, 1960.
6. E. M. Everton, oral interview.
7. James A. Haakerson, oral interview.
8. Boyce House, *Were You at Ranger?* (Dallas, 1935), p. 116.
9. Boyce House, *Oil Boom* (Caldwell, Idaho, 1941), p. 32.
10. *New York Times*, May 9, 1923.
11. *Oil Investors' Journal*, II (June 1, 1903), 5.

12. J. K. Barnes, "Doctor Cook's Discovery of Oil," *World's Work,* XLV (April, 1923), 611-17.
13. "Investing in Oil," *Review of Reviews,* LXIII (April, 1921), 443.
14. *Oil Investors' Journal,* III (October 15, 1904), 7.
15. House, *Oil Boom,* p. 26.
16. *Oil Investors' Journal,* III (May 3, 1905), 9.
17. Barnes, *op. cit.*
18. *Current Opinion,* LXX (April 21, 1921), 545.
19. *Literary Digest,* LXXVII (December 8, 1923), 11.
20. *Baptist Standard,* May 2, 1901.
21. "Investing in Oil," *op. cit.,* pp. 443-44.
22. *New York Times,* March 9, 1924.
23. *Fort Worth Star-Telegram,* January 15, 1922.
24. House, *Oil Boom,* pp. 56-57.
25. Barnes, *op. cit.,* pp. 614-15.
26. House, *Oil Boom,* p. 31.
27. James A. Clark and Michel T. Halbouty, *Spindletop* (New York, 1952), p. 87.
28. House, *Oil Boom,* p. 31.
29. Carl Coke Rister, *Oil! Titan of the Southwest* (Norman, 1949), pp. 185-88.
30. Wirt Hord, *Lost Dollars, or Pirates of Promotion* (Cincinnati, 1924), p. 13.
31. Rister, *op. cit.,* p. 394.
32. *World's Work,* XXVII (November, 1918), 510.
33. *New York Times,* April 7, 1923.

Folksay of Lawyers

HERMES NYE

IN THE DRAMA of folklore and folksong, the lawyer and the judge make frequent, if minor, appearances, but (perhaps unaccountably) they never attain the major roles of cultural hero or archetype.

The lawyer usually displays the Reynard-like characteristics of cleverness and dishonesty, and by most accounts is unscrupulous, grasping, and shrewd. For all his wit, however, he seldom appears to be rich—and in criminal cases at least his cause is almost invariably lost and his clients end up on the gallows or in being transported for life. His professional status is pretty well recognized; we find, for example, in Burl Ives's "Chivalrous Man-eating Shark,"

> A doctor, a lawyer, a preacher
> He'll gobble one any fine day;
> But the ladies, God bless them,
> He'll only address them
> Politely and go on his way.

References to counsel in folksong are frequent and so well known that only one or two instances will suffice.

The bawdy seventeenth-century French "party song" called "My Mother Chose My Husband," which has been so ably translated by Katherine Anne Porter, tells us that

> My mother chose my husband, a lawyer's son was he,
> And on the wedding night he came to bed with me.

Of the lawyer himself, the father of the bridegroom, we hear no more, but the mishaps of the bride are dealt with in considerable detail.

"The Durant Jail" casts a disdainful light upon the counselor:

> Now, here's to the lawyer, he'll come to your cell
> And swear he will free you in spite of all hell;
> Your money he'll get before he will rest,
> Then say, "Plead guilty, I think it is best."
> It's hard times in Durant Jail;
> It's hard times, po' boy.

The judge as well usually appears in an unsympathetic role, in a typical situation sentencing a mother's only joy to be hanged by the neck till dead. This is the case in most outlaw, bad-man, or gallows songs. "Po'Boy," or "As I Sat Down To Play Coon-Can," tells us,

> The jury found me guilty, Po'Boy,
> And the judge says, "You must die."

The old British broadside, "Botany Bay," the ancestor of "The Boston Burglar" and its progeny, states,

> At the Old Bailey Sessions, the judge to me did say,
> "The jury has found you guilty, lad, you must go to Botany Bay."

The exploits of Judge Roy Bean and his law west of the Pecos are too well known to be chronicled here.

Witness also the numerous jokes in which the counselor and the judge are shown in an unfavorable light. Here are two hoary examples.

A man observing a gravestone with the legend, "Here Lies Sam Jones, an Honest Man and a Lawyer," observes wryly, "There must be two men in *that* grave."

The young lawyer in court, on being asked if he was trying to show contempt of court, replies blithely, "No, Your Honor, I'm trying to conceal it."

Layman's law, or, as we might call it, *Corpus Juris Populi,* is a fascinating blend of fact, fancy, and half-truth. A few examples of popular assumptions, mostly fallacious, come readily to mind:

1. A lawyer should never defend a client whom he knows to be guilty. This blindly disregards the fact that every accused person has certain constitutional rights, such as the rights to counsel, to have witnesses subpoenaed in his behalf, and so on. In addition, this stricture would most certainly condemn at least 95 per cent of the criminal lawyers to a condition of perpetual starvation.

2. A check written on Sunday, or a check written in pencil (and, *a fortiori,* a check written on Sunday *and* in pencil), is invalid.

3. Oral testimony is not proof and just barely constitutes evidence. A frequently heard statement in this connection is, "He'll never prove it, it's just his word against mine."

4. An employer must give an employee two weeks' notice of termination of employment. The opposite, of course, is never the case.

5. Likewise, a landlord must always give a tenant one month's notice to vacate.

6. Every law firm, and especially every Irish law firm, numbers among its ranks at least "one smart Jew," so as to keep affairs on a sound commercial basis.

7. The "unwritten law," that a man may kill his wife's paramour, is, to the surprise of most lawyers in other jurisdictions, actually a part of the statutory law in Texas.

8. The *corpus delicti* is an actual human dead body. This is true in the case of murder or manslaughter, but it is far from being the case in arson and other crimes not involving the person.

9. If the defendant's address is unknown, it takes seven years to get a divorce. This is based on the assumption of death after seven years' disappearance.

FOLKSAY OF LAWYERS 95

10. "I had a good case but the lawyers sold out on me." This is a frequent plaint of the disappointed litigant and unfortunately is too often true. The selling-out usually takes the form of sloth or neglect rather than of downright dishonesty, but to a loser the distinction is too fine to detect with the naked eye.

11. Lawyers are students of Blackstone. Sir William Blackstone (1723-80), a highly unsuccessful English barrister, found his true vocation and a knighthood in the bargain by his teaching and his written *Commentaries*. That book was used, along with the Bible, Shakespeare, and Webster's *Dictionary*, as the complete library of many a frontier American lawyer up to sixty or seventy years ago. But not now.

The folksay of the lawyer is generally of a cynical if somewhat ponderous cast and of a punning nature. It may possess a fair amount of symmetry and an impressive though somewhat primitive rhythm:

1. Happus cappus (habeas corpus).
2. Notorious Republican (Notary Public).
3. Driving With Irene (D.W.I., or Driving While Intoxicated).
4. "Now comes Defendant and denies the allegations and defies the alligator" (parody on the phraseology of the general denial).
5. Dry writ (habeas corpus writ, made without bond).
6. "Are you practicing law or just practicing economy?" (question frequently asked young lawyers).
7. "Did you get justice or what you went after?" (query put to a lawyer on the way from the courthouse).
8. Greenback poultice (infallible remedy for the ills of the plaintiff in a damage suit).
9. In the iron (in jail).
10. Eyeball witness (eyewitness).
11. Meat witness (a witness in the flesh).
12. White-horse case (a precedent on all fours, so to speak).

13. Nickel-and-dime policy (automobile policy with five- and ten-thousand-dollar limit).

14. "Can't find his way to the courthouse" (said of inexperienced counsel).

15. "Made one $10.00 fee and several small ones" (popular gibe of depression days).

16. Served a term in college (served a term in prison).

17. "Depends on what the Judge had for breakfast" (the decision can go either way).

18. "A lawyer can't make any money in the courtroom" (belief inspired by the time-consuming procedures of trial).

19. "The ideal client is rich, guilty, and scared" (remark attributed to the counsel of Harry Sinclair in the Teapot Dome trials).

20. Philadelphia lawyer (smart cookie; of colonial derivation).

21. Sea lawyer; barracks-room lawyer; latrine lawyer (in the armed services—any smart clerk who studies the rules for his personal advantage).

22. "The lawyer who represents himself has a fool for a client."

23. "Eating his way to the wool-sack" (from the English Inns of Court, where one must eat a certain number of meals before attaining the upholstered dignity of the bench).

24. "Horseback opinion"—now, in more modern times, "Curbstone opinion" or "Cocktail party jurisprudence" (offhand opinion, costing nothing and usually worth just that).

25. "South side of the docket" (the defendant's position on the court's docket; insurance and other corporate counsel are usually referred to as "being on the south side of the docket").

In the field of criminal law, many of the phrases are lifted from the thieves' argot of the jailhouse:

1. "Maupry" (mythical crime, exhibiting a naked woman to a blind man).

2. "Breaking into jail without consent of the inmates"

(mythical crime, used in kangaroo court to relieve an inmate of his money).

3. "High-Five" (in Dallas, the city jail, now on the *fourth* floor, is still referred to as "High-Five" for the sake of alliteration).

4. "Cross-Bar Hotel" (jail).

5. "Two-time loser" (criminal who has served two terms in the penitentiary; in Texas this is significant because on conviction for a third time, the penalty is life imprisonment as an "habitch," or habitual criminal).

6. "New turnout" (fresh recruit to the field of prostitution).

7. "Free worlder," or "free world" (citizens not confined, and the world they inhabit).

8. "Make the street" (get out on bond).

9. "Hit the ground running" (got out on bond and then skipped).

10. "Put him on the ground" (get him out of jail).

11. "Six-shooter deputy" (constable with ostensible authority; usually the low-arm of a fee-hungry Justice of the Peace).

12. "Push-pull bond" (appearance bond, posted after habeas corpus hearing).

Lawyers' pronunciation, the *lingua franca* of the bar, reflects, according to some authorities, the wretched Norman influence following the Conquest (prior to which, supposedly, barristers spoke only the purest Ciceronian):

1. *Scire facias* is usually heard as "sire-ee faish-uss."

2. *Voir dire* is "vorr dear."

3. *Duces tecum*, it is true, comes off fairly well as "deo-keys tea-come."

4. *Certiorari* takes perhaps the worst drubbing of all, as "sir-show-rare-ee."

Feathered Duelists

HALDEEN BRADDY

OUT IN THE Paso del Norte country you might cuss a man and get by with it, but you would not get by with cussing his chickens, not his big red rooster.

This healthy westerner, close to the earth and in love with living, takes more pride in his fighting cocks than he does in his livestock. Something hot and vigorous in his blood makes him admire a rowdy rooster. He enjoys calf roping, bullfighting, and horse racing, to be sure; but his chest really expands with pride when he keeps fighting chickens. Owning a flock of champion cocks advertises to his neighbors that he has wealth enough to partake of the sweets of life. The cocker is the prince among sporting men.

Cockers who gather on the Texas-Mexico Border to pit their battling roosters bring these entries from far and near. Many come from Old Mexico; others fly the airways to El Paso from New Mexico, Oklahoma, and distant points of Texas. Still others live at the Pass itself, native *Paseños* who claim that the sun and wind of Borderland breed the finest brand of fighting cocks alive today. In the dust-laden air of the gusty Southwest all of the roosters, no matter where they come from, soon develop gravel in their craws, so that championship contests always feature ferocious but evenly-matched roosters. Their brilliant plumage, gleaming brightly as a choker of rubies in the ruff along the neck, derives, not from the soiling wind, but from rich feeding and the radiant sunshine of the southwestern

FEATHERED DUELISTS

winter. The cockers of El Paso walk with a strut. They believe in the prowess of their cocks and will back them with plenty of betting money.

For eight months, from early December to the Fourth of July, cockers live but for one purpose—to pit their cock on a Saturday night in a battle to the death. The cockfighting season opens at a period when outdoor sports have closed for the winter. Spectators throng to the heated indoor enclosures during the cold months of the year, surrounding the fighting pits in a circle of closely-packed bodies. More imposing pits have circular rows of grandstand seats. At these places bettors walk the rim of the pits flourishing fists full of greenbacks. Spectators comprise both men and women. All of them are intent, serious, well-behaved. Drinking, with its attendant merrymaking, is forbidden, because it would be dangerous to stumble into the pit. Cursing and loud talking also come under the ban, for the crowd wants to hear the referee announce the owners of the chickens and the cockmasters who handle the roosters in the respite between rounds. The best way to spend a cold winter evening on the Border is to see a cock fight in a warmly-heated arena.

Until recently, thrilling cock fights occurred in Juarez, Mexico. Now those days may be forever gone, because Juarez has banned the sport and closed its famous Pan-American Cocking Arena. On February 8, 1956, Ponciano Humberto Solorzano, a federal district attorney, went himself to the doors of this arena and personally shut them. He placed government seals on the locks. Then he ordered the manager, Abel Soto, arrested. This Mexican closure disappointed many cockers, as both Americans and Mexicans had frequented the Pan-American pit.

Immediately the enthusiasts turned their attention to the north banks of the Rio Grande, to the New Mexico pits adjoining El Paso. Here cockers brought their families, the women and children. Youngsters displayed zest for the sport, rallying the roosters with loud outcries. "Stick him in the heart!" some of them yelled, while others, more at home in Spanish, said, "Picale en el corazon!" All the time, the bettors kept shouting their odds in a pitch louder than the children. "Ocho a cinco!" (eight to five) announced one gamester, holding his money above his head as he walked about the ring. Somebody took that bet. Then the bettor became fevered with the gambling lust, for he saw his chicken beating its opponent. "Dos a uno! Dos a uno!" (two to one) he repeated frenziedly. This time there were no takers. The one-sided fight had suddenly ended. The bettor's chicken had sliced the throat of its adversary.

The appeal of novelty has nothing to do with the popularity of cockpitting. Border enthusiasts had their counterparts in the long ago. As old as civilized mankind, the sport entertained the Athenians of ancient Greece. Prince and populace attended the fights throughout that land. Soon enthusiasm for the sport spread in various directions, to Asia Minor, to the island of Sicily, and to cities like Alexandria, Delos, Rhodes, and Tanagra. The Romans at first pretended to despise this Greek diversion but in the end adopted it enthusiastically. They boosted cock fights as morale builders for their far-roaming legions. As they roamed northward, they introduced the pastime to other European races. Rooster fighting thus attracted devotees in all the major countries of Europe—in England, Germany, the Low Countries, and Spain.

Cockfighting probably entered the British Isles with Caesar's invasions in 55 B.C. and 54 B.C. or when Britain became a province under Agricola in 80 A.D. At first only the conquerors indulged in the sport; later the natives adopted it along with other Roman pastimes. In the English language the word "cocking" (fighting) was current *circa* 1230. The anonymous author of *How Goode Wyfe* (about 1450), in the Ashmole MS of the British Museum, warned his readers to stay away from the fights. "Ne go thou not to no wrastlynge," he said, and added, "Ne yet to no coke fyghtynge." Other moral writers and church dignitaries railed against the sport. Nonetheless fights occurred annually in early Britain on the school grounds under the supervision of the Masters. At the finish, the dead birds went to the schoolmasters, as noted about 1565 by N. Carlisle: "The said Schoolmaster shall... have use and take the profits of all such cock-fights... as are commonly used in Schools." By 1684 Charles II had a Royal Cock-Pit at Windsor. Kings like Henry VIII, James I, and both Charles I and II had royal cockmasters who presided over the pits at Whitehall.

Cocking entered America with the early British settlers, although New England always frowned on it. Today the United States has long had a prohibition against the sport, but it continues to be popular down South. Portable pits have been invented to avoid police raids. Since its founding by Richard Martin in 1824, the Society for the Prevention of Cruelty to Animals has vigorously opposed cockpitting. Its illegality has not stopped the cockers. Their vulgar colloquialism, "to beat cockfighting," has come to mean "to surpass everything else."

A fact not generally known in the United States is that cockfighting, not bullfighting, is the national sport of the Republic of Mexico. Mexican devotees include *peones* working on isolated ranches where staging a battle of roosters is much easier, much less expensive than fighting the bulls. Throughout South America cockfighting is a pastime of the people, not of the Latin aristocrats who have vigorously opposed it. In Argentina it gained serious criticism and recently was pronounced unlawful. Paraguay has prohibited it also. But the cocks have their partisans in spirited Puerto Rico, where it is the favorite pastime of poor and wealthy alike. Cuba also has recognized the strength of folk opinion by legalizing the sport and putting its operations within municipal approval.

At the Pass of the North, where two cultures meet, cockfighting has long been an established custom. At the end of the nineteenth century the notorious Juan Nepomuceno Cortina, King of Cattle Thieves, who had robbed Texas Border ranchers blind, was everywhere touted for being addicted to gambling and cockfighting. Probably no place in the world offers such a variety of breeding stocks and cockfighting skills as the twin cities of Juarez and El Paso. Here congregate the fowl-fanciers, *peones* from below the Rio Bravo, oilmen from Oklahoma, or foremen from the farspread King Ranch of South Texas. Here the gamblers and promoters flourish. Here the chicken trainers play and toil.

Al Pandelides, or "Lefty," is one of the really superior trainers on the Border. To put his cocks in fettle, he wraps miniature boxing gloves around their spurs, encouraging them in the art of sparring. So protected, the birds do not damage each other but get needed exercise in the fundamentals of cockfighting. The single largest factor in "Lefty's" success with the fowls derives from his own knowledge of the prize ring. For two years, 1954 and 1955, he held the title of middleweight boxing champion of Mexico.

There are plenty of Border men who "have taken the feather," or succumbed to the spell of cockpitting. Salvador Fierro, of Sahuarita, Arizona, has long been a devotee. So has Pablo Viramontes, of Las Cruces, New Mexico. So also has Chico Chavez, once the sheriff of Juarez, Mexico. Max Slade, of Tulsa, Oklahoma, has likewise won renown with his flocks. A frequent winner in Border derbies is M. L. Davis, of Alpine, Texas. Equally renowned cockers, who nomadically travel to mains from Arizona or Oklahoma to New Mexico, are Buckheister, Cunningham, Garcia, Kelly, O'Neale, Prichard, Royster, and Sanders. Their signatures on the pit blackboards become familiar names to cockfighting fans. George Simpson and "Bull" Adams, two of the wisest chicken men in El Paso, have trailed the sport for years. They travel to Oklahoma and various southern states to see champion roosters fight. Mr. Simpson and Mr. Adams know well the lingo of the pit and have bred many champion fighting fowls.

Beginning breeders choose their favorite color and select

a family of chickens that will breed true. A farm or a few acres in the country will provide the necessary facilities. Fowls need a place to fly and to range; they also require access to water. Gamecocks ordinarily enter their first mains when between one and two years of age. Before they go into the pit, they undergo intensive training.

The most important experience of the young stag commences when his trainer moves him from his solitary cage and places him in a hennery. There he bosses his harem of hens, living and learning the meaning of his cockhood. Later, when the trainer takes him away from the pullets, the cockerel turns into a bird of Mars. Now he has a lust to fight, his lust arising from his strong sex drive. For no other creature displays as much jealousy as the gamecock. In Shakespeare's *As You Like It,* Rosalind says to Orlando, "I will be more jealous of thee than a Barbary cock-pigeon over his hen." Jealousy and an instinct to fight are synonymous with the gamecock.

Pedigreed roosters cost a lot of money. A fine untrained cockerel may bring as much as fifty dollars. A trained cock, one who has graduated from muffs to lethally-pointed steel gaffs or long and razor-edged Mexican slashers, will sell in the hundreds. Few "Rocky Marcianos" survive repeated settings in a cocking main, where a "K. O." means curtains for the losers. Even when victorious, fowls often lose parts of their combs and one of their eyes. Birds who have won five or more fights may sell for $15,000. Usually a proved champion retires from the pit in order to become a brood cock in a hennery. Cock fanciers eagerly gather eggs from a breeding cock's hens. Then the gatherers pay "high" to farmers to hatch these prize eggs for them.

Ordinarily a gamecock needs no encouragement to fight. The folklore of fowls, however, contains ignoble instances to the contrary. When a beaten gamebird decides to withdraw from the battle, he lifts his hackle, showing to the spectators the white feathers underlying his ruff. This act gave rise to the famous expression, "showing the white feather," which symbolizes cowardice. When a rooster refuses to continue the fight, his handler places him breast-to-breast with the other chicken. Sometimes, to stimulate him, handlers force pellets of marihuana down his throat. If he still will not fight, it is ruled that he has forfeited the contest, and therefore his adversary wins.

Professional cockfighting is not for the poor man or the piker. Tall tales never appear in the legends of its gamblers; the plain truth is enough. In the big mains, wagers sometimes go as high as $5,000 on a single match and $10,000 on the main itself. The novice had better keep his eyes open and stay alert. An experienced fan never pays his bet until the birds are carried out, because a cock supine on his back may give a vicious slash and kill his opponent, or a bird that looks like a winner may awkwardly slice his own throat when threshing his feet about.

Cockfighting has no rival for excitement. It can forge men's nerves into steel. The primal release of pent emotions at the moment of the kill, springing from dark recesses of mental frustration, floods the spectator with a needed sense of relief. And so Chanticleer must die. Man's fascination with the kill goes deep; his passion for it, steady and abiding, is the same as that of ancient man. The average sportsman, who relishes a fight by creatures born for that purpose, hates to see the cockfighting season end.

Before Juarez banned cockfighting, an outstanding battle occurred across the Rio Grande. This contest may serve to explain how an actual fight takes place. It caused a lot of excitement among Border gamblers. The bout pitted the inexperienced but much-heralded cock *El Negro* against the veteran rooster *El Blanco*. Scheduled at three o'clock on a Sunday afternoon, the bout was to determine who was champion of the Juarez chicken pens.

El Negro, proudly owned by Juan Carlos Lopez, tipped the

scales at five and a half pounds, which is heavy for a fighting bird. His feathers gleamed black as jet. His whole appearance, from the bristling ruff about his neck to the belligerent stance of his strong gray feet, was so similar to that of a bird of carrion he might with full reason have borne some such name as "The Vulture."

El Blanco, the prize rooster of Seymour Miller's pen, had won many fights, enough to establish himself as a ruler of the roost and the chicken to defeat before any other could be named the champion. Spotlessly white in color, *El Blanco* weighed about the same as his opponent. He looked strong and durable but not so fierce of mien as *El Negro*.

Both roosters wore Mexican gaffs on their spurs—that is, double-edged, razor-like blades nearly three inches long. The two owners handled their birds soothingly, awaiting the signal from the cockmaster that would start the contest.

All at once came the word, "Pit!" The cockers immediately turned the birds loose at each other. Their beaks were keen as sabers; their combs stood erect. The small knives fixed on their spurs tore their flesh as cruelly as lances. Soon both cocks bled freely. Early in the test, gore accumulated on *El Blanco's* white feathers, turning them a vivid red. Between rounds, the owners patched up the wounds on their birds as best they could. Once or twice the men pursed their lips and blew hard on the feathers above the rumps of the birds. The hot, moist air served to stimulate the whole blood stream of the cock when the handlers blew strongly on this vital area. The men also applied their mouths to the injured necks of the birds, sometimes "creasing" them as they ran their lips up and down the necks. At other times they accepted the cock's head into their mouths to massage the wounded areas. After these procedures, both cocks re-entered the fray with quickened fervor, training their bright eyes fixedly on each other.

Midway of the fifth pitting, *El Blanco* tottered to the ground with a gaping hole in his head where the black one's spur had sunk. Groveling in the gravel, he shook spasmodically once or twice, and then he died. Digging his tired talons firmly in the hard earth, *El Negro* upreared himself, swelling his lungs with air, and let out a shaky clarion of victory. Exhausted as he was, he had grasped the fact that he was the winner and new champion.

Old Thurber

C. RICHARD KING

IN THE DAYS when locomotives burned coal, Thurber, in Erath County, Texas, was a company-owned town where thousands of miners dug coal during the day and sought relaxation at night. Thurber was a melting pot in which the ingredients refused to blend—the home of Poles, Germans, Italians, Mexicans, and others who built their own communities within the barbed-wire fence that surrounded the village. These peoples lived to themselves, and kept their old-country customs. Having come from countries where beer and wine formed a part of the daily diet, they drank liberally. They recalled with fondness and nostalgia the folk dances that they and their forebears had been accustomed to on the cobblestone squares of their native villages, so they held public dances.

To their conservative neighbors Thurberites brought lifted eyebrows. The mining community became known as a tough town in an area long devoted to agriculture and ranching, a wet spot on a dry plain.

Yet the very customs which caused concern among neighbors were those which gave Thurber its color, its particular flavor. Among the Anglos the calico ball was popular. Mrs. Hazel Miller, Stephenville, has in her possession an invitation her husband received at the turn of the century. The note tells of a calico ball to be held in the pavilion, a 120- by 40-foot structure built as the center of Thurber recreation. The invitation read:

For the giddy whirl
You will find the girl
Whose dress will compare
With the tie you'll find there.

A dollar bill
Dropped in the till
Will quite suffice
For music and ice.

Additional use of the tie for matching off couples was made popular at the apron-and-necktie parties. For these entertainments, each woman designed an unhemmed apron and matching tie. Each man received a tie as he entered the dance hall, and by matching his tie with an apron found his partner for the party. The couple continued to wear apron and tie, but part of the fun was a hemming contest, with a prize, often a cake, going to the man who did the neatest job of hemming his partner's apron.

The actual digging of the coal was done chiefly by Polish and Italian immigrants, who lived on Hill Number 3. A railroad which served the mines bisected the hill and the Europeans—putting the Poles on the south side of the track and the Italians on the north. Polander Hill had its own dance hall, and on the Italian Hill residents built their own recreation center. Each group retained its own folkways.

One of the most celebrated occasions in Thurber was a Polish wedding. For the exchange of vows, the Polish couple rode to the church in an open buggy, and behind the polished vehicle danced friends and attendants. An accordion player perched in the back of the buggy played traditional Polish wedding songs, and the entourage following the music danced and sang from the bride's home to the church. Dressed in their best—the bride usually in traditional white but always covered with a full white veil, and the groom in black—the couple made this ride to show off wedding finery, a part of the celebration. Although most of the services were held in the Catholic church, they often were read by a Protestant minister.

Following the exchange of vows, the couple again mounted the buggy and, followed by friends, rode to the home of the bride's parents for the wedding feast. Here hundreds of guests were served three meals a day so long as the celebration lasted. Pastries, beer, wine, whiskey, meats, and traditional Polish dishes were kept on a plank table throughout the affair. Antoine Dudko, a resident of Thurber, describes this spread of food as resembling a smorgasbord—an array of pastry, a variety of meats, breads, salads, and fruits. A family of means took this method of displaying affection for their daughter—the greater the wealth, the greater the display of food at the reception.

Night meant a wedding dance in the home of the parents or in the Polish Dance Hall. Joe Martin of Sinton, a former Thurber resident, recalls, "The Poles would eat, drink, and dance for three or four days. Sometimes wind up in a battle royal too, and I believe the weddings were sometimes arranged by the parents. You know the matchmaking, like European royalty." Music usually was presented by an accordion player familiar with native folk tunes as well as current hits.

One tradition of the wedding called for the bride's furnishing a large number of inexpensive dinner plates. These were stacked in one corner of the dance hall, and before any man could dance with the bride or one of her attendants, he had to throw a coin upon the plate with such force that it shattered the dinnerware. A silver dollar was the recommended coin; often the man who tried smaller denominations of change discovered that the task had proved more expensive than if he had used the dollar in the first place. No matter how many times he threw a coin and failed to break the plate, he could not regain any of the money.

"If you didn't break the plate, the bride got the dollar," writes Martin. Dudko comments that the money was used for the bride to set up her new house or to help her parents pay the expenses of the wedding feast.

In her thesis, "Thurber: Life and Death of a Texas Ghost

Town," Mary Jane Gentry writes: "It was not uncommon for the newly married couple to receive three or four hundred dollars by the time the celebration was over. If the bride was pretty and popular, and if she chose her attendants with care, the 'plate breaking' income would often be more."

Martin writes that "the bride danced with guests for a silver dollar. I heard of one bride who danced till she died."

Dudko remembers that music for many of the wedding dances was furnished by anyone who could play—a violin, a jew's-harp, anything. He used to play the jew's-harp.

Although the weddings were the big celebrations for the Polish people, they also observed traditional wakes at funerals, remaining with the bodies two or three nights. Graves were dug at night. Burials often were followed by dances as soon as the grieved members of the family returned home. Mrs. Henry Latimer recalls that when one of her Thurber neighbors lost a child, the family returned from Graveyard Hill, rolled back the rug, encouraged the accordion player, and held a dance.

Not to be outdone by their southern neighbors, the Italians also held big celebrations at their weddings. Usually a band provided music the first day, and an accordion player was retained for the remainder of the observance. A special rice dish called *rizzotto* was served to wedding guests. For many Thurber weddings, the rice was cooked in a large washtub, into which were poured gallons of chicken broth, chicken giblets, tomato sauce, and grated cheese. Along with *rizzotto* was served a salad, a variety of meats, and barrels of wine.

As the wine and beer kegs were emptied during the feast, they were stacked on top of each other. The success of a social event was measured by the size of the pyramid of empty kegs.

The eve of the Lenten season was celebrated by many of the Italian families with a miniature Mardi Gras. Men dressed in costumes and masks, going from house to house entertaining children. Each housewife in whose home the jesters visited would serve wine and *crostoli*, a special pastry which took almost a whole day to prepare. To make it, the Italian wife mixed flour dough, eggs, and brandy. Rolled into an extremely thin layer, the dough was cut into strips which were tied into bowknots. These bowknots were fried in deep grease, then dipped in sugar and cooled.

The Italian women were famous for their homemade bread. Each Italian home in which there was a boarder had an outdoor oven made of brick, stone, and clay, resembling an Eskimo igloo in shape. Many Italian women served boarders, who lived in tents outside the homes. "They would build a big wood fire in the oven and when it was white hot, pull the fire, clean off the brick or stone and put in bread or even pies or meat," writes Martin. They baked once a week, the average oven holding from fifteen to eighteen large, round loaves of bread. The baking produced a yeasty odor, especially when the corrugated iron doors of the ovens were opened. Dudko recalls that large wooden paddles or spatulas were used for inserting the loaves into the hot ovens.

"New bread and old wine" went together in the minds of Italian miners, so their homes had large iceboxes built to hold kegs of beer and wine. Saturday night called for the tapping and drinking of several kegs. Neighbors who assembled for these evenings contributed toward the cost of the drink.

Sunday also meant beer, but it ushered in another pastime, *boccie*, a game similar to bowling. Any number of men could play so long as the sides were equally divided. Solid wooden balls about the size of Texas grapefruit were used, one side possessing balls marked with two small grooves circling the ball and the opposite side using balls without grooves. Although the game score was usually set at twelve, it could be increased by mutual agreement of participants. A small ball, called the "balline," was thrown to the end of the alley, and players tried to hit the balline with the big balls. Each hit on the balline counted as a score. If no player hit, the large wooden ball nearest the balline scored.

If several wooden balls were an equal distance from the balline, each was allowed a score. Naturally, players tried to knock opponents' balls away from the balline and to shove partners' balls closer. Martin writes that the game often was played in singles and that the balline was gray or white for identification.

Members of the losing team bought a round of beer for the winners, and another game got underway. Often only darkness could bring the match to a halt.

Italian and Polish folkways gave Thurber her color, but it was the badger fights that brought her fame. The *Texas Mining and Trade Journal* of March 3, 1900, contains the statement that "more distinguished personages have yanked the ferocious badger right here in Thurber than in any other town in the badger-fighting state," and the *Dallas Morning News* once tagged Thurber the "Bayreuth of Badger Fights." Such tribute probably was due to the interest and enthusiasm that Edgar L. Marston, president of the Texas and Pacific Coal Company, held for the sport. Seldom did he visit Thurber without introducing a Yankee guest to the thrill of a badger fight.

Much of the success of the sport depended upon Marston's glib description and his ability to create within the innocent northerner the desire to witness a badger fight. Throughout his description of the affair, Marston took every opportunity to mention that badgers were becoming scarce and soon would be extinct in that part of the country. He would assure the eager Yankee that he would wire colleagues in Thurber a request that they search for a badger. Inevitably, the answer followed that the fiercest badger in history had been caught and that the dog was straining for a chance to fight him. The telegram would encourage Marston to describe to his associate a famous white bulldog, Old Dewey, that had scrapped with more badgers than any other animal in the mesquite-covered hills. Often ripped open by the claws of the ferocious badgers of the past, his body now contained dozens of scars.

By the time Marston's special railway car arrived in Thurber, his guest was well briefed in the traditions of the West and he longed with all his heart for the badger fight to begin. Comments about the spirit of the badger, tossed about in his hearing, further whetted his appetite.

By nine o'clock, the usual hour for badger fights to begin, miners had crowded into the smoke-filled Opera House, their voices tinged with excitement. The Yankee could not keep from observing that on the well-lighted stage sat none other than Old Dewey himself, growling and snarling and straining. Near by was a barrel covered with a "tote sack," and from it snaked a long rope. The visitor could only guess that the rope was tied to a badger, which would have to be pulled from his barrel.

The *Thurber Journal* of January 8, 1901, describes a fight:

> A large crowd assembled ... and everyone was anxious to bet a few dollars upon the result. The bulldog was fierce and had many backers, but the badger was not without friends who had the money to back their judgment and many large bets were made.

The newcomer was warned to place no bets until he was more familiar with the sport, so he had to be content to listen to the frenzied voices around him and to watch the excitement with which last-minute wagers were made. As fight time approached, search was begun for someone to pull the badger from the barrel. This part of the fight was recorded in the *Thurber Journal* of May 22, 1908:

> Quite a contest came up as to who should pull the badger from his hiding place and several strove for the honor, but were disqualified on account of having money on the result. Several minutes were consumed in finding someone who did not have anything wagered on the result.

That someone, naturally, was the Yankee, who qualified with unanimous approval. Tension mounted as he climbed to the stage. Through his mind ran visions of how he would relate the experience of the badger fight to his New York friends.

Old Dewey tugged, growled, and groaned for action. As the Yankee hesitantly grasped the rope, a miner yelled, "Jerk the blame thing's head off! My money's on the dog!"

When the signal finally came, the Yankee pulled with all his might. Out of the barrel and on stage rolled the badger, the force of the pull drawing it near the feet of the Yankee. He stood amazed. Speechless. Instead of exposing the animal he had expected, he had drawn an ordinary household article from the barrel. And Marston had been truthful when he had commented upon the rarity of the item, for it had indeed become scarce with the installation of indoor bathrooms.

The "fight" over, the miners adjourned to the Snake Saloon, where kegs of beer had been iced for the occasion. Here, around a horseshoe bar which Thurberites boasted was the largest and busiest between Fort Worth and El Paso, spectators commented upon badger fights of the past. "The visitor then became a life member of the famous 'Badger Club' whose members are scattered all over the world, but whose initiations took place in Thurber," observed a writer in the *Thurber Journal* dated May 22, 1908. And here the enamelware chamber pot was autographed by friends who had witnessed the initiation.

SOURCES: Interviews with Mrs. Wanda Newman, Mrs. Hazel Miller, Mr. and Mrs. Henry Latimer, Mrs. M. L. Ballard, all of Stephenville, Antoine Dudko of Thurber, and Joe Martin of Sinton; files of *Texas Mining and Trade Journal* and *Thurber Journal;* clippings from *Dallas Morning News;* and thesis by Mary Jane Gentry, "Thurber: Life and Death of a Texas Ghost Town" (University of Texas, 1946).

Ghost Stories From a Texas Ghost Town

TUCKER SUTHERLAND

WINDING beneath the drooping willows, overflowing the flat prairies of mesquite and huisache, and curving beneath age-old live oaks, the muddy Nueces River has watched history pass by. This river, once a highway for the Lipan Apache Indians, later became a disputed boundary between Mexico and Texas; and today the lusty river feeds rich black land and waters a city of almost 200,000. A huge dam in San Patricio County has spanned its banks and a tremendous fresh-water lake is forming. The lake is already crowded with summer homes and developing industrial sites—the modern world is making a home along the old river.

But there is one place, a few miles below the big lake, that time has overlooked. This is the ghost town of San Patricio, which was once the county seat of a county that extended from a hundred miles north of Corpus Christi all the way to the Rio Grande. It was a flourishing settlement of Irish immigrants where adventurers of Mexico and the United States met, gambled, settled, and often fought. However, San Patricio de Hibernia, as it was called in 1828 when founded by John McMullen and James McGloin, is no longer filled with the bustling activities of the frontier. The railroad passed up San Patricio, and as a result so did history. Yet many years after the decline of San Pat, the ghosts of Mexican soldiers, Irish immigrants, and other early adventurers are still seen and discussed.

It was in the brush country around San Patricio that I spent many happy hours of my childhood—swimming, hunting, camping, and listening to tales of years gone by. I can remember as though it were this very night sitting by a campfire of crackling mesquite listening to ghost stories while waiting for the yelp of the coon hounds. I gulped down every word as the gospel truth and every shadow was a spook on those moonlight nights.

Years later I found ghost stories still interesting. My interest in ghosts was more objective, however, and I became a ghost hunter. Phantom stories no longer served as just entertaining tales; now they became psychic phenomena which interested me greatly. I questioned and searched. From a volume entitled *Ghosts Vivisected*[1] I learned the most popular types of ghosts and read case after case that could be backed up by substantial evidence. The book had taken a formula for investigating ghost stories from Professor G. J. Romanes, a noted Canadian physiologist. I adopted this method as my own with one change. Professor Romanes would not accept stories secondhand; however, since seeing ghosts seems to have gone out of style in this materialistic world, I am forced to accept the secondhand versions. Most of the exciting stories can be verified by the friends and children of those who have seen phantoms, and so it is the thirdhand version that I strive to rule out. But, no matter what the source, ghost stories fascinate me and I often overlook their implausibility.

I have been able to find some people still living who have seen ghosts and can furnish a firsthand version. One of these is Blas Pérez, a man of Mexican descent, who was raised on a farm close to San Patricio. Blas and his two older brothers—Juan and Santos—often hunted the thick brush for deer and other game to feed their family. The boys usually finished their chores about dusk and headed across the fields with their rifles, hoping to get in place along a fence row before the deer came into the fields to feed. Deer usually feed all night under a full moon, and so it was one of these moonlit nights (a favorite time for ghosts) that they settled into their hiding place. The boys adjusted their eyes to the dim light and began scanning the brush line directly facing them. Everything was still when suddenly something white moved in the brush slightly to their left. Thinking it was the flash of a whitetailed deer, they yanked up their rifles and waited for the deer to walk into the clearing. Then before their wide eyes two men, dressed completely in white, walked out of the mesquite tangle. It was a long walk to the nearest neighbors and while the boys lay still and puzzled, the strangers dressed in white came nearer. Blas said a chill ran down his spine when the strangers approached and the brothers held their breaths and flattened closer to the ground because the figures before them *had no heads.*

"They walked past us and right through the closed gate in the fence, as if nothing were there," Blas said. "Then we watched them cross another field, and go through two more gates that were closed, turn right and disappear into the brush. I wanted to shoot them but my brother Juan wouldn't let me."

Blas said that on another occasion when hunting in the same field the boys saw a light moving toward them from an adjoining field. They watched it slowly move around in the field directly to their left. Finally they got up enough courage to investigate. As they approached, the light flew into the dark sky and disappeared into the brush at the same spot they had seen the two headless men emerge. Blas said that later they saw the light several times, but every time they approached it flew into the woods. They finally stopped hunting in this field.

Although the headless ghosts seen by Blas Pérez are interesting, they are a type that can never be backed up by substantial evidence, since the ghosts actually had no motive. This is often the case with stories of headless and other weird forms of phantoms.

One of the most popular types of ghosts is the type which presents some premonition. The stories of this sort can very often be substantiated. Take the story told to me by Rachel

Bluntzer Hebert, who has written a book of poems and other material about San Patricio.[2] Her story is about McMullen and McGloin, the empresarios of San Patricio. It seems that after the town was settled McMullen moved to San Antonio, which is about 120 miles from San Patricio. One night while McGloin was sitting by his fireplace he looked up and saw his partner McMullen standing in the firelight. McMullen's shirt was covered with blood and McGloin was shocked speechless for a few moments. Here was his friend, whom he believed to be more than a hundred miles away, now standing before him in a bloody shirt—and he had made no sound when he entered. Finally, McGloin got hold of his senses and said, "What do you want, John?" McMullen looked at him a moment more and disappeared without a word.

The next morning McGloin saddled up his horse and headed to San Antonio, because he was certain something was wrong. On the way to San Antonio he stopped at his nephew's house to tell him of the occurrence. This nephew, Pat McGloin, verified his uncle's story and thus established very substantial evidence for a ghost story that had a motive. For when McGloin arrived in San Antonio he found that his friend had been murdered the night before at the same time he had seen his bloody ghost a hundred miles away in San Pat.

Another story of an event which took place in the town of San Patricio has long been talked about. However, I have never received a firsthand version, and I prefer to present the tale as I got it from several sources. The startling event took place sometime after the Texas Revolution. A group of men were passing through on their way to opening parts of Texas south of the Nueces. In those days the river was crossed by a toll ferry. The men arrived at San Pat late and decided to spend the night camping out, intending to cross early the next morning. The group made camp near the graveyard and turned in early. During the night they were awakened by loud noises coming from the direction of the cemetery. All the men awoke and listened to the sounds, which they decided sounded like men fighting. Then in the dark above the graveyard they saw a battle raging between Texas frontiersmen and Mexican soldiers. The visitors packed, saddled, and quickly rode to the home of the ferry captain, demanding that he take them across the river immediately. Their wish was granted.

Blas Pérez told me of another legend that lives among the Spanish-speaking people of the area. About three miles downriver from the town there was at one time a ford. As he tells the story, a group of Spaniards were hauling a huge wagon of gold to Mexico when they were attacked on the bank of the river by bandits. The robbers murdered all of the Spaniards and killed their mules, then hid the gold until they could return. However, the treasure was never recovered, and now the area is thickly grown over with brush. But the ghosts of the murdered Spaniards still roam through the sky in their phantom wagon looking for their gold.

Blas says that he and his brothers have heard the rumble of the ghost wagon and the shouts of the Spaniards. He says it sounds as if the wagon is right on top of you; the shouting men pass overhead and off across the river. This story is not one of the distant past, for people still report hearing the wagon in the sky, according to Blas.

Another familiar ghost which has been sighted too many times in the area to be just a product of the imagination is the ghost rider of Lookout Hill. Rachel Hebert furnished me with a secondhand version of this story which she got from her mother, Mrs. Bluntzer, who saw the ghost. Mrs. Bluntzer, a Negro boy, and a ranch hand were on the way to San Pat from Mathis, where the boy and the ranch hand had met Mrs. Bluntzer's train with a buggy. Mathis is about ten miles from San Pat, and Lookout Hill, the highest point of ground in the area, is about halfway. Mrs. Bluntzer and the ranch hand were in the buggy and the Negro boy was riding out to the side on a horse. They reached the hill about dusk. Suddenly the horses reared and dashed forward in fright. Racing toward them from the left was a man dressed in Mexican charro clothes with a big sombrero. The rider was on a big gray horse that made not a sound on the ground as it sailed toward the buggy. Then, much to the amazement of the passengers, the horseman rode directly into the wheel, then emerged in the dust behind the buggy and raced off across the hill.

The legend that goes with the ghost rider of Lookout Hill began many, many years ago. A Kentucky gentleman riding a dappled gray mare arrived in San Patricio one day carrying bags of gold, with which he planned to buy a ranch. The man left San Pat, rode on across the Rio Grande, and returned a month later. On the night of the full moon the man decided to ride out of town. When he left from Sullivan's general store he was wearing gray charro clothes and a big sombrero. Later the same night a rough-looking rider drew up at Sullivan's store wearing gray charro clothes and riding a dappled gray mare. He said he had won the mare and the clothes gambling. The Kentucky gentleman was never seen again, unless it is his ghost that rides Lookout Hill.

One of the ghost stories I have not been able to substantiate is that of the first and only woman ever hanged in Texas. Since my boyhood days I have heard that the ghost of Chepita Rodriguez haunts the people of San Patricio because they hanged her. Whether her ghost has ever really been seen or not I cannot prove, but nonetheless her story is interesting.

Chepita was the daughter of a Mexican citizen who had fled the ruthless dictatorship of Santa Anna to join the rebel force of Texas. During the fighting her father was killed, and Chepita was left in the new land alone. She took up with a Texas cowboy and was soon the mother of a son. In time the cowboy deserted her, taking the son with him. Lonely and brokenhearted, she moved into a small shack in the northern part of San Patricio County. The frontier was booming, and many travelers who were overtaken by nightfall in the middle of the forest found this humble cabin a welcome sight. A number of gamblers and cowboys who frequently came this way made it a habit to stay the night at Chepita's place. For a small sum Chepita fed the visitors and carried their water, but her life was without happiness.

One day John Savage, a local cattle rustler, rode up to Chepita's shack carrying five hundred pieces of gold in his saddlebags. While she was fixing supper for him another horseman approached. Chepita looked out the door and jumped back in amazement. "It was her old lover, the father of her child. But no, the rider is too young to be him. But it looks just . . . it must be, . . . it was . . . her son."

The new visitor brought back many sad memories; after finishing the supper (she did not mention to the visitor who she was) Chepita walked out behind her cabin and sat down on a live oak stump reminiscing. A scream woke her from her sad dreams and she ran into the house. No one was there. She heard a horse gallop off and looked outside. There lay the bloody body of John Savage. He had been slaughtered with Chepita's ax, and his saddlebags were gone. So was her son.

Chepita was brought to San Patricio and charged with the murder of John Savage. Chained to the wall inside the new courthouse, she refused to talk about what had happened. There she stayed until the day of her trial. Many women and children came to visit her, and some brought food and tobacco. When the trial came Chepita said only one thing: "I am not guilty!" But she was found guilty and sentenced to death by hanging. Only one person ever heard the true story of the murder and that was Mrs. Kate McCumber, but she was sworn to secrecy until after the hanging. They hanged Chepita without a blindfold from a mesquite tree overlooking the Nueces. Her body was dumped into a wooden crate and buried in a shallow grave. They said she killed Savage for his gold, but it was later found intact in the saddlebags. For a long time the fate of Chepita weighed heavily on the minds of San Patricio citizens, and it was rumored that sometimes her ghost could be heard crying along the river bank.

No collection of ghost stories would be complete without one about a headless horseman, and who ever heard of a ghost town without one? John Bluntzer was riding from the Odom ranch to the Bluntzer ranch, through territory which was reported to hide just such a ghostly horseman. It was about dusk as Bluntzer plunged into the thick brush. As he rode along he thought he heard another horse. He stopped. The noise stopped. He rode on and the other hoofbeats continued. He stopped again. The noise stopped. Each time Bluntzer galloped ahead the noise moved at the same pace. He peered back through the brush, but in the pale light he saw nothing alarming. Then he saw a slight movement in the trees. He yanked his gun from its holster and fired. He moved back cautiously, and this time there were no hoofbeats echoing those of his horse. Slowly he edged toward the spot where he had seen the movement. And there the ghost lay before him: a prize stud donkey, which belonged to the Odom ranch, with a bullet through its head. And according to Mrs. Loree Russek of Mathis, who told me the story, this was the end of one headless horseman who haunted San Patricio.

1. Anna Maria Diana Wilhelmina [Pickering], *Ghosts Vivisected; an Impartial Inquiry into Their Manners, Habits, Mentality, Motives, and Physical Construction* (New York, 1958).

2. Rachel Bluntzer Hebert, *Shadows on the Nueces* (Emory, Georgia, 1942).

Old Days at Cold Springs

WILLIAM HENRY HARDIN

A PERSON traveling along the highway from Temple to Gatesville, Texas, will notice a side road to the left just after gaining the top of the hill on the other side of the Leon River. This side road descends into Owl Creek Valley. A few miles up this valley is the site of the old Dunn school, which was called "county line" because it marked the boundary between Bell and Coryell counties.

Perhaps a mile above this point the traveler will cross a bridge over Preacher's Creek. Just on the other side of Preacher's Creek is a wooden gate barring further progress. It has a sign on it stating that beyond that point is a military reservation. If, however, the spirit of adventure has brought the wayfarer thus far over this rough and unimproved road, mere signs upon a gate will not deter him. The gate is not usually locked, and, if it should be, a bypass around an isolated gate on the Fort Hood reservation is not too hard to find.

About a mile farther up Owl Creek is a bare "lover's leap" cliff or "bluff" (as it is called locally) looming up on the south side of the creek. This bluff once overlooked the thriving town of Seattle, Texas. Formerly a cotton gin, a blacksmith shop, and several business establishments were located here. It was here that all manner of community transactions were accomplished, the spring seed bought, and the fall cotton sold.

If it were not for the "lover's leap" cliff, the site of Seattle would be very difficult to find because the few foundations that now remain upon it are hidden by rank growths of weeds and thickets. Less than a mile upstream lies another historic site. Here was located Cold Springs. In the vicinity of a well-nigh everliving spring of cold clear water were once a school, a church, a Farmer's Union store, and a few residences. All that remains now is the spring, fully as vigorous as it ever was, and a crumbling stone wall that was once a part of the church. The few concrete foundations, the "lover's leap" bluff, the crumbling church wall, and the bubbling cold springs are all that physically remain of what was once the Cold Springs community, but the folk who once lived here still cherish their memories of the place.

A short way downstream from the springs was the Old Baptizing Hole where the Baptist preacher, Jack Hardin, baptized his converts early each summer. (It was said that the Baptists *had* to hold their revivals early in the season, because the baptizing hole in Owl Creek always dried up later in the summer. After all, it did not take much water for the Methodists to sprinkle their converts.) One thing that Uncle Jack could be sure of during each summertime camp meeting held at Cold Springs was that Ludy Whitmore would find some pretext to renew her religious enthusiasm and take part in the baptizing.

She would become reconverted every summer and be a zealous churchgoer for a few months. She never missed an opportunity to testify for the Lord—even to the extreme of doing it during the revivals held by the Methodists, usually later in the season than the Baptists' evangelical meetings. Ludy's religious fervor would die down as the winter progressed, and by the time of the next Baptist revival, her spiritual status would have reached its lowest ebb, and she would be ready to repeat the entire sequence of events again. After baptizing Ludy for the third summer in a row, Uncle Jack remarked to a confidant, "If I ever get another chance at her, I'll hold her under till she bubbles!"

It was in a brush arbor which was built beside the church each summer that Uncle Daniel Bundren, a deacon in the Cold Springs Baptist Church, was taking his accustomed nap during the sermon—undoubtedly dreaming of the double-header baseball game that certainly would be played somewhere in the community that afternoon. Preacher Hardin was concluding his sermon. He fervidly demanded of his congregation, "How can a sinner get to Heaven?" With greater emphasis he repeated his query. "How *can* a sinner get to Heaven?" The increased pitch of the preacher's voice awoke Uncle Daniel from his nap and, before realizing where he was, he shouted, "Slide! You son-of-a-gun, SLIDE!"

Aunt Bell and Uncle Dick Glass lived in a house within a stone's throw of the church. They were ardent prohibitionists, but Aunt Bell kept a bottle of bourbon on hand for medicinal purposes. Uncle Dick was subject to spells with his heart and whiskey was the only remedy. People doctored themselves pretty much in those days. Doctors usually did not get around then unless you were really dying, and most of the time after you were dead. Folks were always making remarks about Uncle Dick's "playing off" on Aunt Bell just to get a dose of his medicine. She took little stock in these remarks, but she did keep the "medicine" under lock and key in her trunk to insure that it was used only in emergencies. Still and all, Uncle Dick had an awful lot of fainting spells when a new flask of medicine was on hand.

One fall they were gathering the potatoes. Uncle Dick was working the turning plow and the rest of the family and a couple of neighbors were doing the picking. Suddenly Uncle Dick pulled a faint and collapsed down on the newly plowed ground. Aunt Bell was scared nearly to death. "I'll declare to goodness!" she hysterically cried, "I don't know what I'm gonna do! We ain't got a drop of whiskey in the house!"

Upon this announcement, Uncle Dick's eyes quickly flicked open. He slowly got up from the ground, gathered up the reins, and started plowing up potatoes again. He muttered as he slowly trudged off down the row, "No more whiskey—no more faint."

All the members of the Cold Springs Baptist Church felt that they were very tolerant and wholly without prejudice toward the Negro race. Of course everyone was expected to keep in his place! However, there was only one Negro family in the entire community and all of its members were fully used in servile capacities. Old Ed Sims, the father of this Negro family, worked for everyone in the community during the harvesting season, and was employed for the most part the remainder of the year as a stable boy for Uncle Jack Hardin. Uncle Jack was awfully embarrassed one time when old Ed decided that he wanted to join his church.

"Now, look here, Ed," Uncle Jack advised in answer to the old Negro's request, "why don't you take a few days off and go over in the Whitehall community and join the colored church over there? I hear tell that's a lively congregation."

"Nah, Uncle Jack," Ed insisted, "I'd much ruther b'long to your church."

Well, Uncle Jack hemmed and hawed and finally passed the matter off by advising old Ed to pray to the Lord for guidance. "You'll always find the answer to your problems if you take them to the Lord in prayer," Uncle Jack opined. Thus the matter rested for some time. The crops were laid by and Uncle Jack held one revival over at Pidcoke and then a real long one over at Hurst Springs. When it was about time for all the cotton picking to be finished, he returned to the old home place to rest up from his evangelistic labors. One day he saw Ed Sims and wondered how his religious problem had turned out. So he called old Ed over to the gallery where he was resting in the shade and began to talk to him. After innumerable pleasantries of a variegated nature, Uncle Jack finally turned the conversation upon the matter of old Ed's finding a church home.

"Did you take it to the Lord in prayer?"
"Yassuh."
"Well, did the Lord answer your prayers?"
"Yassuh."
"What did you ask for?"
"I ax the Lord," replied old Ed, "if'n He wouldn't pervide a way fer dis ole nigger to be 'mitted to Uncle Jack Hardin's church down in Cold Springs."
"What did the Lord say?" queried Uncle Jack. "Was His answer rewarding?"
"The Lord say," replied old Ed solemnly, "go on, nigger! I'se been trying to get in there *myself* for twenty-five year and *I* ain't made it yet!"

One day while Uncle Jack was going in his buggy down to Leon Junction to meet the train, he saw Pete Sims, a ten-year-old member of Ed Sims's family. Pete was walking along barefooted and carrying a basket. Uncle Jack picked the lad up and let him ride on into town with him. The basket was covered with a white cuptowel, but Uncle Jack was soon made aware of the contents. "You want to buy a cat?" Pete asked almost as soon as he had seated himself in the buggy. Removing the towel, he revealed six young kittens probably about a week old. Uncle Jack did not succumb to the boy's efforts to sell him a cat and, arriving at the depot, he dropped the lad off. As Pete trudged on down the dusty road toward Cavitt's store, Uncle Jack heard him mumble, "Guess these little old Mefdist kittens ain't worth much no how."

The boy's statement intrigued Uncle Jack considerably, and about a week later he picked young Pete up again while going toward Leon Junction. As soon as the lad was in the buggy, he asked, "You want to buy a Baptist kitten?"

Uncle Jack eyed the boy sharply and said, "What do you mean by Baptist kittens? Last Saturday you said they were Methodists."

"That's right," Pete quickly agreed. "But that was *last*

Saturday. The kittens' eyes is opened now and they has seen the light. Naturally, they is now Baptists."

Uncle Jack bought two of the Baptist kittens for fifteen cents and took them home.

Keeping the wolf from the door was a continuing problem for the old Negro stableman who worked for Uncle Jack. While old Ed worked all the time, as did all of his children who were big enough to do so, it seemed that there were always just more mouths to feed than there was food to place in them. Despite the help of his many white friends and all the intensive efforts of old Ed himself, things became quite desperate one winter. Ed talked the situation over with Uncle Jack and received the usual stand-by advice: "Take it to the Lord in prayer; ask and ye shall receive."

So, with no other solution in sight, old Ed repaired to the barn to engage the Lord with his request. One of Uncle Jack's boys eavesdropped upon the old Negro's entreaty to the Almighty. Old Ed found himself a secluded place in one of the back horse stalls, knelt down, and bowed his head. "Lord," he reverently implored of the Deity, "I've tried for a long time not to bother you with my troubles, 'cause I know these white folks keeps you busy enough as it is. So, Lord, if you'll just take care of this one order upon your bounty, I'll shore try to let you alone at least through next year's crop. Send me a barrel of flour, and a barrel of 'lasses—a barrel of sugar and a barrel of salt—and a barrel of pepper and... Naw, Lord, hold *that* one. That's *too damn much pepper!*"

It is rather hard to look at one of the staid pillars of the local Masonic lodge and deacons of the Cold Springs Baptist Church today and associate this same character with his cuttings-up fifty or more years ago. Now take Jack Palmer, who is just as conservative and dignified a man as you could imagine any human being—a good neighbor, pays his debts, and would not say "Hell," even if he had a mouthful. When he was a young'un, though, he was a caution.

The first day he went to school to Cousin Richmond Hardin down at the Cold Springs school, Jack was a strange boy, and Cousin Richmond naturally wanted to break the ice and become friends with the child.

"What's your name, son?" he kindly inquired.

"Jack Palmer."

"Jack Palmer," Cousin Richmond repeated. "Now *that* is a name! Can you spell it?"

"Hell, no!" little Jack exclaimed. "This is my first day in school."

A short time later in the school term, Jack was standing with several other primer students at Cousin Richmond's knee, calling out the letters of the alphabet as they were pointed out to him. After he had called off several of them including A, B, C, and D, Cousin Richmond indicated a letter entirely out of sequence away down the line. Jack looked up at the teacher very solemnly, as if this were not quite fair, and impatiently exploded, "Jesus Christ! *You* guess that one!" Young Jack, in this instance, immediately became acquainted with the requisite stimulation to his learning processes applied by means of Cousin Richmond's teaching aid, a willow switch.

Jack's mother, Mrs. Minnie Palmer, who is now over eighty-four years old and is still living on the old home place located just outside the Fort Hood boundary along Preacher's Creek, likes to reminisce over the doings of her nine children and their friends. Her favorite saying is that there were just as many juvenile delinquents in the old days—but not as many got caught then as today.

The elder Palmers were regular members of the Cold Springs Baptist Church, but this fact did not deter their children, especially the curiosity-seeking boys, from attending the preaching services and revivals of the other denominations. During the summertime the parents habitually kept their bed on the front gallery, and the children would usually make down pallets out there, too. One hot summer night when Jack was about fourteen years old, he came in from attending the Unknown Tongues revival with his brother T. J. The parents had retired hours before, but when Jack came in he brought a quilt out on the gallery and bedded down for the night. Noticing that his father was apparently awake, Jack began talking to him.

"Paw?" Jack asked, to ascertain if his father was really awake.

"What?" Mr. Palmer answered.

"T. J. joined the Holy Rollers tonight."

"He did!" the father exclaimed, surprised that his son would depart in this manner from the way of his ancestors.

"Yeah," returned Jack, "and I would of too, if I'd had a new pair of pants."

"Well, I'll be damned!" old man Palmer exclaimed; and he turned over and went back to sleep. But the next day he went down to the store and bought young Jack a new pair of trousers. He certainly was not going to let the matter of clothing interfere in the religious development of his children.

John Rider was an ill-tempered old man that all the practical jokers in the community liked to heckle. When his peaches were ripe or his watermelons were in season, old John would guard his property with his double-barreled shotgun—simply daring anyone to try and swipe his crop. One time long after nightfall, Jack Palmer and some friends reconnoitered the situation. They located old man Rider's stake-out. Then, Jack took a cowbell and went through the cornfield rattling the bell in a manner to simulate a cow in the corn patch. Old man Rider angrily took off after the sound of the bell to get the damned cow out of his precious roasting ears. While he was being led by Jack to the far end of the corn patch, the remainder of the gang pillaged the peach orchard.

At another time Jack sneaked up to old man Rider's hiding place and, finding the old man asleep, swiped his shotgun. After the boys had taken as many ripe melons as they wanted, Jack crept up close to the sleeping guardian of his sacred property and awakened the old man by discharging both barrels of the gun into the air. Then he dropped the gun and madly made his escape into the cedar brakes before John Rider could recover and reload. On another occasion Jack sneaked up on Rider when he was asleep on guard (which from all accounts seems to have been quite often), and the old fellow was awakened from his slumber by half of a very juicy overripe watermelon being shoved down over his head.

Another annoying habit the boys had during this mischievous period was stealing chickens and then having a barbecue down on the banks of Owl Creek. On one occasion they managed to get plenty of chickens, but there was not a knife to be had among the entire gang. This deficiency did not deter the boys, however, in their proposed feast. They used sharp flint rocks in a truly barbarian fashion, and, Jack later declared, these particular chickens tasted much better than any of the others. Maybe Grandma Palmer was right. "Kids ain't gittin' worse, they're jest gittin' *caught*."

Somehow the tales of the Cold Springs folk seem to have a different flavor from the ones ordinarily heard. There were preacher tales, outlaw tales, schoolteacher and school child anecdotes. All of these stories, once having a definite sense of reality, are gradually fading from the memories of people who were actual participants in the creation of the legends. Soon, no doubt, the tales which were distinctively of Cold Springs origin will fade and can be related about any old rural community.

On the other hand, some of the tales which seem to belong to Cold Springs and which are told as true are readily transferable from one place to another, and it is all but impossible to discover where they originated. The "too much pepper" story, which is perfectly localized in Cold Springs, once had wide currency over the old South; it came in from the outside, and no doubt some of the other stories did too, such as the one about the kittens who became Baptists when their eyes opened.

Prayer Meeting at Persimmon College

JOSEPH T. MC CULLER, JR.

ONCE UPON A TIME, in North Carolina, there was a Persimmon College. It was an academy which not only offered intellectual leadership to its namesake (the local community) but also provided a center for its social and spiritual life. "And the location of Persimmon College?" you ask. Thirty miles due south of Bentonville Battleground. "But I've never heard of that either," you perhaps object. To parody Enobarbus, I wish to suggest that your travels are incomplete if you have never visited Bentonville Battleground. With pride, old-timers in that area used to boast: "Here we fit Yankees right on after Gen'ral Lee had done an' give up."

One reason for the howling success of prayer meeting at Persimmon College was its spiritual leaders. The most famous of these was old Brother Clute Sampson. Come Wednesday night, you could hear him a mile away from the meeting house: "I'm aclim'ing, I'm aclim'ing, I'm aclim'ing up Zion's hill!" When he darkened the door, the whole house rose to sing and shout. But he could sing louder and shout longer than the best of them. "My cup runneth over," he often declared. And it did, practically all his life.

The one exception was the time old Brother Clute fell from grace. He had a big bunch of cattle which he decided to sell because of a dry spell. The night before his sale he fed the cows all the dry peas they would eat, and next morning he drove them down by a creek. Bloated when they reached the market, they looked fat and brought a handsome price. After they shrank in the hands of a butcher, however, he spread the news about Brother Clute's swindle. That was more than the old fellow could stand. For months he was ashamed to return to prayer meeting, and it almost died for lack of leadership.

In time Brother Clute did come back, though, and gave the meetings such zest as they had never known before. He went back because anxious neighbors not only forgave him but also convinced him that it was his spiritual duty to "come home." Brother Clute himself was a bigger success than ever, for to others he was "that hundredth sheep who had strayed from the fold." When he sang "I once was lost but now I'm found," nobody could keep his feet still or his mouth shut.

After old Brother Clute died, his mantle fell on Uncle Nath Ward. Emotionally he was more stable than Brother Clute. In fact, Uncle Nath insisted on beginning prayer meeting with solemn readings from the Scripture. One Wednesday night he stood up and, adjusting his spectacles, began: "Now, sisters an' brethren, I aim to read you a chapter from One-Eye John."

He stopped short and demanded, "What chu laughing at?"

Uncle Ely James was not laughing but was ready to set Uncle Nath straight. "Hold your horses there, Nath Ward," he said. "It ain't One-Eye John. It's First John."

Angered by the correction, Uncle Nath retorted, "Now look ahere, Ely James, are you gonna stan' there an' dispute the Word of God? See for yourself what the Good Book says: John with a big I. An' look over here at this other John; he's got two I's."

Lest you jump to the wrong conclusion about prayer meeting at Persimmon College, I had better remind you that the congregation was made up of followers as well as leaders. You wouldn't go wrong if you said that everybody who went there took part in one activity or another. Take Robbin Tripp's Jane for instance. One night while the folks were up shouting, Jane waltzed up and down every aisle in the house. She looked fit to enter the Pearly Gates on foot. Jane suddenly clasped old Miss Sindy Jackson and screamed: "Hallelujah! Sister Sindy, I don't care if nobody else goes to heaven or not—jest so long as you an' me gits there. That's all I want, Glory to God!"

Another time, Miss Sindy rose to testify: "I could walk on air," she said, " 'cause I got religion all over!"

Jane stood up, more timid than usual, and had her say: "Well now, I ain't zactly blessed that much, but I have got it here an' there."

And there was Jack Barefoot, who usually attended prayer meeting just to look around. What he was really after was girls. That was why he wore his Sunday clothes, even though prayer meeting was on Wednesday nights. Uncle Nath Ward didn't particularly like Jack's fancy duds because, in his opinion, homespun was good enough for anybody. One night Uncle Nath talked about clothes and the part they play in the devil's work. Jack Barefoot fidgeted in a sweat till the shouting began. Then he jumped up, snatched his necktie out by the roots, and cried victoriously, "You've helt me down long enough!" After a few more leaps, he ripped off his starched collar and flung it out the window. Ordinarily you might think that would be enough, but this was Jack Barefoot. He wanted complete freedom. Pausing by Uncle Ely James, Jack announced just how far he would go: "I'll pull off these breeches too, if the Lord say so!"

"Hold on there, Jack Barefoot," Uncle Ely cautioned him. "One pair of breeches won't keep a fool like you out of heaven."

Robbin Tripp also grew happy sometimes, especially when it was time to testify. One night it looked as if he would set a new record for enumerating personal blessings. Here, at least, is the way he started out: "I got so many things to thank you for, dear Lord, I don't know where to commence. My crops, my cows, my chickens, my hogs . . . Only Monday my ole sow had a litter of thirteen pigs . . . and every one of them as plump as the rats that eat my corn! Got my health an' strength too.

But what I thank you for most of all is the times I courted Janie in the briar patch. That's where we..."

"Hold your tongue, Robbin Tripp!" Jane interrupted. "Can't you never keep nothing straight? It was under the rose arbor in back of Ma's house. They were rosebushes, I tell you, an' my Pa set them out."

Robbin was too happy to quibble over details: "Praise the Lord for His servant that planted them rosebushes, no matter who he was!"

Folks did a lot of praying during prayer meetings at Persimmon College too. Some prayers were short, and some were long. I reckon you could say some were just middling. At prayer, as elsewhere, neither old Brother Clute Sampson nor Uncle Nath Ward would be outdone by anybody else. Brother Clute prayed as loud as he sang, and one night just before his "Amen" he lifted both his voice and his hands to heaven: "And now, O Lord," he pled, "wash away all our sins an' make us white as the crimson snow!" Praying for an ailing member of the congregation, another evening Uncle Nath Ward petitioned the Almighty: "Let your healing hand touch the body of Sister Marthie, Heavenly Father, an' bless all her relatives too—white an' black!"

Some prayer meetings were devoted to special problems, such as a needed rain. Let two or three weeks pass without rain, and the folks at Persimmon College would meet to do something about it. That was the way the situation stood one night when Brother Clute bombarded the firmament with this petition: "Open the floodgates of heaven, blessed God, an' send us a gully washer!"

Uncle Ely James, who was easily upset when anything threatened to get out of hand, decided it was time to amend that request. His faith was pretty steady anyway, and more than once he warned his neighbors first to decide what they wanted and then to ask for it.

"We all know how good an' powerful you are, dear Lord,"

he prayed calmly. "Brother Clute there knows too; he's jest likely to overdo it a mite. So please, Lord, don't send us no gully washer. What we're really asking for is jest an all-night drib-drab."

Uncle Ely was right, not only about the rain but also about the people in general. They all wanted pretty much the same things because they were basically alike. Practically every one of them had descended from Britishers who settled that area during the eighteenth century. They were happy enough to see strangers passing through and welcomed them—for a day or maybe even a week. But new settlers aroused suspicion. They might bring new ideas, or maybe even try to impose them on the community. Resistance was evident, and prayer meeting was the time when—as a group—the natives could make intruders feel it.

Now and then outsiders did settle at Persimmon College— not many, but enough to cause trouble. Karl Baum bought a farm and was soon growing the best tobacco in the neighborhood. Some folks admired him and some envied him. To everyone he was suspect, however, when he began to appear regularly at prayer meeting. You might say they were right, for he did suggest changes. The first notion he tried out was to increase the congregation by bringing in people who lived in a near-by swamp. Karl sent his own wagon to haul them; then he himself assumed responsibility for reviewing the fundamentals of religion on their behalf.

To one of the women, Karl posed this question: "Sister, don't you know who died for you?"

" 'Course I do," she snapped. "Ole Dyce Jacobs dyed fer me up till last fall. Seeing how she's passed away though, now I ain't sure who in the devil I'll git."

Somewhat taken aback, Karl changed the subject: "Where is your husband tonight, sister?"

"Dang'd if I know where the ole loafer is tonight nor any other time, now that fishing season is here."

"Do you and your husband stand in fear of the Lord?" Karl asked.

"God knows I don't," she laughed. "But John must. Last time I seen him, he was headed 'cross the lowgrounds carrying a double-barreled shotgun."

Karl dropped the catechism right then and there. "Maybe it's better to start from scratch," he said. So he began relating stories from the Bible. He did his best to keep the stories so simple that nobody could get mixed up; still, when he paused, up rose a swamp man: "Come again, preacher," he demanded. "Which un did you say died fer us—the ole man, or his son?"

Karl admitted failure in his efforts to make the swamp people an active part of prayer meeting, but he didn't give up. His next proposal was that Persimmon College should sponsor a foreign mission. To support his plea, he told about work going on in China and Africa. He achieved emphasis by reference to what, by good rights, ought to be done in parts of America. "No matter how you look at it," Karl said, "you can be a heathen anywhere."

Karl had no more than sat down when Uncle Nath Ward took the floor. "Karl Baum," he said, "it 'peers to me you're a decent sort of fellow. Leastways, you got a dandy farm, an' you don't mind pitching in to help out a sick neighbor. We all respect you for that. But when it comes to prayer meeting, you ought to set back an' listen. Take them swamp rats, for instance. Anybody who growed up around Persimmon College could'uv told you about them from the start. 'Tain't likely it would have done no good though; you had to find out for yourself an' we let chu do jest that. But with this talk about missions, you're going too far. Speaking for myself, I always give generously to any worthy cause—ask anybody in this house. Still, that don't mean I'm agoing to get mixed up in this mission business. Nosiree. Fact is, if I had this here hat full of twenty-dollar gold pieces, I wouldn't give them dad burned ferriners one red cent!"

Karl backed down a second time but didn't shed his conviction that prayer meeting at Persimmon College could stand a change. So one night he turned up with the idea of inviting preachers to visit the community. "This has got to work," Karl said. "Nobody in his right mind is going to argue with a preacher."

The first preacher to come was a boy Karl had known up in Pennsylvania. This young man rode the train to the nearest town and rented a buggy, confident that he would reach persimmon College by nightfall. He would have done just that, if he had known where he was when he got there. He didn't know and had to spend the night three miles beyond his destination.

Next morning about five o'clock the preacher heard someone knocking on his door: "Preacher," a small voice called. "Git up, Preacher. Ma wants that sheet for a tablecloth."

The preacher did not feel very spry at the breakfast table, certainly not up to the fare of a working man: roasting ears, ham, rice, tom thumb, and sweet potato pie. He excused himself for refusing food, until he noticed a pair of small eyes looking clean through him. Then he decided to compromise for biscuit and a rasher of ham, but he decided too late. "Ma," said the little boy, "why don'chu fry that fool an egg, an' see if he'll eat that?"

The preacher finally found his way back to Karl Baum's. He stayed there about a month. On Sundays he preached and on Wednesday nights he conducted prayer meeting. Folks listened politely enough while he talked; then they tried to have prayer meeting the way they liked it. But there was no spirit in it. They sang without enthusiasm, and there was not enough shouting or testifying to talk about. Sensing a general coldness, the preacher decided to leave Persimmon College.

Miss Sindy Jackson was a sympathetic old woman, one who hated to see anyone come and go without a word of encouragement. "Well, Parson," she said, "we shore are going to miss you. To tell the truth, we never knowed what sin was till you come amongst us."

The second preacher Karl engaged decided to turn prayer meeting into a regular revival. You might say he was the evangelical type. He preached every night, till all the old people just stayed home. The young ones attended because he attracted the girls, and the young men were there because they didn't like it. Finally they decided to take that preacher down a peg or two.

Somehow the young men found out what text he was going to use one night and, during the day, pasted leaves in the Bible together. Ready to deliver his sermon, the preacher opened the Bible with his usual confidence. He read to the bottom of a page which ended, "And there was a green bay . . ." He turned the page and continued: "horse!" Flipping the pages back and forth, he exclaimed, "Well, I'll be damned if it ain't horse!"

The young men roared with laughter. The girls blushed silently, but that didn't help the preacher very much. Next morning he sent word that the Lord had called him to work a vineyard down in Georgia.

The last of Karl's preachers was another northerner. He made his way to Persimmon College all right, but didn't stay around long enough to do any damage. One laugh at his expense was all he could handle. He got that at a country store, where most of the farmers around Persimmon College had stopped to blow during the noon heat. The individual closest to him was an old slave-woman.

"Good morning, lady," said the preacher. "Could you give me a little information?"

She threw up her hands and grinned. "Lawdy, no suh! I'z done an' got too ole foh dat bizness, specially wid white folks!"

INFORMANT: For these tales associated with Persimmon College, I am indebted to Annie Lee Gore—one of the few surviving alumnae of an old academy located in Sampson County, North Carolina. The writing is mine, but credit for the survival of lore from that area is hers.

The Frontier Hero:
Refinement and Definition

ROBERT H. BYINGTON

ANYONE ATTEMPTING yet another analysis of the Frontier Hero in these days when even the most hardened Western fan develops an occasional saddle sore feels—like the author of a new English composition text—an urgent need to justify his presumption. We will recognize that the textbook author, whatever his other motives, hopes also to make some money; and we sympathize with *this* ambition, base as it is. The analyst of the Frontier Hero, however, cannot reasonably entertain such a hope, and he finds that the area of his interest has been, if possible, even more heavily exploited than the textbook market. Why, then—when the Frontier Hero has already been discussed and interpreted, at great length and often competently, in many types of publication from the newspaper to the folklore quarterly, and from a wide variety of viewpoints including the psychiatric and even the theological—why, then, presume? The answer lies not so much in the possibility of a spectacularly new approach, but in the confused image of the Frontier Hero that has resulted, in part, from the very abundance of commentary about him. Interpreters do not always have the same hero in view, their deviations in this respect being reflected in the various terms ranging from Phaëton to the Typical Texan they use to designate the hero; and such deviations are understandable when one considers that the media of popular culture do indeed present different versions of the hero, so different at times that they resemble each other only superficially.

There is, for example, the two-dimensional Rover Boy in chaps who captures the rustler gang, saves the mortgaged ranch, and has an annoyingly sanctimonious habit of ordering lemonade at the only saloon in town. He sometimes croons ersatz cowboy ballads, and is invariably assisted by a rustic buffoon of one kind or other. A second type is the picaresque hero like Maverick who appears in farce or comedy as well as melodrama, acts the role of clown or engaging rogue as readily as he does everything else, and stoops at times even to parody of competitors in the genre. Still another type is illustrated by the various gun-fighting marshals, wanderers, and special agents that have proliferated on television in the wake of *Gunsmoke's* success. This hero portrays more fully than most the characteristics of the traditional Frontier Hero—whose main habitat has long been the Western novel and the feature-length movie derived from it—but he does not do it consistently, and the portrait is never complete.

It would be possible to extend this list of types, but I feel sure that the variation occurring in popular portrayals of the Frontier Hero is sufficiently obvious. This variation, while probably refreshing to the television watcher, complicates the problem of interpretation. It also gives rise to skepticism when one realizes that the psychoanalyst who considers the Frontier Hero's main function to be the symbolic resolution of unconscious oedipal conflicts,[1] the theologian who finds in the hero's story "the eternal dialectic of pilgrimage and rest,"[2] and the folklorist who speculates about the hero's origins[3] are none of them looking at the same hero. The confused impression that one necessarily receives from such commentary would clarify if we could settle upon one type as the Frontier Hero par excellence, of which the others are variations or dilutions; and it seems to me there is ample justification for doing this.

The candidate I would advance—to no one's surprise, I am sure—is the hero one finds embodied in such memorable characterizations as Lassiter in Zane Grey's *Riders of the Purple*

Sage or, to cite a more recent example, Jack Schaefer's Shane. This is the lone, gentle-voiced, and inherently scrupulous killer who rides in out of nowhere, reluctantly disposes of whatever evil adversaries circumstances force upon him, and then rides sadly out again—scourged by some inner torment that gives him no rest. Slight variations occur from story to story, but the basic image or pattern of characterization is remarkably consistent; and if any type is worthy of the designation "classic" Frontier Hero, it is this one.

One reason for considering him as the archetypal Frontier Hero is the fact that in the multi-million-volume world of hard and paperback Western fiction—long the chief disseminator of Western myth—his presence has become almost ubiquitous; and the significance of this is underscored by the fact that, among the many interpreters of the Western Hero, those who are seriously interested in him as an index to and reflection of cultural values[4] invariably focus their attention upon the type under discussion here. Secondly, his history is a long one and begins almost with frontier fiction itself. In earlier incarnations he did not of course sport the gun-belt and spurs that form so prominent an aspect of his most familiar role, but among the vaporing genteel heroes and doughty sons of Ol' Kaintuck that dominate the pre-Civil War border romance appears occasionally a deadly, soft-spoken frontiersman or Indian Hater who in every essential respect is the counterpart of his descendant in the age of horses and six-guns. Indeed, it would be as simple to define the hero on the basis of his appearance as forest scout were it not that his role as cowboy/gunfighter is better known and therefore more suitable for purposes of reference and illustration. The type was fully developed in popular fiction long before the post-Civil War era of westward expansion.

Less tangible but perhaps more important as evidence is the fact that, among those who respond to the image of the Frontier Hero at all, this gentlemanly killer type appeals the most. He is more fully developed, more self-contained than any of the others, but at the same time he is less righteous. There emanates from him what Dixon Wecter has called "the salty, sacrificial taste of disappointment and tragedy," and we respond to this aspect of his image as we respond to it in Abraham Lincoln. He conveys an impression of hard-won maturity that other types fail even to suggest. As a result, he is admirable while the others are merely active; and this is as it should be, for *he* is the hero. The others approach herohood only as they take on from time to time aspects of the true hero's definitive image.

Well, just what is this image? It has been generally described often enough; but before the highly speculative business of interpretation can justifiably proceed, it is necessary, I feel, to define the Gentleman Killer type with rather more precision than has yet been attempted. I propose to attack the problem by breaking down the heroic image of the Gentleman Killer into its component parts and considering each separately. These component parts are, variously, basic character traits, attitudes, or narrative elements frequently enough associated with the Gentleman Killer to characterize him; and on the basis of this frequency they may legitimately be called motifs.

There are five primary motifs to the figure of the Gentleman Killer; but since each of these can manifest itself in more than one way, the primary motif is actually a generic title for a cluster of motifs each of which expresses a different manner. In order for the hero to achieve full stature it is necessary that this characterization include at least one of the sub-motifs in each of the five major groupings.

The first primary facet of the heroic image is reflected by what might be called the CAIN motifs. These motifs result from the inescapable fact that the Gentleman Killer, as the name given him explicitly states, is a killer of men. To take human life, and to take it violently, is his ultimate function in whatever context he appears. That he may occupy himself in other ways a good part of the time does not matter; that he may kill reluctantly and then with apparent justification is beside the point; that the bloodletting may be highly ceremonial with his own life placed in jeopardy and his victim given every chance does nothing to alter the grim, unavoidable truth that he *is* a killer. On those rare occasions when he does not actually kill anyone within the actual context of the story, it is made perfectly clear that he *has* killed and is quite capable of doing so again. There is about him, even in his most beneficent moments, a subtle suggestion of potential menace which evokes a faint, indefinable awe from the other characters—their unconscious tributes to the terrible responsibility and power that are his.

For his power is extraordinary. Rather than great physical strength, or mental superiority, it takes the form of skill in the handling of weapons. In fact it sometimes appears that he *is* a killer largely because his remarkable skills fit him for the role to such a superlative degree. By way of emphasizing the importance of the weapon to the identity and function of the Gentleman Killer, the writers call it constantly to our attention; in fact, our first hint that a character being introduced is a potential Gentleman Killer may be the almost loving care with which his weapon—be it long rifle, knife, or six-gun—is described. The amount of space—or screentime—devoted to picturing the appearance, manipulation, loading, sharpening, or cleaning of these weapons seems disproportionate until we realize that the weapon is the clear symbol, the constant reminder, of the hero's death-dealing capacity. The weapon may be out of the ordinary in no way other than the marks it bears of long, hard use and devoted care, or it may have distinctive features that immediately stamp its owner as no ordinary man; but at one point or another it will be thoroughly described and its significance as an index to its owner's character clearly established. In certain stories the owner is metaphorically identified with and known by the weapon he uses with such awesome proficiency, as if he were merely a human extension of the weapon rather than the contrary; and in other stories, while the owner may die or disappear, his near-miraculous weapon passes down through time finding owners in successive generations capable and worthy of using it as it should be used.

In the Western, where what we might henceforth call the Weapon Motif appears most elaborately and insistently, the weapon sometimes assumes an almost mystical significance, as if it were the badge of the demigod. When a hero, who for one reason or another has been made to appear without his weapons, buckles them on again, it is made perfectly clear (the reader is often explicitly told) that an extra dimension has been added to his character, that some special transformation has taken place making him taller, more remote and inaccessible, but somehow *right*. There are suggestions that Nemesis has materialized before our eyes, and the atmosphere becomes charged with vague but dreadful portent. Such atmospheric buildup points up quite dramatically the importance of the weapon to the proper performance of the Gentleman Killer's role.

As if it were for some reason important that we know of the Gentleman Killer's proficiency with his weapon before he is called on to use it in earnest, it usually happens that in addition to the initial description of the weapon, we are provided with a demonstration of the hero's competence in its use that precedes whatever climactic death-dealing is in store. This phenomenon occurs frequently enough to be considered a motif —the Preliminary Demonstration Motif. It may take the form of a shooting contest, knife-throwing lesson, or even actual gunplay, but its purpose is not the meting out of justice or the resolution of any major difficulty; it serves merely to identify the Gentleman Killer further and to give notice that, whatever the circumstances, he is a man who can dominate the play should he be so inclined.

Once either of these two motifs has appeared, regardless of other identifying marks the hero may bear, he takes on an awful appeal; for we recognize him now as a man who has the requisite skill to compete with the forces of evil on their own terms, a man who has the power to kill other men, and who is likely to do so before the tale is told.

The second primary facet of the Gentleman Killer's image is reflected by what I have termed the ISHMAEL motifs. "And he shall be as a wild ass among men; his hand shall be against every man, and every man's hand against him." This prediction of the Biblical Ishmael's fate is rather too extreme to be an accurate description of the Gentleman Killer's relations with organized society; but an essential element in his makeup is the fact that he is a loner, a solitary individual, more often than not a wanderer, who—despite the role of Community Savior he frequently plays—invariably embodies a repudiation of civilized values.

This antagonism toward the settled order may be implicit or it may be overtly displayed; it may be faint or strong. But it *is* consistent, and it takes various forms. In the first place, the Gentleman Killer's very nature insures a conflict between what he represents and what organized society traditionally stands for. Whereas individuals in society are interdependent and mutually involved in a complex network of services and obligations, the Gentleman Killer is autonomous; while the individual in society must observe statutory law and patiently abide the workings of judicial process, the Gentleman Killer is neither governed by the former nor reliant upon the latter; whereas the individual in society is weighted down by invisible clogs that restrict his activity and keep his nose to the grindstone, the Gentleman Killer goes free. He is the antithesis of what the individual in society *must* be to *live* in society; and therefore our admiration for him necessarily implies a criticism, if not an outright rejection, of the general values and responsibilities of community living. If we consider these qualities along with the facts that his function—killing—involves the most antisocial of all acts, and that he is frequently a wanderer with no permanent home, we understand how easily the figure of the Gentleman Killer, without explicit statement or overt demonstration on his part, acquires subversive, social antagonistic overtones. In certain stories, again without any intimation of hostility on his part, he is rejected or scorned by society for one reason or another and becomes a literal outcast with "every man's hand against him"; and as our admiration for him increases, what sympathy we may have had with the representatives of civilization correspondingly wanes.

As often as not the Gentleman Killer gives voice to his antisocial feelings in very explicit terms. When he does so, his criticism usually falls into one of three categories. The first of these, which we shall term the Subversive Motif, has for its target the official representatives of law and order—hence, by implication, law and order itself. This criticism is sometimes evoked by corruption and inefficiency on the part of legally constituted authority and should, perhaps, be considered more salutary than subversive—but it rarely stops there. More frequently the whole machinery of due process is indicted for its utter ineffectuality, the result not so much of corrupt officials but of its own monolithic inertia, or—and this, although vaguely justified, is always strongly put—its unsuitability to the areas in which the Gentleman Killer operates. The representatives of law and order, particularly the enforcing authorities, are so immobilized by legal restrictions that their good intentions come to naught, and evil prospers. The hero would and does substitute for the slow, erratic cranking of the judicial mill what in other contexts is sometimes referred to as "Colt justice"—i.e., the individual hero takes unto himself the weighty, godlike functions of judge, jury, and executioner and resolves the issue forever with one decisive act.

Another category of antisocial expression on the part of the hero—that appears most frequently in his role as forest scout or mountain man—is what we might call the Fugitive Motif. This is the familiar "Flight from Civilization" theme that Henry Nash Smith and others have found to be an important element in the mythic haze which has enveloped some of our earlier frontier heroes, real and fictional; and while it is just as strong as, if not stronger than, the Subversive Motif, the criticism it expresses is vaguer, less explicit. What the hero finds objectionable here is not law and order, or anything else *specifically,* but rather "the sound of axes to the eastward," the presence of people in general. The Fugitive Motif expresses an almost compulsive dread of overcrowding and confinement, and, at the same time, a hunger for the pristine, the untarnished quality of the virgin wilderness. This attitude or feeling should not be confused with Rousseauistic primitivism, which is a more or less rational philosophy activated by moral disapproval of social and institutional corruption; the Fugitive Motif is not motivated by the hope of moral regeneration through Nature and the simple life. Rather, it is more like the desire of the caged animal to be free, the desire for unshackled liberty of action, which becomes impossible the moment anything approaching social organization enters the picture. It is also the rather selfish desire of an Adam who wants Eden all to himself, and who, when unable to resist encroachment, flees to the uttermost limits of the Garden.

Still another phase of the Gentleman Killer as outsider and social critic is what we might call the Anti-Populistic Motif. This is a tendency to place the normal everyday people, the townsfolk, the average citizens—with whom the Gentleman Killer gets involved—somehow in the wrong. The hero naturally appears to advantage when compared with ordinary people, but the Anti-Populistic Motif results from more than the natural inferiority of mediocrity to the superhuman. It is the deliberate characterization of average citizens and their leaders as cowardly, hypocritical, cruel, mercenary, sanctimonious, or unthinking—as, on the whole, a decidedly unpleasant group. This characterization is sometimes explicitly uttered by the Gentleman Killer, usually in a few barbed or bitter statements; but more frequently it is implicit in the behavior of the citizens themselves. That the Gentleman Killer at the risk of his life usually saves one or all of them from the forces of evil in no way mitigates the impression we receive of their essential unworthiness to *be* saved. They are invariably in the wrong for the basest or pettiest of reasons, and we cannot help regarding them as mean-spirited because that is how they are presented to us. This is a curious feature of the American frontier story and one that has been present almost from the beginning.

Each of these three sub-motifs, all of which rarely appear in the same story, serves to emphasize the Gentleman Killer's essential lack of kinship with the rest of mankind. He may make friends, he may join and assist group activity, he is rarely sullen or unapproachable; but there is a gap which cannot be bridged separating him from others, and eventually he will loosen what ties he has made and move on, another of "those untethered wanderers who have appeared so often on the popular horizon."[5]

The third primary quality of the hero's character is conveyed by what might be called the RENUNCIATION motifs. It is these motifs, perhaps more than any of the others, that elevate the perfectly crystallized Gentleman Killer above the level of lesser heroes. In order for him to be what he is and maintain the purity of his own ethos, and in order, also, to emphasize his godlike isolation, it is necessary for him to give up much of what other men hold dear, and what he himself would like to have. This renunciation varies in degree from Celibacy to actual Martyrdom. The true Gentleman Killer, through his own volition or the operation of circumstances beyond his control, is denied the joys and solaces of domestic life and the delights of woman's love. It is not that he has no desire for closer, permanent relations with women or that he arouses no affection in their breasts—quite the contrary; it is merely that, for one ostensible reason or another, before the play is over, he will be alone again. The plots unfold that way. Sometimes, because of approaching middle age, perhaps, celibacy will seem proper and his renunciation will take some other form; at times he will love and be loved in turn, but *something*—his guilt feelings for the blood on his hands, the death of his beloved, or even some obscure point of personal honor—will insure his return to his solitary way of life. It is the price he pays for the power that is his.

The ultimate renunciation, of course, is that of life itself; and upon occasion the Gentleman Killer will make this last, noblest of gestures. Almost inevitably he will have met and overcome his adversaries before expiring, thus liberating the individual or group in whose interest he died, and enshrining himself in their hearts—in this way he can be said to have received his reward. Once in a while, however, he dies for no good reason—because of accident, treachery, or a cause unworthy of his sacrifice—and then his death seems bitter indeed.

Whether the close of a particular story leaves the Gentleman Killer sprawled motionless on his face in a dusty street, or—in another role—somberly nursing a martini in an empty bar as his love walks out the door and out of his life forever, his renunciation is emotionally affecting to those who respond to the image at all, and it intensifies his heroism. That it should do so is, of course, no cause for wonder. Such sacrifice is an ancient mythological motif characteristic of demigods and gods from Prometheus to Christ, and its appeal hardly requires explanation.

Yet a fourth aspect of the hero's image is reflected by what I have called—perhaps inaptly—the HAMLET motifs. These form a natural corollary to the preceding motifs and derive from the unobtrusive but deep-set melancholy that envelops the Gentleman Killer like a cloak, and establishes him immediately as a man set apart by Fate. It is variously suggested that he is a man with bitter memories, a man out of love with himself and disillusioned by the world, a man gloomily obsessed by some dreadful purpose, or simply a man who is unhappy because his day is over; but sadness of one sort or another has marked him for its own, and he wears it like a badge of identification. It is as much a part of his personality as his weapons; it is always an appropriate quality; and it is probably the heaviest, symbolically, of his various characteristics.

The last primary trait of the Gentleman Killer is established by what might be called the PATRICIAN motifs. Our hero is intrinsically a natural aristocrat of the highest type. Like Richard Cory, he is "a gentleman from sole to crown," and he makes it apparent in at least one and sometimes all the following ways. He is inherently kind and gentle, and this is especially —indeed *only*—manifest in his treatment of the weak or abused. He is infallibly courteous to women in a natural and unostentatious way as if he had been accustomed to yield such deference from the time he could walk. His essential kindness is even more evident in his relations with children, animals, old people, or the put upon. If, let us say, a child or a dog is being neglected, cruelly treated, or—in the case of the former—denied sympathy and understanding, the Gentleman Killer will console, protect, or sympathize. It is one of the ways by which we recognize him.

Another aspect of the hero's essential gentility is his self-restraint. He is a stoical man whose mind and will are in absolute command of his emotions—at least to the extent of their outward manifestation. This trait is suggested more than anything else by his *quietness*. A strange, fragile stillness—like that in the eye of a hurricane—envelops him. Where other men are loud, boisterous, filling the center of the stage, the Gentleman Killer is unobtrusive, withdrawn, chary of involvement. This quietness is frequently interpreted as weakness by unperceptive characters in the story, who proceed to take advantage of it. At such moments we discover that the Gentleman Killer is quiet, but quiet as a set trap is quiet. Nothing is more characteristic of the Gentleman Killer than the impression he conveys of dangerous energies held tightly in check. It takes a great deal to disturb his disciplined calmness, to provoke him into a display of his awful power; and when he does make a move, it is not so much a loss of control as it is a deliberate release of directed energy.

A less dramatic but perhaps equally revealing aspect of the Gentleman Killer's self-restraint is his taciturnity. The fully developed hero, although by no means speechless and without giving the impression of being sullen or inarticulate, invariably has less to say than the other characters in the story. He is a silent man, as befits his nature—a man of action rather than a man of words—and when he does speak, he speaks softly, briefly, and to the point. He is not a philosopher or a moralizer (although the pertinence and brevity of his remarks gives them an epigrammatic quality that may help to convey this impression), and he never talks merely to hear himself talk or even to express himself in any basic way. The softness of his tone when he does speak is frequently accentuated by the loudness or excitement of those with him; and, again, the impression he conveys is that of a powerful engine carefully throttled back. Like his self-restraint in moments of great provocation, the taciturnity of the Gentleman Killer intensifies our sense of his power; and it also helps to convey an impression of good breeding.

Another "aristocratic" feature of the Gentleman Killer is what we might call the Leisure Motif, the fact that he does no work in the ordinary sense of routine labor, mental or physical. He is most frequently a wanderer of some sort, a drifter with no fixed responsibilities to anything or anybody other than himself. He does not rise reluctantly to work in the morning, or fall dulled and exhausted into bed at night; he neither sows nor reaps, in the popular sense of the phrase; he does not have a steady job. He may be ostensibly employed in a particular capacity as a hunter, scout, guide, peace officer, or private detective; but these are all occupations that the normal person considers highly romantic and in no way associated with the routine drudgery in which he himself is probably involved. The Gentleman Killer seems detached from the economic necessities of ordinary life, and this suggests yet another aspect of traditional gentility—its freedom from the demanding influence of "Trade" and other plebeian activity.

By far the most important patrician characteristic of the Gentleman Killer, however, is the fact that he is, above all, a man of honor. He keeps his integrity hard and intact, without reference to group values, by close adherence to an inner, personal Code—the details of which are not always clear to the observer but which is obviously active in all the Gentleman Killer's decisions. The Code manifests itself in various ways, but is most clearly illustrated by the familiar Western tradition that in the "shoot-out" or "walk-down" (the climactic gun-duel between hero and villain) the hero never draws first; he chivalrously allows his opponent that split-second advantage of making the first move. This motif, if it can be considered such, is so inevitable in all Westerns that, if one is in any doubt as to the respective roles of hero and villain, one need only wait to see who first goes for his gun in the final duel—*he* will be the villain. The fact that the hero's skill is such that he can grant this advantage and still triumph in no way weakens the impression of *noblesse oblige* his gesture conveys.

Another less explicit manifestation of the Code Motif is the Gentleman Killer's motivation for doing what he does. Most of the time the story line offers a plausible *apparent* reason for the hero's participation in events—self-defense, the deliverance of the oppressed, vengeance, the enforcement of law and order, etc.—but there are a substantial number of stories (and these have a tendency to be the more subtle and artistically developed) in which the hero places his life in jeopardy and/or performs his blood-spilling function when every rational consideration impels him to avoid the issue. At such times the hero himself is at a loss to justify the risk he takes to the prudent and sensible characters who urge his nonparticipation; and the explanation he usually offers is that he *"has* to." The sensible characters in the story find his attitude incomprehensible, but the reader or audience knows intuitively why the hero "*has* to"—his honor demands it. Rational considerations to the contrary notwithstanding, the hero must conform to that indefinable conception of manhood and individual responsibility called honor; for if the hero does not conform to this imprecise but deeply imbedded notion of how it is a man behaves, then he ceases to embody that notion, and ceases to be the hero. If we would know what this "honor," this gentlemanly Code, is or was, we must observe the actions and rationale of the Gentleman Killer, for it may be he is the last representation of it to be found in our culture.

At any rate, the cumulative effect of these PATRICIAN motifs (or, to a lesser degree, the single effect of one of them) is to give the figure of the Gentleman Killer a refined, aristocratic cast; and with this quality the catalogue of those primary motif-groups which define the hero concludes. There are other peripheral characteristics—such as the hero's physical appearance or his near-anonymity in many stories—but these occur too sporadically to be considered definitive. The primary motifs associated with and defining the Gentleman Killer archetype of the Western Hero appear in a variety of combinations from story to story, and *all* of them rarely appear in any one story. When they do, however, we have the Frontier Hero full-panoplied; and it is this figure that the interpreter can discuss most profitably.

The Gentleman Killer is, of course, wholly unrealistic. As a movie advertisement of a few years ago so aptly put it, "There never was a man like Shane." And there never was. The Gentleman Killer is a mythical archetype, a special combination of character traits and behavior patterns which the American folk have found consistently appealing and which they have imposed —largely through their popular writers—upon any number of real-life individuals and types, from the backwoodsman to the private detective. A heroic image so persistently popular over such a long period of time—from the early part of the nineteenth century to the present day—cannot be without its significance, and a systematic study of its origins, its history, and its meaning has been long overdue.

1. Warren J. Barker, "The Stereotyped Western Story," *Psychoanalytic Quarterly*, XXIV (1955), 270-80.
2. Alexander Miller, "The 'Western'—A Theological Note," *Christian Century*, LXXIV (November 27, 1957), 1409-10.
3. Joseph J. Waldmeir, "The Cowboy, the Knight, and Popular Taste," *Southern Folklore Quarterly*, XXII (September, 1958), 113-20.
4. As opposed to the narrow expert who uses the hero only as a framework for a highly specialized exegesis in terms of his own discipline, or the glib journalist who is indifferent to the absurdity of his interpretation just so long as it is entertaining.
5. Constance Rourke, *American Humor* (New York, 1953), p. 174.

Belle Starr and the Biscuit Dough

JOHN Q. ANDERSON

BELLE STARR, the notorious woman bandit of North Texas and Indian Territory, had occupied a unique place among frontier outlaws for almost a decade when my father saw her with her hands in biscuit dough. Such a domestic role was indeed strange for "The Queen of the Bandits," "The Lady Desperado," "Wild Woman of the West," and "The Petticoat Terror of the Plains," names eastern newspaper editors had been calling her for several years. But the end of my father's story about the biscuit dough fits perfectly into that sensational portrayal, as does his account of how she was eventually killed. Though both stories may only add to the confusion surrounding the biography of Belle Starr, they are worth telling because they illustrate so well how hopelessly tangled are folklore and fact.

The story of Belle Starr and the biscuit dough is set in the eastern part of Indian Territory, near Wilburton, where my father was born, the son of a small rancher and stock breeder.[1] Belle and her gang—made up of her Cherokee Indian husband, Sam Starr, his numerous kin, and other fugitives from justice—were hiding out on Winding Stair Mountain in the Kiamichi range between robberies and horse-stealing raids in the Territory and North Texas. Though the band included murderers and thieves, these criminals never molested the local white and Indian farmers and ranchers. The natives knew that the outlaws preferred robbing banks, holding up the mail, and taking money elsewhere from people who had more of it than the struggling backwoodsmen did. Belle and her gang were so neighborly, in fact, that they spent a great deal of their stolen money in the towns in the area where they stocked up on provisions and ammunition, and in the Robin Hood manner, it is said, gave money to the poor. Those who opposed such neighborliness might regret doing so, as did the proprietor of a general store who showed some reluctance when Belle, sitting on her horse in the street in front of his establishment, ordered him to sell her all the ammunition he had. When he refused, she rode her horse up on the boardwalk in front of the store[2] and flirted her hand momentarily over her pearl-handled six-shooters. The man soon had the ammunition ready.

Natives of Indian Territory who had nothing that the outlaws wanted sometimes took advantage of their hospitality and when in the vicinity of their camp stopped and passed the time of day or even took a meal cooked over the campfire, doubtless experiencing a thrill in being near such evident lawlessness in a generally lawless country. One afternoon late my grandfather and my father, then a boy of about ten, were passing the camp of the outlaws and stopped to call, as was customary. The camp was spread in an open glade, the horses were tethered to one side, and the evening meal was being prepared over a campfire in the middle of the opening. Belle herself was busy with the cooking and did not look up when the callers arrived. Off to one side the young men of the gang were amusing themselves with target practice, shooting at a knot in a tree. The visitors watched with interest, though guns were by no means strange to them since all men in Indian Territory at that time wore them and could use them. Naturally the outlaws were all experts, but an argument developed over whose bullet had been placed where in the tree. Tempers flared, heated words were exchanged, and a fight was brewing when an arresting command came from the area of the campfire. The voice was Belle Starr's. She had been making biscuits in a pan of flour, stirring the dough with her hands. Slowly she stood up and wiped the dough off her hands with a rolling motion, as though she were pulling off tight gloves. She walked over to the group and gave her hands a last swipe on her riding skirt. "I'll show you who can shoot," she drawled. From their holsters, she drew both of her pearl-handled six-shooters and methodically, hand over hand, emptied them into the knot in the tree. The argument was settled.

If there was more to my father's story, I cannot now recall it. More is not necessary; the story is dramatically complete. This tale, which thrilled me so much as a boy, compares favorably with versions of Belle Starr's life in its emphasis on her guns and her proficiency in handling them. The story indicates that her much publicized marksmanship and her flair for fancy guns were not merely the creation of eastern newspaper editors and hack writers. Burton Rascoe, her chief biographer,[3] could find no evidence that Belle ever killed a man, though he says that she early developed a liking for guns and melodramatic costumes and actions. He does not, however, go so far as Glen Shirley, who maintains that she was an "expert horsewoman and a deadly shot with pistol or rifle" by the time she was fifteen.[4] Though I am not persuaded that the circumstances of the Civil War made Belle an outlaw, as Shirley appears to maintain, she did indeed grow up with guns and violence.

Guns were part of the everyday life of the Missouri frontier where Belle was born Myra Belle Shirley in 1848, and as a girl during the opening years of the Civil War she knew the violence associated with weapons, whether or not she, as legend has it, served as a spy for the Confederates. And then in the Dallas area in North Texas, where she came with her parents in 1863 at the age of sixteen, guns were also common. In fact, by the time Belle was twenty she had fallen in love with outlaw Cole Younger, a fugitive from Missouri, and had had an illegitimate daughter by him.[5] When Younger deserted her, she took up with another gunman, Jim Reed, and lived with him in Texas and California until he was killed trying to escape the law in

1874.⁶ Shortly thereafter, Belle, on her own as an entertainer in a Dallas dance hall and later as professional dealer of poker and faro, affected a brace of pistols as part of the costume that became her trademark. Rascoe says of her at this time:

> She dressed spectacularly, but entirely within the conventions. She wore a high-collared bodice jacket and long flowing skirts, which she knew how to drape prettily over a side-saddle made especially for her at a cost of one hundred dollars . . . high-topped boots and a man's Stetson hat turned up in front and decorated with an ostrich plume . . . around her waist she wore a cartridge belt from which two revolvers were suspended in holsters.⁷

The guns were merely decoration; Rascoe found no proof that she ever used them. The story of her killing a Colonel Nichols on the streets of Dallas is a fabrication, he says; it was John Younger who killed the Colonel.⁸

Evidently pleased with the sensation created by a woman wearing guns, Belle improved on that theatrical touch when in 1880 she married Sam Starr, a full-blood Cherokee Indian, and took up residence in eastern Indian Territory at a place she named Younger's Bend after her first lover. According to reports, she then affected "a brace of ivory-handled Colt .45 revolvers in holsters especially made for her." Within a short time she was a familiar figure on the streets of Fort Smith, Arkansas, the metropolis for eastern Indian Territory. She rode a fine black mare named Venus, owned a highly-decorated side-saddle, and "liked to drop into barrooms, drink with the men and play the accompaniment on the piano for the popular cowboy and sentimental songs of the period."⁹

In February, 1883, Belle's notoriety became national when she and her husband were arraigned in the federal court of "Hanging" Judge Isaac Parker at Fort Smith on a charge of horse stealing.¹⁰ The first woman defendant ever to appear in that famous court, Belle was specifically named in the indictment as the "leader of a band of horse thieves,"¹¹ and the local newspaper described her in detail as a horsewoman without rival and "an expert marksman with the pistol." When news of the trial went out over the telegraph, rewrite men on distant metropolitan dailies gave Belle the sensational titles that she afterward bore in the national press.

Though Belle and Sam were sentenced and spent nine months in a federal prison in Detroit, they were soon back in Indian Territory, where stories of Belle's guns and marksmanship continued to grow. In 1886 she was again in court in Fort Smith, charged with robbery, and again news stories emphasized her beautiful horse, saddle, and guns. The *Dallas News*, for instance, on June 7, 1886, carried a story with a Fort Smith dateline which mentioned "her two trusty revolvers, which she calls her 'babies' " and stated that "Belle is a crack shot, and handles her pistols with as much dexterity as any frontiersman."[12]

As a consequence of this publicity, Belle Starr was by the time my father saw her in the late 1880's widely known as a marksman with an affection for fancy guns. Published stories, though they furnished no proof of her proficiency with firearms, were evidently based on fact, even if exaggerated. My father saw her put twelve bullets into a knot on a tree. He was, it is true, a small boy at the time and was quite likely influenced by the tales then current about her, and his subsequent retelling of the story was doubtless colored by published accounts of her after her death. For instance, my father remembered her guns as being *pearl*-handled, though Rascoe says she carried specially decorated guns and once refers to them as having *ivory* handles. To accord with the flamboyant Belle Starr legend, they *should* have been pearl, even if they were not.

Whatever Belle's firearms were like and however she handled them, the six-shooters accompanied her body on its last earthly journey. She was wearing her famous guns in 1889 when she was ambushed and killed. She was shot in the back and had no opportunity to use the guns. When she was buried in the grave dug by the Starr brothers near her cabin at

Younger's Bend, her hand clasped one of the famous guns. Some of the Cherokee neighbors, doubtless mystified by the white squaw who wore guns and otherwise acted in such an un-squawlike manner, placed small pieces of cornbread in Belle's coffin, carrying out their ancient death ritual.[13]

How Belle Starr came to that inglorious end is another story that my father told, an East Oklahoma version which agrees with none of the published accounts. (In his old age he learned of the Rascoe version and disagreed with it completely.) My father said that in the late 1880's the federal government, which alone had jurisdiction in Indian Territory, instituted a campaign to clean up that haven of fugitives from justice in response to the pleas of the upright citizens, both white and Indian. Federal authorities in Fort Smith assembled a sizable force composed of deputy U.S. marshals, citizens, and troops; the small army pursued the outlaws into an isolated part of the mountains and trapped them in a horseshoe bend of a flooded river. They sealed off the neck of land and waited.

Belle Starr's gang, which included her eighteen-year-old son Ed Reed, was trapped with the rest. As acknowledged head, Belle called a council to decide what was to be done. On three sides of them was the flooded river; on the neck of land waited the law to take them in, some of them for rewards, dead or alive. Escape seemed impossible; tension mounted; quarrels arose. Most of the gang, including Belle's son, favored surrender. Belle, who declared that she would never surrender, proposed that they attempt to swim their horses across the swollen river. Despite assurances that she would never succeed, she mounted her horse and called for those who were not cowards to follow her. No one moved. Alone, she rode toward the river. Just as she plunged her horse over a bluff into the dark water, a shot rang out and she crumpled in her fancy saddle. Her own son had shot her in the back. When her body was recovered, he claimed the reward and eventually received a lighter sentence for his own crimes because of his betrayal.

This version of Belle Starr's death is an appropriate end for the legend of the woman outlaw because it raises a melodramatic and sordid life to the level of the heroic, portraying the unconquerable individual betrayed by his own flesh and blood. However, this dramatic ending in no way resembles the facts. The simple truth is that in February, 1889, Belle had accompanied her current husband, Jim July, alias Starr, down the road to Fort Smith, where he was going to appear in court on a larceny charge; she was returning home alone when she was shot in the back from ambush by an unknown assailant. Her body was found by a neighbor, lying face down in the mud of the road where she had fallen from her horse. As soon as he heard the news, Jim Starr returned from Fort Smith and over Belle's freshly dug grave pulled a gun on neighbor Ed Watson, who reportedly had quarreled with Belle over some land, and accused him of killing her. Watson was later tried for the crime, but Belle's son, Ed Reed, refused to testify against him; neighbors swore that Watson was not a troublemaker and he was freed.[14]

Though he could find no evidence, Rascoe found a widespread belief in East Oklahoma that Ed Reed, Belle's son, was the killer of his mother. Reed, the offspring of Belle's alliance with outlaw Jim Reed, was born in California where his father and Belle had fled after Jim Reed had murdered two men in North Texas, and the son already had a criminal record at the time of his mother's death. Some people hinted strongly to Rascoe that an incestuous relation existed between Belle and her eighteen-year-old son and that he killed her after she had horse-whipped him for riding her favorite horse without her permission. Frank Dalton, one of the outlaw Dalton brothers, also alleges that Ed killed his mother. In his published reminiscences Dalton states that Ed, who had been in hiding from the law, returned to Younger's Bend and waited in the brush near Belle's cabin to go in after nightfall so he could get money from her. In the dusk he saw what he thought was an officer of the law peering about in the yard. He fired into the shadows and hit Belle, who, dressed in men's clothing, was looking for a hole in the fence where pigs had been getting into the field. A. W. Neville, who recounts this story, says that it sounds imaginary.[15]

Finally, Glen Shirley believes that Belle's current husband, Jim July, alias Starr, killed her, for fear that she would learn of his infidelity. In the twenty years after Jim Reed's death, Belle married or lived with younger and younger men. Sam Starr, for instance, was four years younger than she. After he was killed in 1886 in a gunfight, in which he also killed the law officer who had been trailing him,[16] Belle had a series of younger lovers,[17] and eventually she married Jim July, who was twenty-four when she was thirty-eight. He probably changed his name from July to Starr at Belle's insistence because she had kept that name all along, perhaps because she liked the dramatic sound of it. Shirley says that Jim July was being unfaithful to Belle and was afraid she would find out and kill him; so he killed her first.[18]

Though my father's account of Belle Starr's death agrees with none of the numerous other versions, it does contain one verifiable motif, if a borrowed one. Belle's death-defying leap on her horse into the flooded river was derived from a story about Sam Starr, her former husband. In 1886 Sam, who was being chased by a posse, jumped his horse off a twenty-foot bluff and swam the river to escape. That dramatic act was transferred to the Belle Starr death legend.

Within a few months after Belle's death, a book entitled *Bella [sic] Starr, the Bandit Queen, or the Female Jesse James* was published by Richard K. Fox Publications, New York. The work of a hack writer, it purported to be a biography, employing realistic narrative and dialogue, and incorporating an alleged diary. Published in paperback and sold for twenty-five cents, the book, according to Rascoe, "does not have a single essential fact correct."[19]

Even so, my father's stories about Belle Starr illustrate that the popular imagination was also at work on the available material in making a legend of her while she still lived. The story of the biscuit dough demonstrates the skill with guns an outlaw is supposed to have along with the cold calm to make that skill effective. The defiant death of Belle in the other tale has the grand manner about it, and as in the endings of other outlaws' lives appeals more strongly to the emotions than to logic. Thus such tales as these are the folk method of making heroes larger than life and enabling them to triumph over the harsh frontier environment in a way that is not possible in real life.

1. My father, Albert Slayton Anderson, son of Berry and Martha Henson Anderson, was born near Wilburton, Indian Territory, February 10, 1882. After he married, he moved to Old Greer County, Texas (now Harmon County, Oklahoma), and thence to Wheeler County in the Texas Panhandle, where he died October 20, 1956.

2. Loraine Epps Anderson, my wife, says that when she taught school in Northeast Louisiana at Delhi she heard a Mr. Gholson tell about Old Man Younger, father of the famous outlaw brothers, who came to Delhi on his old white, bullet-scarred horse and rode up on the wooden sidewalk and into the open door of a mercantile store, frightening the clerks and the Negroes. According to Frederick W. Williamson, *Northeast Louisiana* (Monroe, Louisiana, 1939), pp. 95 and 103, Jesse and Frank James and the Younger brothers were in Northeast Louisiana for a time after the Civil War. There is a "Jesse James house" in Delhi; it was built by Captain Jared, an uncle of the James brothers. Because residents of Northeast Louisiana suffered at the hands of the Yankees during the war and because the outlaws were said to have aided the Confederacy, the James and Younger brothers were accepted in the area and children were named for them.

3. Burton Rascoe, *Belle Starr* (New York, 1951).

4. Glen Shirley, *Law West of Fort Smith: A History of Frontier Justice in the Indian Territory, 1834-1896* (New York, 1957), p. 86.

5. Rascoe, *op. cit.*, pp. 115-16.

6. *Ibid.*, p. 118.

7. *Ibid.*, pp. 154, 177-78.

8. *Ibid.*, p. 188.

9. *Ibid.*, p. 214.

10. Shirley, *op. cit.*, p. 86.

11. Rascoe, *op. cit.*, p. 215.
12. *Ibid.*, p. 234.
13. *Ibid.*, pp. 242-43.
14. *Ibid.*, pp. 247-48. See also Carroll C. Holloway, *Texas Gun Lore* (San Antonio, 1951), p. 154, who accepts the story that Ed Watson shot Belle Starr.
15. A. W. Neville, *The Red River Valley, Then and Now* (Paris, Texas, 1948), p. 53.
16. Shirley, *op. cit.*, p. 94.
17. Rascoe, *op. cit.*, pp. 194 and 210. These were said to include the outlaws Jack Spaniard, Jim French, John Middleton, and "Blue Duck." Jesse James reportedly spent several weeks in hiding at Belle Starr's Younger's Bend cabin. Called "Mr. Williams from Texas" by Belle, he was unknown to her husband, Sam Starr.
18. Shirley, *op. cit.*, p. 92.
19. Rascoe, *op. cit.*, p. 15.

Legend of the Lad

ELEANOR MITCHELL BOND

IN THE CHRONICLES of the North Texas Panhandle, probably no single character is now more vividly remembered than a certain salty, flannel-mouthed cowboy of the Box T Ranch by the name of Georgie Sennitt. You probably won't recognize him by that name. Hardly anyone ever does. He was known in every corner of the vast Texas cow country as The Irish Lad, "the dancin'est, whiskey-drinkin'est cowpoke between Wolf Creek and the Canadian River." So thoroughly representative was he of his time and section that his story has become a part of the folklore of the flat, limitless plains of the West.

No one seems to know when The Irish Lad was born—or where. He himself said he had no idea how old he was, or who his parents were. And if he did have any pertinent information of this sort, he was reluctant to tell it. No one seems to remember when he made his first appearance in the little town of Higgins. He was always just a part of the scene—one of the mainstays of the sparsely settled frontier. The only thing that stuck Higgins together at that time, most folks said, was "whiskey and sandburs," and The Lad certainly did his share with regard to the whiskey. There is probably more fact than fantasy in the tale that most of his salary, reputed to be from eighteen to twenty dollars a month, was spent on Saturdays in the Ranch Saloon, the only saloon in town in the early days. It is undisputed fact that hardly a Saturday went by that he was not seen with his foot on the brass rail, drinking everybody else under the table, and holding his liquor like a man. The amount of whiskey which he is purported to have consumed at one sitting grows with each telling. In fact, bending an elbow was the cause of his being fired on numerous occasions from the Box T. But as hands were scarce and The Lad always had a way with a fractious horse, he was always rehired on the promise of good, sober behavior.

There was the time Pat Doyle, then manager of the Box T, sent The Lad to plow a fireguard inside the pasture fence, which ran along the road a quarter-mile north of the town. The Lad had made two or three rounds with his walking plow when he suddenly decided that the Gray place also needed a little protection. The E. C. Gray place was just across the road, south of the Box T. Furthermore, it adjoined the town on the northeast. So when The Irish Lad got within sight of the saloon, all good resolution about work left him. He merely drove the team into town without lifting the plow from the ground, hitched the horses at the saloon, and set 'em up for the boys. After all, it *was* Saturday. It was only after he was well into the second bottle that he suddenly remembered the unfinished job. Swinging through the saloon door, and unhitching the team, he began to plow long and deep furrows up and down the street. One might call them "whiskey furrows," for just as firewater does nothing for a man's equilibrium, it did nothing for the evenness of those rows. For weeks after, a buggy ride down Main Street could be recommended only for a body with a strong constitution.

My father, Grover C. Mitchell, lived in the little town of Higgins from the time he was seven. His remembrance of The Lad is clear and keen. He says: "In 1899, when I was not quite eight, I put The Irish Lad in a special category, and I've kept him there ever since. Mother had a red-headed Irish girl who did the housework, and every time The Lad was in town, he would come by the house to court Stella. It was a rather mild and very blushing romance, but on his frequent visits

The Lad never failed to bring two sacks, a little one filled with chocolate candy for the lass—and a gunny sack filled with empty beer bottles for my brother and me. No present could have been more welcome: Billy Adams, who ran the old Ranch Saloon, paid two cents apiece for the little beer bottles, and five cents for the large quart sizes. It must have taken The Lad all week to find the ten to twenty bottles he brought us. Maybe he even drank them empty, but every Saturday the wooden buckets in Winsett's Store were pretty well emptied of lemon drops and 'lickrish' sticks because of his generosity. We sure were glad he liked Stella."

Another old-timer of the Lipscomb County community, Harry Zollers, now of El Paso, told me of The Lad's love for square dancing. He said that while he was as homely as a throwback to gorilla days, he could always cut a pigeonwing with a pretty girl, a couple of good fiddlers, and a pint or so of red-eye for inspiration. Mr. Zollers said, "He would and could, and I have seen him, jump high and pop his heels together twice before hitting the floor again—and all in time with the music."

Hardly anything was big enough, or important enough, to keep him from going to a dance. He was on his way to a square dance late one Saturday afternoon when Wolf Creek was on a rampage. After a gully washer, the creek was always dangerous to "man, buggy, and beast," but The Irish Lad was not one to turn back because of a raging torrent. According to Mr. Zollers, "He spurred Old Red into the yellow flood, which seized them both in its sandy clutches. The Lad, who was all dressed up in bright silk bandana, made-to-order boots, plaid shirt, and the corduroy breeches he always wore to social affairs, was a heavy chunk of a fellow, and he had to slide from the saddle, hang onto the horn, and swim frantically, or both he and the horse would have drowned. The next day, some cowpunchers found him and his horse away down the river where Wolf Creek joins the north Canadian, wet, bewildered—with his boots full of sand, his corduroys smelling like a skunk—and still asking where the dance hall was located!"

The Lad loved to dance, but he generally "paid the fiddler" next day. Mr. Zollers recollects one such "morning after": "One morning, when Papa opened the gates of the lumberyard, he heard a great groaning, and immediately began to search for the source. There, on the ground, between two high stacks of lumber, lay The Irish Lad, badly injured with two broken wrists. After bathing his face with water and bringing him back to consciousness, Papa asked The Lad just *how* he had got into the yard, which was surrounded by a six-foot board fence, topped with two strands of tight barbed wire. The Lad told him that he had attended the big dance at Higgins, had danced until the wee hours, and had drunk not wisely, but too well. He had mounted his big bronc and slapped him with his hat, and the last he remembered he was sailing through the air over the fence, and was landing on his hands. The Lad had fine-looking tapering fingers, small wrists, and nice forearms, but after this accident his wrists were huge, crooked, knotty, and terrible to look at. Because of this, he wore gauntlets with long dangling whang strings, and many a lady fair felt the sting of those whangs as he followed the caller and danced the squares in the way that an Irishman was supposed to dance."

One of the best-remembered stories of The Irish Lad is that of the famous horse race between him and that well-known homespun philosopher Will Rogers. At that time, there seemed to be nothing unusual about Will. He was just another cowboy who worked on the Ewing Ranch near the Box T—but he did have a fast horse.

One rainy morning in the spring of 1899, Will and The Irish Lad were talking on the porch of the old saloon. "Talking big," my father called it.

"Why, that buzzard bait of yours is ready for the bone pile!" boomed The Lad, in a curious combination of Irish brogue and western drawl. "Five dollars sez Old Red can outrun your horse from the Grace fence corner to the railroad tracks."

The J. W. Grace corner was a quarter-mile south of the tracks.

Will didn't answer immediately. He took his knife and slowly scraped a piece of mud from his boot. Then, scratching his head in the gesture which was always to be so typical of him, he grinned. "Ah'll take that bet," he said.

"Yee-aay-ee!" somebody yelled, "a horse race!" And instantly everything was confusion. Throngs appeared from nowhere, and everybody within hearing distance rushed for a vantage point on the veranda of the old Higgins Hotel. Before Will and The Lad had carelessly mounted their horses to ride to the starting point, the old porch was sagging with its load of spectators. Men tore past waving greenbacks; stakeholders had money coming out every pocket; and tradition says that by the time the cowboys had reached the fence corner to begin the race, more than a hundred dollars had been placed in quick bets.

All was quiet as the crowd waited for the start. Then suddenly, both men slapped their black Stetsons back and forth on each side of the horses' flanks; mud flew; cowhands yelled; and the race was on! It looked mighty close for about half the distance, but at that point Will's horse began nosing out in front. All the speed Old Red could summon wasn't enough to catch up. When he saw that he was beaten, The Irish Lad stopped slapping his horse, reined up to a trot, and rode up to the saloon.

He hitched his horse and looked at him. Old Red was breathing heavily, and standing ankle deep in mud. "You win," The Lad said to Will, "but my horse never was a mudder. We'll try it again in dry weather. Come on in, byes, tha drinks are on me!"

Life in the early days wasn't all "whoop and holler," however. Old-timers will tell you that among the quiet joys of life on the range was the singing of folksongs on night guard over a herd of skittery cattle. A cowboy who could bring out the sad notes of the old songs with a mouth organ was very much in demand. The Lad always carried one in his shirt pocket along with his sack of Bull Durham. He considered them as two necessities of life.

Among other necessities, The Lad always listed a horsehair rope, bacon grease, and "cow butter."

Everybody agreed that the rope was important. Many of the old-time cowpunchers believed that a rattlesnake would never crawl over a rope made of horsehair, and no cowboy would ever retire to his bedroll without carefully placing his hair rope in a circle around it. He always took care to see that it touched the ground everywhere and did not rest on a cow-chip, weed, or bush, especially if he happened to be camped in a prairie dog town whose population probably included a few rattlers.

And all agreed on the importance of bacon drippings. One of the strange beliefs of the early days was that the wound of a nail puncture didn't especially need doctoring, but the nail should have bacon grease rubbed on it!

But butter was different. Most of the cowboys listed it as a luxury, and when it was not available, resorted to a concoction known as "Charlie Taylor." This mixture of salty bacon grease, lard, and sorghum molasses tasted good spread on sour dough biscuits, but The Lad always complained of it as "a purty pore substitute for real cow butter."

There is no question that while the life of The Lad was full of difficulties, it was also full of the lightness and humor that make a colorful character.

With each generation, the figure of The Irish Lad grows a little more legendary among folks "down in the skillet," until today, in the annals of the famous old Box T, he has become an almost mythical person. Just how much of the tales that are told of him is truth and how much fiction cannot be determined, but the legends of his many escapades have taken the place of historical fact in the prime importance of things.

Folks say he was buried without much pomp in the lone little Lipscomb graveyard—but in the land bordering the 100th meridian, The Irish Lad is not really dead. He lives on in the folklore of the windswept plains, a symbol of the early frontier days; a symbol of his sunburned section; and for that matter, a true symbol of that hard and reckless breed of men who tamed the West because they were tougher than it was.

Stories of Ranch People

STANLEY W. HARRIS

DURING MY childhood I lived for a few years on a ranch and heard many stories told by the ranch people. Here are some of them.

Good Advice

Three men went out West to dig for gold. After many months of digging they had managed to end up with one bag of gold apiece. They started back and met an old man on the road. The old man gave them three pieces of advice that he said would never fail them: first, never travel at night, always stop by sundown; second, never try to cross a flooded river, wait until the river goes down; third, never confide in a woman. They thanked him for his advice and continued on their journey. The sun was almost down when they came to a town and stopped at an inn for supper. After eating and resting for a short time, two of the men decided to resume their travel, as they wanted to reach a near-by mountain top before stopping for the night. The third man took the old man's advice and stayed at the inn. When he awoke the next morning he discovered that a fierce norther had blown in during the night. He decided to go on despite the cold, so he clothed himself appropriately and started up the mountain. When he reached the top he found his two friends frozen to death, so he took their gold and continued on his journey.

He had traveled for days when he came to a river at flood stage. There were some men at the river with a wagonload of gold, debating as to whether they should cross during the flood stage or wait till the river went down. After much talk they decided to cross the river that day. One fellow managed to swim across the river with a rope and the others built a raft to put the wagon on. When they were ready to push off they asked the walking stranger if he wanted to ride over with them to the other side of the river, but he remembered the old man's advice and declined to go. When the men pushed off they were immediately swept into rough water; the raft was destroyed by the current, and the rope the man held on the far bank jerked him into the river. All the men were drowned.

The traveler waited until the river went down and then crossed over. Following the river a short way to see if he could find any sign of the men and their wagon, he soon came across the wagon with the wheels gone; half the gold was still in it. He found a good hiding place for the gold and went on to the next town, where he purchased a wagon and two horses. After going back and loading up the gold, he continued on his journey. Another week of traveling finally brought him to his home town and his dear sweet wife.

Still remembering the old man's advice, he didn't tell his wife where he got the gold, and after a few attempts to find out she quit asking him. But she wrote her two sisters about the matter and shortly they came for a visit. They also tried to pry the secret of the gold out of him, but they too failed. Buying some beer, they persuaded their sister to get her husband to drink it. This started loosening his tongue. The sisters were listening outside the door when he began his story about the gold. When he finished the part about the river crossing, the sisters rushed in and accused him of murdering the men. The sheriff was called and he was thrown in jail. A trial was held and the jury decided he must have been guilty of murder because he wouldn't even tell his wife. He was taken out and hanged and the three sisters took the gold and divided it equally.

The Balking Mule

A rancher wooed and won himself a wife. Driving into town for the marriage, he didn't want to hitch his best horse to the buckboard, so he hitched up a mule he used out on his ranch. After the ceremony he loaded his wife's belongings into the buckboard and started home. When they were barely out of town the mule balked and sat down. The rancher said, "That's the first time." With a little persuasion the mule got up and went on. About halfway home the mule balked again and the rancher said, "That's the second time." The mule was persuaded to get up and go again. Within sight of the house the mule balked once more and the rancher said, "That's the third time." Climbing down, he picked up his gun from the back of the buckboard and shot the mule dead. His wife, who had been quiet up until now, lambasted him for killing the mule. The rancher looked at his new wife and said, "That's the first time." You know after that, that rancher had the best wife ever known in those parts.

The Careless Rancher

A rancher was almost forty before he decided to get married. Having written to all the lonely hearts clubs he could find, he finally settled on a forty-year-old woman who he thought would be a good match for him. He wrote to her and told her to come on out and they would tie the knot. Well, it was the worst choice he could have made. She nagged him from daylight until dark, nagged his cowhands, nagged until she caused all the good horses to turn to bucking and pitching, made the paint peel off the house, and forced the clouds to stay away, creating a drought for several years. This lasted for about ten years until one day she had a heart attack and died. A Model T hearse was brought out from town, but they had to wait because a cloudburst had hit the area the night after the woman's death. The next day the casket was put in the hearse to be taken to town. A bump swing gate was at the edge of the rancher's property; to open it you had to bump it with a vehicle. The rain had caused it to be tighter than usual and when the hearse bumped the gate it jarred the casket, shaking the dead wife's heart into renewed activity. She regained consciousness and immediately wanted to know why she was there, why the ground was so wet, and why, why, why.

This time the cowhands moved to town, the horses ran off, and drought returned to the earth. After another ten years the wife died again. Again it rained. After three days the weather cleared up and the casket was loaded into the Model T. As the hearse neared the bump gate the old rancher called a halt, yelling, "Stop this contraption and I'll open the bump gate. No need to take any chances!"

Short in the Saddle

Riding out on the range one day, a cowhand came upon a rattlesnake. His horse got excited, started pitching, and took off on a wild stampede. They hadn't gone far when they came to a barbed-wire fence, where the horse made a sharp turn, throwing the cowboy astraddle the top wire. The horse was going so fast when he threw the cowboy, and the barbs were so sharp, that he was split clear up to his Adam's apple. Not to be fazed, the cowboy got up, lengthened his stirrups to fit his situation, and continued on his journey.

The Smallest Paisano

[This story is hard to tell in print because of the emphasis that is put on certain words and the lowering of the voice as you progress to the last word, which is spoken with all the lung power you have.]

The first Paisano on earth was about the smallest bird that existed. Why our present-day hummingbird is large compared to the first Paisano. She had the smallest wings; they were real small. Real tiny feet and a short tail. She was just the smallest little bird that existed. Well one day she laid an egg, and man! was that egg ever small. Why an English pea is large compared to that egg. One day that egg hatched out [here you begin to lower your voice] and man oh man!! you can't imagine how small that little bird was. Why that Paisano was so small that when he ran out on a highway he could run under a walking turtle without ruffling a feather. The wings of this baby bird were the teeny weeniest of the teeniest. The feet of this Paisano—why ant legs are big compared to them. They were real teeny, weeny, tinesy. The body and head were only a tenth the size of a newborn hummingbird. That Paisano was so small that the mother kept losing him in the nest. And do you know what the very first word of the baby Paisano was? [short pause] *MAMA!*

Tall Timber Tales

EDWIN W. GASTON, JR.

TO THE STOREHOUSE of folklore, the sawmill life of East Texas has contributed its full share. Tall tales and true, as well as songs, chronicle the activities—economic, religious, social—of the people associated with the timber industry in the counties of Angelina, Nacogdoches, Polk, Sabine, and San Augustine. The representative materials that I have selected for presentation here may be classified broadly as pertaining to animals and to people.

Among the tall tales about animals are two involving hogs. The sawmill "front," or logging camp, naturally lay near the forest, where, in East Texas at least, livestock owners were oblivious of property lines—particularly in the absence of fences—in letting their animals forage for food. At one "front" near the Sabine River, a hungry hog chanced one day upon a woods crew working with dynamite to clear stumps off a railroad right-of-way. The hog caught the crew's collective back turned and gobbled up a stick of dynamite, percussion cap and all. Before it could get clear of the blasting area, however, the swine paid the price of pilferage: the woods crew set off a charge, which, in turn, ignited the dynamite eaten by the boar. When the debris settled, the astonished workmen found two smoked hams, a generous supply of fried pork chops, and some barbecued ribs.

Another hog in the area of a certain sawmill made a pig of itself by eating everything in sight, especially pine cones.

Vexed with the swine, company employees one day caught the animal and sold it to a near-by butcher. When the butcher rendered the meat he got not lard, but turpentine.

Another tale is that of the unfortunate dog that wandered into a sawmill and came regrettably close to a circular saw. Before the dog could disengage itself, the saw had cut the animal into three equal lengths. At that very moment, fortunately, the sawmill doctor happened along. Seizing the opportunity for an experiment in anatomy, he snatched up the three pieces, sewed them back together, and, miraculously, restored life to the dog. But in his haste, as the doctor soon discovered, he had sewed the hind third on the front part of the trunk and the front third on the back part. Ever since that time the dog has chased its nose with its tail.

Among the tall timber tales about people is the one of the false teeth that gave a woods crew a helping hand in loading a particularly heavy log. The "chain gang," as the loading crew is known, was struggling with the log, which stubbornly refused to be budged into place on a railroad flatcar. Every member, including a large man with false teeth, strained to his utmost —but to no avail. Now it so happened that the fat man's teeth didn't fit and that he often carried them in his hip pocket, particularly when he was away from home and out of earshot of his wife. Such was the case at this time. Just when it seemed that the log would never be prodded into its proper place, the man accidentally backed into a tree. The pressure exerted on the false teeth in his back pocket made them clamp on to a sensitive spot of his anatomy, giving the man such a start that he heaved against the log with superhuman strength. It fell into place.

Then there is the story of an unusual sawmill marriage. A Negro wife of a "chain gang" employee appeared one Monday before a judge who had only the previous Saturday married the couple. She wanted a divorce. The judge naturally inquired as to the reason for the woman's hasty action. "Well, jedge," she replied, "hit's lak dis: ah only met dat man on Frid'y." Taken further aback by this disclosure, the judge pressed the woman for more reasons. She answered: "Lak ah said, ah only met him Frid'y. And ah mean to tell yo' dat he was de mos' ovah-introduced person ah evah come to know!"

In passing from the tall tale to the true, I should note what appears to be a rather significant feature of sawmill lore. Apparently timber folk have failed, in East Texas at least, to create the mythical hero. Davy Crockett, Mike Fink, Pecos Bill, Paul Bunyan, and John Henry, as I have found, are known among sawmill circles. And Bunyan and Henry, it is true, are associated with logging and railroads. But no truly indigenous legendary figure has been called to my attention by Piney Woods sources.

The representative examples of true tales and other folklore elements that I have chosen from tall timber life may be grouped broadly into those relating to the job and to the home. To the former, or the occupational, belong stories and songs bearing on success, business deals, and language. To the latter, or the domestic, may be assigned stories and songs touching upon medicine, religion, recreation, superstition, and folk wisdom.

Songs on the job frequently enabled workers to do their chores in a helpfully rhythmical manner. For example, the "steel gang," which laid railroad ties and rails from the mill site to the "front," often did its work to the rhythm of songs of its own composition. As members of a crew picked up rails, they would sing out: "Pick 'em up and lay 'em down." Then, as they aligned the rails, they would add: "Jint 'em back." Finally, as they spiked the rails, they would conclude: "Swing 'em high," referring, of course, to the sledge hammers. The entire song would ring out with the collective steps of the operation:

> Pick 'em up and lay 'em down;
> Jint 'em back;
> Swing 'em high.

Another song sung by the "steel gang" is the widely dispersed play-party song, "Old Joe Clark," including some stanzas of apparently local origin:

Ole Joe Clark makin' ties,
Ole lady Clark a haulin',
All little Clarks sittin' in a row
An' half of 'em a squallin'.

CHORUS:
Roun' an' aroun' the ole Joe Clark
Roun' an' aroun' I say,
Roun' an' aroun' the ole Joe Clark,
I haven't got long to stay.

Once I had a han'some gal,
I brought 'er from the South,
She ate so many butterbeans
'Til you couldn't see 'er mouth.
    (repeat chorus)

Took 'er to the blacksmith shop
To have 'er mouth made small,
She opened up so doggoned wide
That she swallowed shop an' all.
    (repeat chorus)

Went to see ole Joe Clark
An' he was sick abed;
I rammed my hand down in his throat
An' pulled out a chicken head.
    (repeat chorus)

Went to see my gal one day
She met me at the door,
Shoes and stockin's in 'er hand
An' 'er feet all ovah the floor.
    (repeat chorus)

Although saloons were not allowed on most sawmill property, these houses of hospitality still entered prominently into the business, as well as the social, life of the sawmill. Near one particular mill, an enterprising saloonkeeper frequently cashed pay checks. A casual sort of fellow, he did not bother to present the checks to the company for payment until he had a large number on hand. Once when his accumulated holdings of checks totaled more than $1,300, he attempted to redeem them at the company commissary. The commissary manager was short on cash at the moment and sought to persuade the saloonkeeper to retain the checks for a while longer. In disgust, the saloonkeeper—undoubtedly a pragmatist—sought to take out the checks in barter. He suggested: "Jes' give me $1,300 wo'th of Star chewin' tobacco."

Another folklore element at sawmills was the special language that developed out of the work, including such terms as the following:

(1) "Loader man," one who participated in the operation of loading logs on flatcars or wagons;

(2) "Quarter boss," a company-employed law enforcement officer, who held a Ranger's commission;

(3) "Steel gang," a group which laid ties and rails for railroads from the mill to the "front";

(4) "Crummy," a railroad caboose that derived its name from the fact that laborers used the facility as a place for eating their lunches and generally dropped crumbs of food on the floor;

(5) "Chain gang," a group which loaded logs on flatcars and wagons for transportation from the woods to the mill (its name deriving from the fact that it worked with log chains);

(6) "Chainman," a member of a chain gang;

(7) "Skidman," a member of a chain gang whose job was to skid logs from where they fell to the place where they would be loaded;

(8) "Roll-down man," a member of a chain gang whose task was to roll the logs into place on the flatcar or wagon;

(9) "Loc'y man," a member of a railroad operational crew;

(10) "Tongue-steering yoke," "swaying yoke," and "lead yoke," the oxen that dragged logs from the forests to the railroad cars or wagons for transportation to the sawmill.

Part of the sawmill language, of course, included more colorful expressions, such as the inference that a mill operator does not "have enough credit to buy a string of lace leather." And the language, by virtue of the fact that much work was performed in the presence of continuous noise, included signs made by the fingers and hands. A finger touched to the nose, for example, meant, "I don't know." One touched to the ear signified, "I can't hear you." A finger jutted with emphasis toward the ground indicated, "Go to hell!"

In the home at a sawmill, medicine naturally was important. The larger mills had their own doctors, who dispensed recognized medicaments. But often the housewife depended upon home remedies, and even the doctors themselves sometimes resorted to the use of unusual treatment. Such a treatment occurred in the case of the wife of a sawmill hand who was having difficulty in giving birth to a child. The regular mill doctor failed in an attempt to induce birth and called upon an older colleague. The second doctor "snuffed the patient," holding a bottle of snuff under the woman's nose and having her inhale. As a result, he successfully delivered the baby.

Also in the domestic category of medicine was the fact that, in addition to officiating at the birth of a baby, the sawmill doctor often was called upon to name the child. One doctor with a sense of humor suggested for a girl baby the name "Placenta." To his astonishment the physician later discovered that the parents, ignorant of the anatomical meaning of the term, had followed his suggestion.

Unlike those of northern and western logging camps, the recreational pursuits in East Texas sawmills did not usually include such contests of skill as logrolling. Baseball was a popular sport among men and boys. But in one camp the diamond sport was short-lived. After clearing an area and building a baseball park, the men and boys engaged too enthusiastically in the game and its sidelights. Drinking and fighting broke up a game, and the sawmill owner, a rather narrowly moral man, immediately ordered the park closed and replaced the diamond itself with a truck garden.

Holidays in sawmills provided recreational opportunity for the entire family. In many camps the Fourth of July especially was important, with the company sponsoring a free barbecue for employees and their friends. But the "friends" began to abuse the privilege in one camp at least, some coming from as far as fifty miles to partake of the food and entertainment. The free barbecue was discontinued in this camp.

Of the superstitions around the sawmill home, the belief in "charms" seems to have predominated. Various charms were worn to ward off disease and to prevent accident. Still another indication of the power of charms is the story from a Nacogdoches sawmill camp where there lived a rather old Negro employee who had a young wife. One day he asked the foreman for permission to get off from work in order to go to Humble, Texas. When pressed for his reason, he explained to the company official that he needed to have the power of a little blue stone charm recharged. He said that he had obtained the charm from a man in Humble and that he would have to take it back to the same person to get it recharged. He needed it to keep younger men from calling on his wife during his absence from home.

East Texas sawmill life, with its humor and pathos and its ignorance and wisdom, is summed up in a true story, again from Nacogdoches. An old Negro woman served as cook and housekeeper to the mill foreman and his wife. Among her countless virtues was the ability to bake an apple pie unrivaled in the area. This pie, as well as all of her tasty dishes, the unlettered old servant prepared without the aid of cookbook and sans any apparent science. One day the foreman's wife inquired: "Mary, how in the world do you always manage to make perfect apple pies?" The cook replied: "Why, ma'm, de Lord helps me." Trying to hide her amusement, the mistress inquired further: "Well, then, why doesn't the Lord help me with my cooking?" And the old cook, with a look that reflected the wisdom of the ages, answered: "Because, ma'm, yo' kin read."

INFORMANTS: Dave Kenley of Lufkin, Texas, and D. D. Deveraux, Robert Weeks, and Clyde Thompson, all of Diboll, Texas, sawmill employees; Clyde J. Woodward of Nacogdoches, Texas, sawmill foreman; and Dr. G. F. Middlebrook of Trawick, Texas, sawmill doctor. Certain materials from the files of the late Dean T. E. Ferguson, Stephen F. Austin State College, Nacogdoches, also have been helpful.

Anecdotes of Two Frontier Preachers
ALVA RAY STEPHENS

ONE OF THE unique characters produced by the American West was the frontier preacher. He was typically a man of strong character and often of ready wit who had been converted to religion and called to preach after reaching manhood.

The stories about Andrew Jackson Potter and Lorenzo Dow presented here were secured from the late Stuart Killough of Pflugerville, Texas, on November 1, 1958. Killough was eager to talk about these two men whom he had admired ever since the days when his father, also a frontier preacher, would tell stories about them over and over. Before relating the incidents for the tape recorder, Killough would rehearse in order to get the details in their correct places. He had the amazing ability of telling a long, detailed story once and then repeating it almost verbatim while adding a few salient points not mentioned in the rehearsal.

Andrew Jackson Potter, first of the two preachers discussed by Killough, was born in Missouri on April 3, 1830. His father died in 1840, and Andrew, thrown on his own resources, began earning a living with race horses. Perhaps gambling also helped, for it was said that he was better at playing cards than at spelling. He attempted to enlist in the expeditionary forces for service in the Mexican War, but was rejected. He was, however, accepted by the commissary department. In 1852 he arrived in San Antonio, where he married the following year.

Converted at a camp meeting in 1856, he became a Methodist preacher. He drove a herd of cattle to Kansas in 1861, and the next year joined the Confederate Army, in which he served throughout the Civil War. The remainder of his life was spent largely on the Texas frontier; he was the first preacher to deliver a sermon at Fort Concho. He dropped dead in his pulpit October 21, 1895. See *The Handbook of Texas*, edited by Walter Prescott Webb (Austin, 1952), II, 400-401.

It is interesting that Killough refers to the second preacher, Lorenzo Dow, as an early Texan. This is a good example of how tales travel and become part of the folklore of a people. A New Englander by birth, Dow became a circuit rider in 1794 and preached in many places. He made three trips to the British Isles before his death in 1834 and spent much time in the southern United States. Natchez, Mississippi, was as far west as Dow came. Many of Texas' early settlers migrated from regions in which Dow had preached, however, and brought stories about him with them. See *Dictionary of American Biography*, edited by Allen Johnson and Dumas Malone (New York, 1943), V, 410.

Here then are the tales and anecdotes of two frontier preachers in the words of a master storyteller.

This is Stuart Killough. I'm going to tell you a story that was told to me by my father back in 1900 and he personally knew Andrew Jackson Potter and worked with him some himself. Now Andrew Jackson Potter was a gambler down in Bastrop, Texas, to start with. He was a rather successful one. Well, like all gamblers he liked to see bigger towns, so he decided to go to San Antonio on a spree, and he went to San Antonio. And, of course, the first place he went to was the saloon. The next thing he did was get drunk. Then the next thing he did was to get into trouble with the policemen, and he was a pretty tough man and they had a pretty hard time getting him to jail. He knocked four of them down. But finally [they] got him in jail and when they got him through the police

ANECDOTES OF TWO FRONTIER PREACHERS 187

court he didn't have much money left. But he had a little bit and he went down to the printing office and had a lot of handbills struck and a great French singer was going to come to San Antonio to sing. And he also made arrangements at the Opera House. Well, he was up on the stage. He had a thin curtain on purpose so they could see his shadow through the curtain and he was back there and the crowd got to cheering him to come out. Well, he would have had a big audience if he had of stayed back a little longer; but, he couldn't stand the cheering so he came out and he began to sing and he couldn't sing and the audience soon found it out. Well, they had some young, smart fellow in the audience. He came out with his gun and wanted to know who he was. Potter threw his disguise aside and covered him with two guns. He says, "I'm nobody but Andrew Jackson Potter," says, "I think that I've got even with your police courts." Well, the cowboys and others in town they all gathered [around] him, took him down to the saloon and they had a big time all night.

Now just how Andrew Jackson Potter became a preacher I don't know. But, anyhow, he became a preacher in time to be a chaplain during the Civil War in the southern army. Before battle he could always be found exhorting his men, and when the order came to charge he grabbed the gun and led the charge. Well, after the war was over with he came back and went on into the ministry and they knew he was a tough man and they saved him some tough places.

Well, down on the coast somewhere in the Corpus Christi to Brownsville country they had a bunch of smugglers somewhere down there and they sent him down there to start a church, and he found a little schoolhouse isolated and he found the trustees and they said he could preach there. Well, the people around there, they didn't want no preaching so they got together and was going to have a dance at the same time that he was to preach. Well, he came in at the proper hour and they were all there. They had their guns and he walked in,

Winchester in his hand. He stood it up against the table that he used for a pulpit. He laid a couple of pistols down on the table and he said, "Well, folks," he says, "I've made legal arrangements to use this schoolhouse to preach in at this hour." He says, "I understand that you've announced a dance here," and he says, "I claim priority." "In other words," he says, "I made arrangements first and I've got a right to use the schoolhouse," and he says, "We are going to have preaching." He says, "We may have a little gun play before we have preaching, but," he says, "if we are, let's get started and have the fight; I never like to begin preaching late." He says, "Don't worry, we're going to have preaching." Well, an old red-bearded fellow down in the audience in the back of the house he raised up and says, "Parson," says, "I didn't know that was your game," says, "now you just go ahead and do all the preaching you want to and I'll take care of the fighting," and says, "I don't think there'll be any fighting."

This is Stuart Killough, telling [another] story about Andrew Jackson Potter, a well-known frontier preacher of Texas. He was a chaplain in the Civil War. He started out at Bastrop as a gambler and he had quite a few experiences. Among other experiences was one down in the Seguin country somewhere down there many years ago. He and a preacher by the name of George B. Killough was sitting down on the rostrum of a church and there was an old drunk man there. Well, the drunk man was fooling around and he was a pretty tough character and there was a young preacher on the floor preaching. He brought out something in a loud voice and an old psycho walked in, I mean this old drunk, walked in behind him in the audience on the rostrum and sang out whatever the preacher said just as loud as he could right behind the preacher. The preacher turned around with the intention of knocking Psycho Smith— I'll call that man's name directly. I say the preacher turned around with the intention of knocking this drunk man down but Andrew Jackson Potter was on his feet before the preacher had time to do anything. He had a walking cane. He grabbed that old drunk man by the arm and drew back his walking cane, says, "Look here you old scoundrel," says, "sit down here and listen to this sermon. That's no way to act in preaching." Well, this old drunk was quite a fighter. To hit him was one thing, to threaten to hit him was another and he knew Potter and he knew Potter would hit him and he was afraid of Potter as well as Potter was afraid of him. So he looked at Potter. He says, "All right, parson, just as you say—not as I care," so he sat down.

Well, a little later on, the church sent Potter out to San Angelo to build a church. Well, a Catholic priest had been able to stay within three miles of San Angelo, and that's about as close as any clergyman ever got to that town before. So Potter was fooling around, going from saloon to saloon, first one thing and another and mingling with the cowboys there, and they all found out he was a preacher and they had an organization to run him out. So he saw the sheriff and got a place to preach down in a corner of the jail in the yard outside, not in the jail. They all came down and they were going to run him out when he started preaching. Well, he had a box of something that he used as a pulpit and he had a long frock coat on and he reached back in his coat-tail pocket, pulled out his Bible, laid it down in front of him. He said, "Well, folks," says, "I'm a Methodist preacher. I come here to preach to you folks," and says, "I presume that you want preaching or you wouldn't have come down here." Says, "Nobody but these fellows in jail have got to listen at me," and he says, "You folks came down here of your own accord," but says, "I understand too that there is some talk of not having preaching here. Well," he says, "I intend to preach to you," says, "I'm pretty sure I'm going to do it by the help of God and these two forty-fives," and he brought out two from somewhere. Nobody knew where he got them at. One in each hand. He says, "I'm going to preach to you fellows," and he preached to them. They knew Potter's record when he was a gambler, with a gun. When he pulled the trigger he didn't miss and they all knew it.

Well, he stayed there four or five days and talked and worked around and finally he went up to one of the larger saloons in town, jumped up on one of the gambling tables and told them that they wanted to listen at him a minute. Says, "I've been here and I've been preaching to you fellows several days and you all know me," and he says, "I need some money to build a church on." He says, "Now I want all of you to kick in pretty heavy." He says, "I'm going to pass the hat." Well, he got a good start on a church right there in that saloon and it wasn't long till they had a church and from that day till this no preacher has ever had any trouble in San Angelo.

This is Stuart Killough again. I have told two former stories about Potter—Andrew Jackson Potter, and this is his wind-up. The best that I know of he started to preaching along about 1860, maybe as early as 1855. I do not know exactly. He served many churches in Texas from that time up till 1900 and he built a church at San Angelo and he served at many tough places, many places where preachers wouldn't go outside of himself and he built several churches. But after he became an old man, somewhat feeble, the church sent him back to the first church that he ever preached at, the first charge. He served it for a year and at the close of the year, he had all of his reports made out, he had his work absolutely completed. He was preaching his farewell sermon. He finished. He got through with it and he was ready to dismiss the congregation. He stopped and looked them over. He says, "Well, folks," says, "I think you've heard my last sermon." He says, "I think I'm going home," and he fell dead in the pulpit.

This is the story of a preacher named Lorenzo Dow. He was quite a noted character in early Texas. He did a number of quaint things. Among other things, one day he was going down the road and he met a little Negro and the little Negro had a tin horn. He asked the little Negro's name. The little Negro said "Gabriel." "Well," he says, "Gabriel, I met you at just the right time." Says, "I'll give you a dime if you'll go down to such and such a church about one mile from here and climb up that tree behind the pulpit there. Do you know where it is?" The little Negro says "Yas suh, I sho' do." "Well," says, "you climb up that tree and listen to me preach and when I say 'Blow, Gabriel, Blow,' you blow that horn for all it's worth."

Well, he went down to the church and preached on the Judgment. Of course, he knew the little Negro was up the tree. He got the congregation pretty well worked up and he hollered out just as loud as he could holler out, "Blow, Gabriel, Blow!" That little Negro gave the horn—blew on the horn for all it was worth. Everybody jumped to their feet and started to run. Lorenzo Dow hollered at them, says, "You fools set down," says, "What would you do if the Judgment was coming? That's nobody but a little Negro up the tree with a tin horn."

Well, Lorenzo Dow went on from there. He would make appointments to preach, sometimes as far as five years ahead of time. He was never known to miss an appointment. One time he made an appointment to preach at a brush arbor in an isolated place, went on a year or so and nobody heard anything about Lorenzo Dow. Well, the date of his preaching came around and the congregation they turned out. They had always turned out to see if he was going to get there. He would make them so far ahead of time and do so many quaint things. Well, they got there and they noticed a horse that looked like he had been ridden a little bit not far from this arbor, but they didn't pay any attention to that and they didn't see no Lorenzo Dow. Well, it went on and eleven o'clock came and still no Lorenzo Dow. They had a big box that they used for a pulpit and it was big enough and almost as long as anybody lying down. It was turned face downward, the open part of the box down. Well, that box began to move and Lorenzo Dow came out from under that box and preached to the people. He came there in the night sometime and he didn't know where to go and he was tired and he took his saddle and made him a bed and crawled in under that box and went to sleep and slept until eleven o'clock the next day and crawled out and preached to them.

And another time he was going through the country and he wanted to stay all night at a place and they said yes he could stay. Nobody there but a woman. Well, shortly after he had got there, there was a man came there, and he soon found that was not the man of the house; in fact, the man didn't belong there. Well, a little later on the woman's husband came in, and he was drunk. As he stepped up on the front porch, the first man came running into Lorenzo Dow's room. There was an empty flour barrel in there, and there was some lint cotton there, and the man jumped in this flour barrel and pulled the lint cotton down over himself to hide himself so this drunk man, the woman's husband, wouldn't find him.

So the drunk man, he began to raise quite a disturbance with his wife and she told him to go on and go to bed, that they had Lorenzo Dow staying with them that night. He says, "Lorenzo Dow. I've always heard that Lorenzo Dow could raise the devil." Says, "He's got it to do." Well, she tried to keep him out of there but in Lorenzo Dow's room he went, shook hands with Lorenzo Dow and told him that he understood that he could raise the devil and he had it to do. Well, Lorenzo Dow tried to quiet him down and he wouldn't quiet down. Lorenzo Dow says, "All right," says, "get you a good club and get there by the door. I'll do what I can. If the devil runs out by you, hit him a good hard lick." But says, "Don't hit him hard enough to kill him because we don't want a dead devil on our hands."

So he took the candle and he went hunting over the room like he was trying to find something till he got to this barrel where this fellow was hid under this lint cotton. He set the cotton on fire. Of course, the man had to come out of there and the cotton was hanging to him and it was a-blazing. He run by this drunk and the drunk was sure it was the devil so he let him have a good hard lick. And he swore from then on ever after that Lorenzo Dow could raise the devil, and he knew because he did it for him once. So that's all I know right now about Lorenzo Dow.

Wolves, Foxes, Hound Dogs, and Men

A. L. MILES

FOLKLORE is as earthy as my mother's favorite description of a stingy man: "Him? He'd skin a flea for its hide and tallow." Duncan Emrich says of folklore, "The material is traditional, but the touch of the individual is upon every item.... It is the difference between pot stew simmering on the open fire and the standard contents of a tin can."[1] It is this touch of the individual that has adapted much of the lore of the Old Country to America. The branding iron came to the Southwest from Spain by way of Mexico. No doubt the use of hound dogs for chasing the fox and other wild animals originated with the English country gentleman of former ages; but, like the Spanish branding iron, it made its way to Texas.[2]

Fox hunting has been carried on wherever English-speaking people have settled. In some areas, as on the North American prairies, similar methods are adapted to the chasing of other animals, such as wolves and coyotes, and even coons and possums. This is where Coryell County and many other sections of Texas come into the picture. And in these areas better and tougher hounds are required than are needed in the old-style British chase.

The chase of the fox with horses and hounds in England during the seventeenth century became surrounded by codes of social usage and legal enactments. Principal "organizations" or "Hunts" were founded in the early seventeenth century. A Hunt requires a pack or several packs of hounds, kennels, and a clubhouse. The Hunt or "Association" is directed by a "Master of Fox Hounds" and several paid employees. The principal of these are the "Huntsman," who arranges and leads the chase for the day, and the "Whippers-in," who see that dogs work properly. These officials and the hunters wear scarlet coats when in the field. Theoretically the expenses are paid by annual subscription for temporary hunting privileges. Subscription fees usually are far short of requirements and must be supplemented. This often becomes the responsibility of the Master of Fox Hounds, who has inherited his dignity and responsibilities from ancestors who founded the Hunt. Anyone may join in the chase, and large numbers of outsiders are often present.

In British hunting districts foxes are carefully preserved, and the haunts and habits of each family of foxes are studied so as to reduce the possibility of not finding them on the day of the chase. Hunts include men and women. When the Huntsman is in the place where he expects to find a fox, he turns loose the pack of twenty-five to forty hounds. Dogs immediately start searching for trails. When a dog finds a trail (in Coryell County it would be when a dog "strikes") he "gives tongue" (in terms of Coryell fox hunters he "opens up") and other dogs join him.

Others in the British Hunt are notified by bugle or cry of "Gone away!" Then the race is on. The Hunt requires fast horses with jumping skill. Hunters follow as closely as possible down roads, through gates, across fields, and over fences if necessary. Later they pay for damages.

Anyone seeing the fox shouts, "Tally-ho!" All huntsmen try to keep as close together as possible in order to be "in at the death." The fox sometimes goes into a hole or takes other cover. This is called "going to earth." When this occurs a fox terrier is turned loose to oust him so that the chase may continue.

Some form of the English pattern of hunting remains in the northeastern United States. It has flourished in New York, but because of popular community feeling against a crowd of human beings taking vicious dogs out to chase a small timid animal to its death, the sport has declined in recent years. There has been no decline in the hunting of foxes with hounds in Coryell County or other sections of Texas; but the pattern, which in my youth had changed greatly from that of the English hunts, has changed considerably more over the years of my observation.

The first hound dogs I remember seeing were owned by "Uncle" Lo Russell, who lived on the Leon River about fourteen miles northwest of Gatesville. He kept them for trailing deer. This was in about the middle 1890's. Uncle Lo hunted deer with a 10 gauge double-barrelled shot gun. The shells were hand loaded with an extra heavy charge of black powder and buckshot. About the best he could do was to get close enough to a deer to shoot it and cripple it. Then the hounds trailed and finally caught the crippled deer. This appeared to be an effective procedure, because Uncle Lo always brought back the venison.

In the late 1890's and early 1900's Coryell County hound-dog men concentrated their efforts on wolf hunts, mostly of coyotes. At that time coyotes were numerous in this area and I deeply regret that they are now all but extinct. Their near extinction, however, is by no means due to the activities of those who engaged in the wolf-hunting sport. I recall much criticism of wolf hunters for never catching and killing a wolf or coyote. In order to remain in the good graces of the owners of the land where they wanted to hunt, the wolf hunters consistently maintained that every effort was made to catch and destroy wolves. A half-century later, now that most of the old-time wolf hunters have passed away, and now that just about all the coyotes have been exterminated, it comes out that little or no effort was ever made actually to catch or destroy a wolf. In their rounds the wolf hunters often discovered dens of young coyotes, but none of the pups were ever destroyed. They were simply left to grow up and make for good hunting next year. All wolf hunters true to the tradition of following hounds bitterly resented the shooting and killing of a wolf.

In the late 1890's and early 1900's there was no formal organization of wolf hunters in this area; yet meetings of confirmed followers of hounds were held to discuss their problems and prospects for good or poor hunting or to rehash the hunt of the night before. These meetings were informal and unannounced, yet they were well attended. The word got around. A few of the favorite places of assembly in Gatesville were Dr. J. R. Raby's office at the First National Bank (he was president of the bank), O. K. Lovejoy's cotton buying office, or the office of C. E. Gandy, who was agent for Wells-Fargo Express.

No doubt the most outstanding hound-dog man in Coryell County was the late Dr. J. R. Raby, physician, banker, rancher, and breeder of registered shorthorn cattle. His show cattle won many prizes at stock shows in Fort Worth, Kansas City, and Chicago. Other members of the informal group of lovers of hounds included thirty to forty individuals representing a cross section of the population of this area, both white and colored. There were physicians, merchants, cotton buyers, mechanics, farmers, ranchers, day laborers, and just about every classification that could be mentioned. Yet they all had one common interest, hounds.

A familiar scene nowadays on a Saturday afternoon in Gatesville is a group of hound-dog men, white and colored, assembled at the southeast corner of the courthouse square discussing hound dogs and fox races.

In the late 1920's or early 1930's hunters in this area formed an organization known as Central Texas Wolf and Fox Hunters Association. After coyotes were ruthlessly destroyed by "government trappers," the organization was reduced to Coryell County Fox and Coon Hunters Association. About all that is left of the wolf-hunting days is old-timers' memories of the men and dogs participating in hunts of the early 1900's. It is quite interesting to listen to these old fellows—the few that are still living—extol the virtues of early day hounds as they consume the barbecue at a meeting of the Coryell County Fox and Coon Hunters Association held annually at Pecan Grove on Coryell Creek. They talk about "Big" and D. Mayberry's "Old Woodrow," Dr. Raby's "Old Major," Arch Boyd's "Old Oscar," Wade Hampton's "Old Rex," Mono Pruitt's "Old Emma," Wade Bone's "Old Bessie," Carl Gandy's "Old Troup," Oce Lovejoy's "Old Big Pup," and others too numerous to mention. These were some of the dogs that made names for themselves around 1913 and 1914 and that still live in the memory of wolf hunters who saw and heard them in action. In fact, there still exists a footprint of Oce Lovejoy's "Old Big Pup" in the cement walk in front of Lovejoy's home, preserved very much in the same manner in which footprints of movie stars are preserved in cement at a famous movie theater in Hollywood, and perhaps with as much respect and admiration. At least "Old Big Pup" was never charged with subversive activities by the association or anybody else.

Coryell County hound dogs have done much to erase racial prejudices in this area. As was true of the Wolf and Fox Hunters Association, the present Fox and Coon Hunters Association includes white and colored. In their meetings there are no signs of discrimination. Both white and colored men sit around the same table, eating their barbecue and discussing the merits and faults of various breeds of hounds, apparently unaware of race or color.

Often one of the high lights of association meetings is the dramatization by a certain old colored hound-dog man of a wolf or fox race. He has the unusual ability to imitate the exact tones of voice of many different hounds. He starts with the "strike" dog first on a cold trail, backtracking at times, and finally picking up a hot trail. He has other dogs "opening" or "coming in" at different times. He also brings in a "babbler," the kind of dog that interferes with the rest of the pack and is a real headache to hunters. Finally he has a whole pack of six or eight dogs, all in the race with as many different tones of voice, until the wolf is bayed or the fox is treed. As he gives almost perfect imitations of the voices or "mouths" of each of the dogs as they come into the race and follow the trail, he keeps his audience in close contact with the chase. He puts on the act with all the professional ability of a Shakespearean actor and always receives tremendous applause.

I might digress here to say that because of what appears to be complete absence of racial discrimination between white and colored hound-dog men, it seems possible that national tension could be lessened and probably eliminated if extremists on each side of the race problem could be persuaded to take an interest in and acquire a pack of good hound dogs. There is a magic something that grips hound-dog men and seems to overshadow and eliminate all forms of discrimination, at least as long as hound dogs are involved.

This does not imply that hound-dog men do not have the sort of petty jealousies and prejudices common to all men. The big farmer is jealous of a neighbor who is a bigger farmer. The rancher who has to make a living for his family, riding the range and personally caring for his own livestock, is jealous of the Johnny-come-lately who owns a ranch purchased and improved with "oil money" and lives in the city and has all ranch work done by hired help. This same kind of jealousy exists between hound-dog men who once owned wolf dogs, those who now own fox dogs, and those who own coon dogs. The man who owns only coon dogs seems to be the low man on the totem pole. Of course, the man who owned wolf dogs in the great days of wolf hunting is top man and the fox-dog man is in between. None of these jealousies, however, stem from race, color, or creed.

Of all breeds of dogs the hound dog is the least glamorous. He is a glum, listless-looking creature when not hunting.

Apparently he does not know enough to try to escape danger. I know of instances where this seeming inability to detect approaching danger has caused the death of some of the best hound dogs. Yet the good-for-nothing looking hound dog has the profound respect and affection of its owner.

Probably the hound-dog man's admiration for hounds is summed up in a statement made by Jim Nichols: "It is a well-known fact that if you get over to a dog what you want him to do, he will be eager and anxious to do it. I've had them stay on trail until they dropped dead in their tracks. Tragic but true."

Former dog sergeant at Gatesville Training School for Boys and now retired, Jim Nichols probably knows more about hound dogs—both hunting dogs and dogs trained for trailing people—than any other man in Texas or elsewhere. Anyhow that is my opinion. He has followed hounds on foot, on horseback, and in automobiles chasing wolves, foxes, coons, and people.

Evidence of Nichols' knowledge of hounds is contained in a copy of a letter he wrote in 1946 to B. F. Sylvester in Omaha. This letter indicates that Sylvester had requested a Texas Ranger named Olson to give him some information on training bloodhounds for apprehending fugitives. Olson referred Sylvester to Jim Nichols of the Gatesville Training School. Nichols' reply was given in detail and covered two and one-half typewritten pages, single spaced. This letter contained the following unusual paragraph marked "off the record": "It is not generally known, but true nevertheless, that dogs trail much better when the fugitive keeps his shoes on. If he abandons his shoes and goes barefooted, the trail is much harder to run." There is no explanation of this statement.

Nichols does not prefer bloodhounds for apprehending fugitives. This is evidenced in a Mexia, Texas, newspaper clipping giving an account of his apprehending two escaped German officers from the Mexia Prisoner of War Camp during World War II. This clipping (no date) states: "A weather-beaten Texas officer—and three hounds of dubious ancestry—shared honors in the capture of two escaped German officers within 33 hours after they escaped."

A letter Nichols has from the FBI at San Antonio indicates the above-mentioned German prisoners were First Lieutenant Hans Sprenger and Second Lieutenant Hans Johannson, who escaped shortly before midnight October 8, 1944, and were captured at 10:00 A.M. October 10, 1944. Nichols has five letters from the FBI at San Antonio, all commending him for his excellent assistance in apprehending these and other escaped German prisoners of war with the hounds he kept at the Gatesville Training School. He says he received many more such letters, but did not try to keep them.

Nichols is equally adept in training hounds for wolf and fox hunts. For this reason he was always selected as one of the judges in field trials back in the 1930's when the Central Texas Wolf and Fox Hunters Association held annual three-day meets in the southeastern part of Coryell County in an area now occupied by Fort Hood. Every autumn, usually in October, wolf and fox hunters from all Central Texas would attend these meets, setting up tents and remaining on the site for the duration of the hunts.

In field trials the best hounds were entered in the competition. These hunts were governed by an elaborate set of rules patterned after the Running Rules and Regulations of the National Fox Hunters Association. The rules specify that a hound shall be scored on (1) hunting, (2) trailing, (3) speed and driving, and (4) endurance. Methods for arriving at a final score for each dog are intricate and very technical.

Every year at the meeting of Coryell County Fox and Coon Hunters Association the hound-dog men have what is called a "drag race." Someone takes a wet coon hide and drags it on the ground in an open field over an irregular path, ending the trail at the base of a tree. Then a live coon is chained in the tree out of reach of the dogs. The dogs entered in the race are brought on leashes to the point where the trail originates.

As soon as the dogs catch scent of the trail they immediately burst into barking and begin pulling on the leashes held by their owners. Their action is like lighting the fuse on a string of firecrackers. The dogs are turned loose at the same time and the first to reach the tree with the coon in it wins the race. The most interesting part of the whole performance is to see how quickly hound dogs are transformed from a state of solemn lethargy to a howling, raging state of uproar and confusion when they catch the scent of the trail.

The enthusiasm of a hound dog in performing the task he is trained for is almost without limit. One story told by Harve Hale, whom I consider strictly reliable, is that of his hound dog's swimming more than three-quarters of a mile across the flooded Leon River bottom to get into a fox race on the other side where he heard other hounds "running." The hound not only swam across the flooded area to enter the race, but swam back across the river to his owner the same night. This occurred in the spring of 1958. Since then I have been told by Bert Richardson of other incidents that parallel this story in detail.

Fox hunting in England was an autumn and winter sport. In Central Texas field trials are always held in the fall season. While I cannot find any recorded reason why autumn and winter are the favorite hunting season, there is a cause. At least there is the almost universal belief among hound-dog men that "nature has a way of taking care of things." They believe it is difficult for the best "strike" dogs to pick up the scent of a wolf or fox trail in the whelping season. When one hound-dog man was pressed for a more logical reason, he apparently was a little peeved and replied rather abruptly, "All I know is that hunting just ain't no good when wolves and foxes are suckling their young."

Here are three stories from what I consider reliable sources that indicate there may be some foundation for the hound-dog man's belief that "nature has a way of taking care of things."

To back up this belief, Jim Nichols says that three or four hunters were out with their hounds one cool spring night and had built a fire under a bluff on Coryell Creek. They had turned their dogs loose. In the pack they had their best "strike" dogs. While sitting around the fire waiting for the dogs to pick up a trail, the men heard a noise near the top of the bluff. They investigated and found a den of five young wolves too small to move around under their own power. They did not disturb the young wolves but went back to the fire and waited about an hour for the dogs to pick up the trail of the mother wolf. After the long wait and failure of the dogs to strike they decided to check again on the wolf den. Much to their surprise the mother wolf had returned and had moved out three of her young. The dogs were still combing the area but were never able to strike a trail. Out of respect for this display of cunning on the part of the mother wolf the hunters called in their dogs and moved on to what they hoped would be better hunting.

Another story that parallels this one is told by Eiland Lovejoy and C. E. Gandy, two very reliable men. One afternoon a farmer out on Dodd's Creek called one of his hunting friends by telephone, told of finding a den of three young coyotes on his farm, and asked the hunter to bring out his hounds and try to catch the mother coyote. That night the hunter and some of his hunting friends took their hounds to the scene of the coyote den. They looked the den over. One of the men took off his coat and stopped up the den so the young coyotes could not possibly get out, and then they turned their dogs loose to try to pick up the trail of the mother. The dogs spent about an hour hunting all over the area but were never able to strike a trail. The men went back to the den only to find that the mother coyote had returned to the den, pulled the coat out, and moved the young to safety. The best "strike" dogs were never able to pick up a trail.

Another story similar to the two above mentioned is told by an equally reliable source, Bob Carpenter, newspaperman of Comanche, Texas. A hunter at Comanche found a den of young foxes near Sidney in Comanche County. He also saw the mother near the den. Within less than an hour he and his companion hunters had thirteen hounds at the scene of the den. The dogs were turned loose three or four at a time. They diligently covered the area for at least a mile in every direction but were never able to strike the trail of the mother fox. When asked how he accounted for this unusual phenomenon, the hunter's answer was, "It is simply nature's way of maintaining wild-life balance."

These stories seem fantastic, but in view of the evidence, who knows? Nature may have a way of taking care of things and maintaining wild-life balance. Folk wisdom, anyhow, repeats, "All I know is that hunting just ain't no good when wolves and foxes are suckling their young."

1. "America's Folkways," *Holiday Magazine*, XVIII (July, 1955), 60-61.

2. In arriving at what is included in this set of rambling remarks I talked with numerous hound-dog men and attended two of their annual association meetings. Some of the most dedicated and outstanding men were:

>O. E. Gandy, county judge
>Eiland Lovejoy, city secretary
>Jim Nichols, former dog sergeant, state training school
>Bill Byrom, retired merchant
>Harve Hale, farmer
>Albert Swindell, retired farmer
>"Big" Mayberry, (colored) retired farmer

All the above mentioned are residents of Coryell County, Texas. I also had a lengthy session with Bob Carpenter, Linotype operator for the *Comanche Chief* at Comanche, Texas. Carpenter is a comparatively young fellow, in his early forties, but shares the same traditional views held by the Coryell County men ranging in age from sixty to well over eighty years of age.

The Magic Art of Removing Warts
GRACE PLEASANT WELLBORN

UNCLE DAN, a rough, illiterate, but generous and good-natured pioneer of Wise County, was best known for his ability to remove warts. Many families brought children in a wagon or buggy across the country ten to fifty miles for Uncle Dan to remove their warts.

Uncle Dan could remove other growths from man and animal. People near Chico had a story about Uncle Dan's saving a ranch foreman from getting fired. The foreman developed a growth on his left foot. For years he had to split his boot or shoe. Finally the growth was so large that he had to cut out a piece of leather about two by four inches so that it could protrude.

No local doctor could be persuaded to operate. Eventually the poor man was so crippled that the owner had to hire an underling to do the walking and riding while the foreman acted as a kind of office manager. When this arrangement did not prove satisfactory, the foreman was in danger of losing his job. Then it was that a stranger who had bought the neighboring ranch brought unbelievable tales about an old man—part Indian—living in Wise County, a reputed magician, who could remove warts and even larger growths. Desperate, the foreman made the three-hundred-mile trek to Uncle Dan's. The magic, or whatever it was, was so effective that the foreman gave Uncle Dan a big white hat, which he wore from that time on.

It was generally known, too, around Chico that the town's

multimillionaire banker, Lee Morris, had shipped a good saddle horse from one of his ranches across the country to Uncle Dan to be healed. On its shoulder this fine horse had a big callus that the saddle kept rubbing and irritating. No horse doctor on the frontier had been able to cope with the callus, and finally the horse had been turned out to pasture. Then Mr. Morris decided to try Uncle Dan, who at that time was living up on Pringle Creek. Details were never reported, but people understood that Uncle Dan restored the horse to its former usefulness. Natives who kept this legend alive usually said that the banker had not even offered Uncle Dan "one thin dime" after the growth had "shriveled up." Some claimed that Uncle Dan wouldn't have accepted money.

Because of what happened to me, I believe these reports about Uncle Dan's magic. Once when I was perhaps eight or nine years of age, a seed wart grew on my upper lip. It was narrow in circumference but the four long "seeds" stood out, stiff and flaring. People seemed never to look me in the eye when I met them but to fasten their attention upon this little brown seed wart, about halfway between the corner of my mouth and the center of my upper lip.

Then—I do not remember exactly how or when—we heard about Uncle Dan. It took little persuasion for my father and mother to load the three of us children into the buggy, with a little board placed across the front and above their feet for us to sit on, and to start the five-mile ride to Uncle Dan's house.

It was late in the afternoon when we arrived at the little unpainted two-room house with a porch on which wires were strung from the ceiling to the floor for morning-glory vines. Through the vines I could make out the lines of Uncle Dan's big body, relaxed and spilling over the sides of a chair.

I was excited, really trembling, when, after my father had told him our business, Uncle Dan called me to come to him. Squaring away his cane-bottom chair, which was tilted back against the wall, he pulled me down on his left leg. He peered intently at the wart with his little squinted eyes—bright blue, but almost closed by their fat, full lids. Their gaze was calm, complacent, a bit mischievous, and they seemed to pierce ordinary barriers. I shrank from meeting them directly.

Looking intently at the little wart, he said, "Wahl, shore 'tain't very big! Let's see."

Then, putting his left arm around my waist, he placed the forefinger of his right hand on top of that little seed wart and pressed hard, following the pressure with a circular, massaging motion. I think I had my eyes closed from fright, but when I opened them after about the fifth circular movement, I was relieved to find his eyes were not on me at all. They had a far-far-away gaze. I wondered what he could see so far away. And he was mumbling. I couldn't make out one word, even though I held my breath to hear better.

The ritual must have lasted several minutes, for I became calm enough to notice his stiff, unkempt, sandy hair and the long, curly, red fuzz on his arms, bare to the elbow. I recall even noticing the dirt on the rolled-up sleeves and being offended by the sweaty odor from his body. Then the circular movement slowed and he paused and again exerted pressure.

Then he said, "Young lady, don't put your hands on it; don't watch tha thing. Fergit it. And you won't have a wart three weeks from now!" These were the last words I remember his saying to us.

It took all the discipline I could exert to follow his instructions; but I remained faithful and honest. Never once did I look in the mirror directly at the wart. Never did I put my hands on it, though I would feel for it with the tip of my tongue. To my continual disappointment I could thus apprehend its presence morning after morning, until I became skeptical and concluded that I shouldn't have expected to get rid of such an ugly thing so easily. But eventually, as Uncle Dan had suggested, I forgot my wart.

Then one day the wart was gone! I examined my lip with

the mirror for the slightest indication of the wart's former location, but there was no visible sign. The disappearance of the wart seemed miraculous to me, and even today I can offer no explanation of why it disappeared. As I grew older this "miracle" grew dimmer in my memory until it all but completely faded.

Many years later, when I was visiting my sister in Amarillo, Texas, that experience came suddenly back to my mind. I saw on my nephew Mike more warts than I had ever seen on one person in my life—thirty-eight! We counted them. My first impulse was to burst out with the insistence that we make the 365-mile trip to see Uncle Dan. Then I hesitated. Did I really believe in him? I refrained from discussing that childhood experience of mine with my sister until the next morning, when I was helping Mike wash his hands. His warts were terrible—rusty, deformed-looking, crusty. I counted twenty-odd of all sorts and shapes. It was then that I suggested that Mike be taken to Uncle Dan. With a chuckle, my sister wanted to know how Uncle Dan could succeed after numerous doctors had failed to remove Mike's warts with oils and acids. She dismissed the topic by changing the conversation, and two or three times the following year she visited my mother in Wise County without calling on Uncle Dan.

Then one summer our families met at a family gathering at Mother's house. Mike still had his warts, and Uncle Dan was still alive and living closer to town; so I insisted on a trip to his house. In fact, I announced that I was going to take Mike myself if the others did not care to go along. The result was that a car full of adults and children in a laughing, disbelieving mood was soon on its way down the country road under Mother's direction toward Uncle Dan's house.

It was a neat little white cottage which he now rented with his pension check. There—almost exactly as on the earlier occasion—were the white yard fence, the porch with the strung wire, the morning-glory vines, the long shadows of the late afternoon, the tilted cane-bottom chair, the chubby Uncle Dan, with the same little blue slits of eyes that seemed to pierce all barriers, the hair still untidy but now white. I had not seen him for years, but I would have known him anywhere.

I had heard that he had remarried after the death of his first wife and that his present wife was part Indian. A woman was standing in the doorway as we approached but mysteriously disappeared before we came close enough for me to see her clearly.

We told Uncle Dan about the warts. Mike was as tense as I had been years before, but I was calmer. I seated myself so that this time I could watch every move that was made. Not half a dozen sentences were spoken before Uncle Dan said, "Come 'ere, son!" The front legs of the chair slid to the floor; Uncle Dan pulled the twelve-year-old boy to a sitting position on his left knee, looked at his hands, and asked if those were all of the warts.

"No, sir; there are thirty-eight," Mike answered in a low voice.

"Gosh, son, whar are they?"

Mike started pointing them out. "Here's the biggest one on my elbow. Here's one on my neck. Oh, and I've got one in my hair just above my ear."

"That's all, son?"

Mike seemed a bit uncertain. Then he started again and hunted and counted thirty-eight warts, pulling up his pants leg to reveal three on a knee, one back of the knee in the bend of the leg. Finally, he kicked off a shoe and sock to point out one on his heel and one on the side of his big toe.

Then Uncle Dan said, "Son, I think I can find all those. If I miss one while I'm hunting, don't say a word; jis point it out. Don't say a word!"

"Yes, sir," whispered Mike.

Then Uncle Dan's eyes wandered to that far-away horizon. It seemed to me that his eyes didn't blink. His lips began to move, but not one sound escaped that I could hear, though I was seated very close to his feet, near enough to be certain that I was not wrong about his peculiar blue eyes, near enough to be certain that his clothes were still dirty and his body unbathed.

The ritual must have required twenty minutes. Throughout, the little porch was lined with three women and three children. Not a chair had been brought out to us. We lounged on the steps or clung to the edge of the porch, except my boy, the youngest one present, who was perched on an old churn turned upside down. Not one word or sound escaped from the group. Only once did Mike interrupt to point out the wart in the bend of his knee. Seldom did Uncle Dan's eyes rest on Mike's body. Usually he just "hunted" the next wart when he had finished with the last one.

When he had handled every wart, he gave Mike the same precautionary advice that he had given me thirty-five years earlier. Then Uncle Dan looked around at each of us, his eyes passing from one to the other, holding our attention a brief second. He smiled and said, "Son, them warts—ever' one of 'em—will be gone in three weeks if you do what I tole ya."

Hesitantly, I offered to pay Uncle Dan. He refused bluntly, though I knew he needed the money. He said that he had been taking warts off for over sixty years and had never charged a cent; he'd be afraid to charge—money might break his charm.

Wanting to know more and realizing that this was perhaps my last chance, I asked him how he ever got started. He said that the magic charm to remove warts was handed down from one generation to the next. A man had to reveal the secret to a woman, and only one woman, or a woman to only one man. His mother had transferred the power to him just before her death when he was ten years old. She was part Comanche Indian, he said. Her father, who had worn his hair in long braids in the Indian fashion, had given her the secret before that.

How was Uncle Dan's art to be passed on? Rumors were that he had no daughters, and he was now in his late seventies. He could guess my unasked question, but his only response was the beginning of a smile. His half-breed Indian wife, standing in the shadows of the doorway, and until now unnoticed, said, "I wan' he give me secre. He wonna."

Uncle Dan dropped his countenance and seemed to fix his eyes upon the floor near his feet. He appeared in serious and deep meditation. The thick, heavy silence was broken by the growl of a dog that lay back of Uncle Dan's chair; a cat had strolled from under the house.

"Stray cat," Uncle Dan chuckled. "Bowser not reconciled yit."

This incident made our leaving natural and easy.

"Gosh, he's sceery!" said Mike as we drove away.

I doubt that a person in the car except me really believed as we drove back to town that Uncle Dan's magic would stand the severe test of Mike's thirty-eight warts.

In a joking spirit I said to Mike as we parted the next day, each family going toward its own home town, "Mike, drop me a card if your warts mysteriously disappear, but be sure not to watch them!"

It must have been at least six weeks later when the letter postmarked Amarillo arrived. Inside I found a brief, scrawled note, "Don't have a wart! Don't know when they left! Just all of a sudden I couldn't find a wart. Hoorah for Uncle Dan!"

That was five years ago. Two years ago Uncle Dan died from a heart attack. I asked Mother last summer when I was in Chico if the old magician had handed down his secret to anybody. No one seemed to know. A big crowd, including many of his patrons from the surrounding towns, had attended the funeral. People said that they had never seen so many flowers in that small country church. It is likely that with the passing of Uncle Dan there came an end to the magic art of removing warts in Wise County.

Arkansas Variants of Some Texas Folksongs

JAMES WARD LEE

BALLAD SCHOLARS generally agree that British ballads, as well as American ballads from the East, came to Texas by way of Virginia, through Tennessee or Kentucky to Arkansas. But when I came to Texas from Arkansas, I did not expect to find the same kind of folksongs; I expected cowboy songs and local ballads, with just a sprinkling of "Barbara Allens" and "Elfin Knights." After looking through most of the Publications of the Texas Folklore Society, especially William A. Owens' *Texas Folk Songs*, I find that there is a great similarity between what has been collected in Texas and what I had collected in the Ozarks. My versions of "The Little Mohea," "The Hangman's Rope," "The Drummer Boy of Waterloo," "Henry Green," and "Rolly True Dum"—to mention a few—were very close to the versions which had been found in Texas.

While comparing my Arkansas transcriptions with Texas versions, I noted how Texans had altered some of the texts. I noted also that one of the songs, a local Texas ballad, had made its way to Arkansas while becoming almost extinct in Texas. The information that I found in Owens' book about the Texas ballad that went to Arkansas[1] led me to reconstruct its itinerary.

On August 7, 1958, Albert Harrison of the Bohannon Community near Hindsville, Arkansas, sang "The Sherman Cyclone" for me. Mr. Harrison, a man in his late seventies, said he learned the song from his mother's sister some sixty years ago. He said he thought the cyclone occurred in Sherman, Texas, on May 15, 1886 or 1888. Mr. Harrison was right about the place, the month, and the day, but the year was 1896. The date, May 15, is given in the song, but the state is unspecified. I was sure that Mr. Harrison had been right about the tornado's having been in Texas, when I read the following account in *A History of Grayson County, Texas:*

> The worst disaster in the history of the county was the cyclone in Sherman on the afternoon of May 15, 1896. A description by an eye-witness follows:
> "The huge, black, funnel-shaped cloud approached from the south about four o'clock. It descended to the ground and hit on what was then known as South Cemetery Street, now Ricketts. It passed just east of the cemetery and traveled north up the little creek. On Houston Street across the creek was an iron bridge which was completely destroyed. During the cyclone the air was filled with mud, dirt, and the cries of victims pierced the darkness and the rain fell in furious torrents. It took only a moment for the cyclone to leave more damage than Sherman had ever known or suffered since. When the cyclone raised, the rain stopped and the sun shone. There were no hospitals in Sherman at that time and only one undertaker's establishment. There were 73 deaths and the property damage amounted to about $50,000."[2]

Still I did not know the origin of the ballad or how it traveled to Arkansas. Owens' *Texas Folk Songs* provided some answers and some food for thought. Owens remembered having heard the song in his boyhood, but was unable to find anyone who knew more than a few lines of it until he learned from Mrs. Nelle Dowd of Denison that the song was written by Mrs. Mattie East of Bells. Mrs. East, who had been blinded in childhood, became a popular singer at church gatherings and picnics. She married a man who was also blind, and after their marriage they traveled in a wagon through Texas, Oklahoma, and Arkansas giving singing programs at churches and schoolhouses.

Around the turn of the century a person wishing to learn a song would get someone to sing it to him while he wrote it down in his "ballet" book. It seems reasonable to assume that Mr. Harrison's aunt or one of her friends had heard Mrs. East and had copied the song into a ballet book. I doubt that the song ever became popular in the Ozarks, because I collected extensively in Mr. Harrison's area and never found anyone else who knew it.

There is, of course, no proof that Albert Harrison got the ballad in the manner that I have described, but the evidence seems to point that way. One thing that leads me to that conclusion is the similarity between Mr. Harrison's version and that printed by Owens. The two versions are almost identical, except that Mr. Harrison omits the last two stanzas. However, Mr. Harrison was trying to recall something he had learned over half a century earlier. In the stanzas that remain, Mr. Harrison's version has only about a half-dozen minor variations.

Another interesting aspect of folksong is local adaptation. Much has been written about the "Ocean Burial–Dying Cowboy" song that begins "Oh Bury Me Not on the Lone Prairie." Another song, also called "The Dying Cowboy," has undergone a similar though somewhat less radical change at the hands of some Texan. It is printed by Lomax as "The Dying Ranger," beginning "The sun was setting in the West / And it fell with a lingering ray / Through the branches of a palmetto / Where the dying cowboy lay." The song is rather common; Vance Randolph has two versions in his *Ozark Folksongs*[3] (another case of a Texas song that went East). Randolph says that this particular song was a western adaptation of a New England song of the Civil War, but he had collected no version of the original song.

In the western version, the cowboy has been wounded in fighting the Indians, "in," as he says, "driving them from our shore." As he lies dying, he tells his comrades of his past life, and how he has left his home in Northwest Texas to answer the call for volunteers. He dies and the cowboys "lay him down to rest / With a saddle for his pillow / And his gun across his breast." Leander Witt of Madison County, Arkansas, sang this for me on July 19, 1958.

Then on August 7, 1958, Miss Mamie Sams, who doesn't live more than five miles from Mr. Witt, sang me the New England version. In Miss Sams's version the situation is the same except that the cowboy—now a soldier—is not from "Northwest Texas, up in that good old state," but from "far away in old New England, in that dear old pine tree state." Instead of driving the Indians "from our shore," he is driving away "the traitors"—presumably the Confederate soldiers.

Apparently some returning Civil War soldier had brought the song back, but had changed it to rid it of its Yankee taint and make it more vivid by giving it a Texas setting. I doubt that a song about a New England soldier would have been popular in Texas immediately after the Civil War. Miss Sams's family had come to Arkansas after the Civil War from somewhere in the North. Miss Sams said the song had been in the family all her life; therefore I assume that they brought the New England version with them. The two songs existed side by side for fifty years without ever coming together. Mr. Witt had learned his version about 1905 from a "tie hacker" on the railroad named Samuels. If Mr. Witt had ever heard Mamie Sams's version, I know what he would have said to her: "Oh yes, I have heered the song, but you ain't got the right words."

Sometimes adaptation becomes so radical that a hearer or reader will not recognize the song unless a catch phrase strikes ear or eye. Radical adaptation in one folksong almost escaped me when I was looking through *Texas and Southwestern Lore*, the 1927 Publication of the Texas Folklore Society. Had not my version had a little bit of interesting history, I would have passed up the ballad that J. Frank Dobie published in "Ballads and Songs of the Frontier Folk."

My acquaintance with the song began one summer when I went out to Combs, Arkansas, to visit Mrs. Martha Hawkins, eighty-five, who had been quite a folksinger in days gone by.

She lived with a daughter of sixty-five who was very solicitous about her mother's health and didn't want Mrs. Hawkins to sing. As you know, an old Scottish lady once told Sir Walter Scott that "these songs are for singing; they're no for reading." And a folksinger will not recite—he looks upon that as some alien kind of art, which it is. It is true that Scott got some of his ballads by recitation, but such instances are very rare; usually a singer will either sing or refuse to perform altogether. Mrs. Hawkins, however, consented to recite one song that began, "At the foot of yonders mountains, where fountains doth flow." She called the song "The Greenbriar Shore." Vance Randolph had collected a less complete version called "The White River Shore," or "Dear Jewell."[4] H. M. Belden in *The Frank C. Brown Collection of North Carolina Folklore* has a version of the same plus an informative headnote.[5] Other titles, says Belden, are "The White River Shore," "The New River Shore," and "The Red River Shore." He mentions that a Texas version had been collected, but he does not publish it. I had forgotten Belden's headnote when I saw Dobie's "On Red River Shore." The first line of "The Red River Shore" began "At the foot of yonder mountain / Where fountain doth flow," but the rest of the song dealt with cowboys and six-guns and broncos. As I began to read Dobie's version I could tell that both rhythm and narration were the same. In the headnote Dobie tells that he learned the song from two Oklahoma boys in 1925. He states correctly that the song is not new. "The narrative element or the absence of it in a cowboy song," he writes, "will go a long way towards determining whether it was composed before or after about 1890."[6] He then conjectures that composition of the song dates at least as far back as 1890. It was, I suspect, composed a hundred years earlier.

In both Dobie's and Mrs. Hawkins' versions a young man who lived "At the foot of yonders mountains, where fountains doth flow" is driven away from the shore by his true love's parents. The girl writes a letter to the young man and tells him if he will come back and get her she will flee with him. The parents learn of the plot and collect an army of—in Mrs. Hawkins' version—"full twenty or more," in "On Red River Shore" "twenty and four." The youth returns and draws his "glittering sword" (Dobie's variant, "six-shooter"), and "some he killed dead, some he wounded full sore"; so he won his own true love on the Greenbriar, or Red River, Shore.

Mrs. Hawkins' version appends a final verse that is also found in Vance Randolph's version. Pure folklore, it was doubtless added by a woman. Although it has nothing to do with the narrative, this last superfluous verse is a good way to end any song:

> So hard is the fortune
> Of all woman kind
> They're always controlled
> They're always confined
> They're controlled by their parents
> Until they are made wives
> And they are made slaves by their husbands
> For the rest of their lives.

1. William A. Owens, *Texas Folk Songs* ("Publications of the Texas Folklore Society," XXIII [1950]), p. 128.

2. Mattie Davis Lucas and Mita H. Hall, *A History of Grayson County, Texas* (Sherman, Texas, 1936), p. 180.

3. Vance Randolph, *Ozark Folksongs* (Columbia, Missouri, 1946-50), II, 196-98.

4. *Ibid.*, I, 307.

5. Newman I. White and Paul F. Baum, eds., *The Frank C. Brown Collection of North Carolina Folklore* (Durham, 1952-61), II, 286-87.

6. J. Frank Dobie, "Ballads and Songs of the Frontier Folk," in *Texas and Southwestern Lore* ("Publications of the Texas Folklore Society," VI [1927]), p. 158.

Owl-Bewitchment in the Lower Rio Grande Valley

HUMBERTO GARZA

WHEN I ASKED Dionicia Fernández of La Feria, Texas, whether owls have strange powers or whether they are like other birds, she had an answer for me: "There are good and bad owls, and the good owls are just common birds of prey that live in palm trees and other places that offer them shelter. But the bad owls are really witches in disguise, or birds sent to earth by the devil and kept as pets by witches."

In the minds of many Texans of Mexican descent owls are associated with *brujas* and *brujería* — witches and witchcraft. It was not difficult for me to collect a number of owl-bewitchment tales in the Lower Rio Grande Valley, for many such tales exist there.

One story was told to me by Antonio Cisneros of La Feria. Mr. Cisneros, who remembers the Valley as it was in the early 1900's, places the time when he first heard this owl-tale as 1908. The incident occurred near what is now Harlingen. Mr. Cisneros and a group of men from both sides of the Rio Grande were working the fields. One day a stranger came to the camp to work. The unusual thing about this man was that he vomited blood on Thursdays and Fridays, although not necessarily every week. As time went by and the men in the camp became aware of the strange illness that plagued the newcomer, one of them, Francisco de Leon, decided to do something about it. He told Mr. Cisneros, who was a good friend of his, the rituals he would go through to rid the stranger of his misery. The man was vomiting blood, he said, because he was bewitched by someone in the town in Mexico from which he had come.

The first thing Francisco de Leon did was to go to a nearby ranch on a Friday for some horsehair. The next day he began the ritual by tying twelve knots in the rope of horsehair and saying a small prayer between each two knots. All the time he was tying these knots he was heading toward two big owls which were making loud noises on top of a large mesquite tree. When he finally reached the tree and tied the last knot in the rope, the two owls fell to the ground and he started to beat them with a stick. Mr. Cisneros says that he and another man went near the place where the two owls fell, and he thinks he remembers hearing voices — but he is not sure.

After the owls were dead, Mr. de Leon told the sick man what to do the next morning so that he could be cured of vomiting blood. He told him to gather all the clothing he had in his possession and build a large fire. He was to wait until there were many ashes left from the burned wood, and then rake the ashes from the middle of the fire to the sides, leaving a hole in the center. Then he was to throw his clothing into the middle of the ashes and cover them up so that they would burn.

The man carried out these directions, Mr. Cisneros said, and never again vomited blood while he was with the group of workers. In order that the vomiting should go away forever, Mr. de Leon told the stranger, he must go home when he had enough money and go through the same burning process with the clothes he had left at home in Mexico.

Mr. Cisneros also told me another story concerning a certain Francisco Cantú and his daughter, Herlinda. It seems that Mr. Cantú, who believed in the supernatural, was thoroughly convinced that his daughter had been bewitched by someone. He read a book on owls and their doings and finally came upon a treatment, or rather a ritual, which would cure her.

Taking a bullet from a gun he had, he marked a cross on its tip. With this bullet he shot an owl that was always perching around his house. Before he shot the owl, he had to say a prayer, *Las Doce Verdades* (The Twelve Truths).[1] Mr. Cantú did not manage to kill the owl, but only wounded him in the wing. He took the owl home. It was horrible, the people told Mr. Cisneros, and truly the work of the devil. It had long hair made up into braids that reached below its neck. Its eyes were those of a human being and its beak was shaped like a nose. Many believed that the owl was really a woman in disguise.

After Mr. Cantú had shown the owl around town during the day, he tied it to a tree for the night. When he went after it the next morning, it was gone. The people said that other owls had come to free it and had taken it away during the night.

Herlinda died shortly afterward. Then Mr. Cantú decided to make a real study of the book on owls so that he might cure other people of what had apparently killed his daughter. And indeed, according to Mr. Cisneros, he did cure a lot of people all over the Valley. But then he died very suddenly, after having cured a man in Matamoros. Many of the people believed that he too had been *embrujado* — bewitched.

Mrs. Cisneros also gave me some interesting information. She told me that a group of *lechuzas* (owls) always numbers seven or less. The owls, she said, gather together because they have something important to discuss, just as people gather when they have something special and interesting to talk about. She added that there is a saint, San Espedito, who is noted for bringing down "bad" owls. "The picture of San Espedito," she said, "is found in the market in Matamoros."

Mrs. Dionicia Fernández, a very old lady, told me a story about a woman who was a witch and who at night would change into an owl and fly around the town in which she lived. Finally, one night a group of people decided to bring down the owl so that they could see who it was. They started to pray it down, and went on until the owl hit the ground. Then the townspeople saw that it was in the shape of a woman whom they knew very well. When they caught her they were going to burn her; but the witch began to cry aloud, begging them to let her go because she had a baby boy to take care of, and promising that if they would spare her she would never again practice *brujería*.

Mrs. Fernández said that the woman held to her promise. When her son grew up, however, he followed his mother's former practice of witchcraft.

Another tale told by Mrs. Fernández concerns a girl who was married but never liked to eat at her own house and was always telling her husband that she liked what her mother cooked better than anything else. One day her husband decided to take her to her mother's house so that she could eat what she liked. When they arrived, the husband said he was going to town for a while. But he did not go; instead, he hid behind the house.

When the mother and daughter thought he was gone, they quickly ran to the back room and opened a huge chest. From inside this chest the girl's mother pulled two large bottles of blood, and each of the women drank one. Meanwhile the girl's husband was seeing all that happened.

When they had finished drinking, the witch told her daughter that they should go for a ride, disguised as owls, for a while before her husband came back. The girl did not like the idea very much, but finally she consented. Then they took the eyes of two cats the mother had in her house, and put their own beneath some stones. But as they were changing into owls, the girl's husband came in. So they quickly changed to human beings again, except that they had cats' eyes instead of their own. When the husband saw what his wife was, he left her there with her mother and never came back.

Mr. Fernández told me about an incident that happened to him. One morning around three o'clock, as he was going to milk some cows, he heard someone laughing and decided to investigate. He had gone along that same path before, but had never heard any strange noises. Searching around, he finally came upon a large mesquite tree, where he saw three big owls that were laughing very loudly. He never again took that path when he went to milk the cows.

Another story concerns an owl and a robber. It was told to my mother, Mrs. Berta Garza, by her father, and she says it is true. As this man was standing outside his home he saw an owl that had been troubling him very much for many days, so he decided to pray to make the owl fall down. The bird finally fluttered down, and he started to beat it with a stick. But the owl suddenly changed into a woman, who begged him to stop hitting her. She promised that she would keep him from being caught stealing. When he heard this he stopped and let the woman go. After that he began to steal; but he was never caught, because when the police were about to get him he would disappear behind some object or into thin air. This man lived to be very old, and then died a natural, nonviolent death.

The next story, which was told to me by Samuel Menchaca of La Feria, took place in Buena Sevi, a small town in Chihuahua, Mexico. During the Mexican Revolution there were many owls' nests on a mountain near Buena Sevi. In the town lived an old woman who cured people with herbs and other remedies. One day a young lady came to see whether she could cure her of facial blemishes. The cure the old woman prescribed was that she go to the owls' nests, gather some eggs, and rub the egg yolks on her face. When this remedy did not work, she went to the woman again, and was told that the owl's feathers made into a powder would cleanse her face. But this time the old woman said that she would get the feathers herself. The next day she left Buena Sevi, and did not return.

Several days later a search party was formed to go find the old woman. They did find her, but what they came upon was mostly bones. Because the old woman's ribs were crushed, the people said that perhaps she had been killed by a bear, and then the owls had eaten her to the bone. When they saw what had happened, the people realized that the owls were a menace, and so they decided to burn the nesting grounds.

After the burning, a strange thing happened. There were fruit trees on the mountain where the owls had lived, but the fruit had always been so sour that it made anyone who ate it sick. But a few days after the nests were burned a man came running down the mountain yelling and shouting with joy. He had had a terrible stomach-ache, he said, but he had met a shepherd who had given him a mango that had grown on the mountain, and when he ate it his pain had disappeared. After this many people went to the mountain to get fruit to cure their stomach-aches. How the fruit got this strange power is still a mystery, but many believe that the smoke made when the owls were burned had entered the trees and their fruit and made the strange remedy possible.

Another story told me by Mr. Menchaca had to do with a very well-known doctor in Mexico who was bewitched by his mother-in-law. She did this by burning some of his hair along with the feathers of an owl. Mr. Menchaca went on to say that many of the doctor's friends as well as other doctors tried for a long time to find out what was causing his strange behavior. At night he would shout in the streets, "Ahí va, ahí va!" ("There it goes, there it goes!"), and point with his finger. During the day he would constantly look up as if he were searching for something.

Finally one day, after many had examined the doctor, a psychiatrist came to see whether he could determine what was troubling him; but he could not find the difficulty either. The psychiatrist did not stop with his examination of the man himself, however; he went to someone to whom the others had not talked — the doctor's wife. She told him that while it might not be of any importance, she had noticed one strange thing: an owl had flown over their house every night since her husband had been ill. The psychiatrist, Mr. Menchaca said, probably knew a little about witchcraft, for he immediately told the doctor's wife that her husband was bewitched.

He told her that he would come that night and would try to bring the owl down by saying a short *oración;* then he would kill the owl and put its head in a jar of alcohol. In this way he would discover who it was that was bewitching her husband, because the person would get a terrible headache the next day and would go to a relative or close friend to seek aid.

Meanwhile the owl, which was a male, flew to the home of the doctor's mother-in-law, where he lived with his mate. The mother-in-law was not there, having gone to get some blood with which to carry on her witchcraft. She had put in the eyes of a cat and had left her own under some stones near the fireplace, with the female owl to guard them. When the male owl came back and did not find the witch, he killed the female owl and then destroyed the witch's eyes.

When the doctor's mother-in-law came home, she was horrified at seeing her eyes all torn. She immediately sent word to her daughter to come at once. When the daughter arrived the mother concealed her cat's eyes and told the young woman to go buy her some sunglasses.

By the time her daughter returned, the witch had prepared an herb to put her to sleep so that she could take her eyes out. But the psychiatrist, who had become suspicious of the mother-in-law, was on his way to her *hoje.* He arrived just in time to save the girl from her witch-mother, who had already put her on a couch to take out her eyes.

After the witch had been sentenced and all her belongings destroyed, the doctor again returned to a normal life.

In general one may say that in stories of owl-bewitchment someone shows signs of being bewitched but does not recognize these signs; then someone else does recognize them and frees the bewitched person. The owl-witch has to be overcome by violence made effective by religious means—prayer or a bullet marked with a cross. Prayer figures as the principal weapon of counterwitchcraft; it can bring the owl to earth so that it can be beaten to death or captured. The witch does not necessarily have to be destroyed; sometimes she can be made to promise to give up witchcraft.

In the last tale related above, a doctor is the victim and a psychiatrist is said to be the deliverer. That a doctor can be bewitched is certainly proof of the power of witchcraft; but he is released by another man of science, who does not make use of either exorcism or psychiatric methods. He suspects the witch and seeks her out just in time. He is a psychiatrist in name only, but in the mind of the storyteller he no doubt possesses a mysterious power comparable to that of the exorcist. Possibly the deliverer is called a psychiatrist because psychiatrists have had to take account of and treat cases of owl-bewitchment.

I do not believe in bewitchment, but I know that many people go through the torture of being "bewitched" by owls. In the Lower Rio Grande Valley the owl is generally feared and is avoided as much as possible. It is not easy to tell "good" from "bad" owls.

1. On *Las Doce Verdades* see Wilson M. Hudson, "The Twelve Truths in the Spanish Southwest," *Mesquite and Willow* ("Publications of the Texas Folklore Society," XXVII [1957]), pp. 138-50.

Tales of the Paisanos

MIRIAM W. HIESTER

A TERM USED by J. Frank Dobie in his introduction to *Tone the Bell Easy*[1] seems the most descriptive of the people about whom the following group of tales were written. He writes of the *paisano* (the countryman), a name which suggests simultaneously the two most outstanding characteristics of these people: their loyalty to their country—Texas—and their Mexican ancestry. The Texas-Mexicans have contributed no small part to the "flavor of Texas" with their delightful folklore and their influence on place names and vocabulary. Regarding this, Mr. Dobie states, "In considering hundreds of legends current among English-speaking Caucasians of Texas, I have found very few that do not evidence Spanish-Mexican sources."[2]

Generations of *paisanos*, who have lived in more or less isolated ranch villages since the "early days," have conserved through oral tradition a distinct folklore. Often reminiscent of the folk literature, customs, and beliefs of the colonial days of Spain and England, it has blended somewhat with that of the Mexican Indian, and even of the Anglo-American, in spite of the isolation and homogeneity of many of the communities. In matters concerning courtship, marriage, and funerals, the *paisanos* have conserved the customs of the Spanish; but the lure of the witch and of the Indian medicine man still persists today among some of the people, and the typical Texan's love for the tall tale is evident in many of the stories. All these elements blend to form an amalgam not found elsewhere.

No one loves a good story more than the *paisano*. On long evenings around the fire in winter, or out under the stars in summer, he enjoys telling tales of witches, of fairies, of animals who talk, and of strange happenings. Some of the myths of the *paisano* date back to the days of his primitive ancestors; consequently, we often find in them remnants of animism or survivals of other strange beliefs held during the childhood of his race.

To trace the origin of the stories would be an impossibility. Aureliano Espinosa, in his *Cuentos Populares Españoles*,[3] expresses his belief that the tales may have originated in India. He contends, however, that the earliest origin of stories is immaterial and that should we trace back to the most ancient version, we would still have no assurance that it is the first form of the legend.

To distinguish among the various racial elements in many of the stories would be equally impossible, for these are often as inseparably fused as the numerous blood strains which run through the veins of the *paisano*. The tales are not entirely Spanish, or Indian, or *Americano*, but are *paisano*.

Some of these tales were written out in Spanish for me by my students in the high school in Mission, Texas; others were related to me either in Spanish or in English and I wrote them later from notes and from memory. José Hernández, an enlisted man stationed at Brooke Army Hospital and a student in the Brooke Hospital Center School where I taught, told me five of them.

They are given here as told to me—vibrant and accompanied by few explanations. For each story I have included in the headnote the name of my informant and the motif number according to Stith Thompson's *Motif-Index of Folk-Literature*.[4] I have also included any facts I may have found concerning probable origin, history, or type[5] of the tale; but I have not done extensive research to determine the earliest possible version or to note the many variants.

El Violincito

The theme of the possession of magic objects is a very old one, appearing in unmistakable form in a Chinese Buddhistic collection of the sixth century A.D., in the Ocean of Story, *of the eleventh century, and in the* Thousand and One Nights.[6] *An interesting variation is that known from the Grimm collection as "The Jew Among Thorns" (Thompson, Type 592). In this the hero has a magic fiddle which compels people to dance. He is eventually brought to court for his misdeeds and is condemned to be hanged. "As a last request he secures permission to play on his fiddle, and he compels the judge and all the assembly to dance until he is released."[7] "La Gaita que Hacía a Todas Bailar" (Espinosa, No. 153) is also quite similar to the following story, except that in the former the goats miss the music to the extent that they all die of a broken heart when the musician leaves them to seek his fortune elsewhere. Rebecca Méndez, a student of mine in Mission, Texas, was my informant in this story. I have translated it from the Spanish. (B700, D1235, D2661.1.2)*

There was a boy who spent all his time herding goats for his grandmother. He became very lonesome during the long hours out on the plains with just the goats for company and asked the Blessed Virgin one day if she would give him a magic violin. She granted his request and from that day on he amused himself by playing on this wonderful instrument. When the goats heard the music, they would dance. They even forgot to eat, so enchanted they were with the music.

When he went home at night, the grandmother noticed how tired the goats were and asked the boy why this was. He said he did not know. She told him to put the goats in the corral, and then she went to get a switch with which to whip the boy, for she knew he was lying. He ran quickly and got his violin and began to play it. Both the goats and the old woman danced to the music and were unable to stop as long as he played. The old woman danced so long and so hard that she fell dead.

When the people in the town found out that the boy had caused his grandmother to dance until she fell dead, they told the *aguacil* to arrest him. He was sentenced to be hanged. He asked that they allow him to play his violin one more time before he died. They brought him his violin, and he began to play the most beautiful music that anyone had ever heard. One by one they began to dance. He continued playing and they continued dancing, unable to stop as long as he played on the magic violin. At length, completely tired out, they begged him to stop playing. The *aguacil* promised him his freedom if he would just stop the playing. Thus he was allowed to go free. Some say that on a moonlight night in a remote spot you can still hear the strains of a violin, and that if you creep up very quietly, you can see a *pastor*, now an old man with a long white beard, playing his violin to his goats, who are dancing and dancing. But you must leave soon before the spell is upon you; for if you stay, you will dance too, and like the grandmother be unable to stop until you fall dead.

El Nagual y la Segua

"*Ancient superstitions which survive to the present time in Mexico and Central America include the curious complex known as* nagualism."[8] *This belief, which appears to be American Indian, centers around a witch who is able to assume animal form in order to wreak vengeance on enemies. José Hernández, an enlisted man on duty at Brooke Army Hospital, gave me the following information about* el Nagual *and his companion witch* la Segua. *He related this and all the other stories he gave me in rapid Spanish, stopping now and then to allow me to jot down notes, from which I later wrote the stories. José, a talented singer, was born in San Antonio, but has lived in Laredo and other towns along both sides of the Rio Grande. His mother was from San Luis Potosí.* (G211.1, D658.1)

El Nagual, a most hideous creature dressed in a black cape, with the body of a man, the face of a dog, and the horns of a cow, wanders forth at night, choosing especially the shadows of trees or houses for his path. Without warning he will pounce shrieking upon a young man who dares to stay out past the usual bedtime hour. But according to legend, he especially likes the *señoritas*, from whom he always steals a kiss before he releases them. It is suspected, but has never really been proved, that young men about town disguise themselves as *el Nagual* now and then to achieve an opportunity to kiss a reluctant *novia*. The thought of a chance meeting with *el Nagual* drives many young men home at an earlier hour than they would prefer.

La Segua, who is the opposite of *el Nagual,* is the devil for the men. It is she who takes them away to some unknown place from which they never return.

Once there was a man named Paco, who had a very frightening experience with *la Segua.* Paco was returning home from the village late one night after a *fiesta*. As he rode along the dirt road on his horse, he could see the white blossoms of the wild olive trees and even the flowers of the *nopal,* for the moon was very bright.

Now everyone knows that a horse is *maldito;* he is especially so at night if there is moonlight. The ox, the mule, the burro, the cow, and the rooster are all *bendito,* for they announce the approach of evil. Remembering this, Paco wished he had chosen to ride his burro instead of his horse.

Just then he heard a cry coming from under a bush. It sounded like a child whimpering for its mother. Paco, convinced that some infant had been abandoned by the roadside, went over to the bush and found there what appeared to be a young child. Placing her before him on his saddle, he continued on his way.

Suddenly, the child turned into a beautiful girl who began to smile at him and flatter him about his looks and his strength. But when he started to kiss her, he discovered that her face had become that of a horse, with long ears and huge teeth which showed as she yelled, "Eeeeeeeeeeee!"

Terrified, Paco managed to drop her off his horse, whereupon she became a *yegua* (mare) who pursued him, all the while neighing the horrible "Eeeeeeeeeeee!"

Spurring his horse forward, he was able to reach home in

time to rush in the house and slam the door shut before *la Segua* caught him.

"Qué te pasa?" asked his wife, seeing his pale color and his frightened face.

"La Segua! La Segua! She's after me!" he shouted in an extremity of terror.

Snatching her rosary, his wife began to swing it back and forth across the door. Soon the shrieking of the creature ceased; and when Paco and his wife opened the door, La Segua had disappeared completely.

San Miguel y el Diablo

José Hernández (A162, V236)

In the days before the beginning of the earth, the Devil and Michael were archangels of God, one sitting on the right and one on the left of His throne. But the Devil, whose name then was Luz Bel (Beautiful Light), was jealous of God's power and wanted to be equal to the King of the Universe. He plotted a revolt with some other angels who were also dissatisfied with their lot. God, of course, knowing all things, was aware of the plan and commanded Miguel and the good angels to throw Luz Bel and his crew out of heaven.

Luz Bel's name was then changed to Lucifer *(Luz de Infierno)*, which he bears to the present day.

Now and then Miguel finds Lucifer wandering around the earth, where by rights he does not belong. With his sword, the good angel drives him back to the lower regions. Once, it is said, Miguel stamped upon Lucifer, whom he found doing a particularly evil deed. On this occasion, Miguel broke several of his toes and burned his feet. For weeks afterward he could be seen limping around heaven. In many pictures Miguel is pictured with his sword in his right hand, the scales on which he weighs the souls of men in his left hand, and his toes tied up with bandages.

El Regalo

José Hernández (V412, D1622.3)

It was Christmas Eve; and in a small town in Mexico the church, which was, indeed, a very beautiful one, was crowded with many people who were attending the *misa del gallo*. The *Niño Jesús*, a particularly prized statue in this church, appeared more splendid than ever, for was it not His birthday that the people were celebrating? His swaddling clothes and tiny sandals, all of pure gold, shone in the light of the candles, and those who looked at Him between prayers felt that a living Presence pervaded the image. They went away from the service with a strange feeling of wonder.

As the church was emptied and the families went back to their homes to open the gifts awaiting them, a child of about ten years—though by his size he seemed much younger—fled into the church. He was barefooted and clothed in rags and was shivering both from cold and from fright. As was often the case, a policeman of the town was chasing him.

Clutching under his arm the small violin with which he earned his living, the waif ran through the church and was directly in front of the statue of the Christ Child before he saw it. Dropping to his knees and gazing up in rapt wonder at the *Niño*, gleaming and beautiful with the candles still burning at His feet, the child remembered then that it was *La Navidad* and that everyone should bring a gift to the Christ on that day.

"What can I give Him," he murmured to himself, "I who am so poor and miserable?"

Then, remembering his violin, he took it up and began to play the best song that he knew for the *Niño Jesus*. As he finished and was standing there thinking dejectedly what a very poor gift he had made, the statue moved slightly and pushed forward one tiny foot, allowing a golden sandal to fall into the hand of the street urchin. Surprised and a bit fearful, the miserable little creature looked up quickly to the face of the *Niño* and observed that He was smiling.

Presently He began to speak. "It is a present for you."

"How beautiful it is!" exclaimed the child. "But I could never take it. The policeman would think that I stole it."

"Have no fear," He insisted. "That will be arranged. I want you to have it, for you have given me the most wonderful present of all tonight. You gave me everything you had."

Joyous, but still a bit fearful of consequences, the waif again ventured out into the street, where the policeman was still waiting for him.

"What have you there?" the big man demanded. "Is it not enough that you steal a loaf of bread at the *panadería!* Must you go thieving even in the church?"

The policeman, of course, would not believe the child's story; he did agree, nevertheless, to give him a chance to prove it. Going up to the front of the church, the policeman placed the shoe again on the *Niño's* foot, and then the urchin played on his violin the same song he had played before. As soon as the last note had been played, the tiny foot of the *Niño Jesús* was again extended; and the golden sandal fell into the hand of the boy.

"It is a miracle!" exclaimed the policeman. "I would not have believed it had I not seen it with my own eyes!"

But there are many who did believe without seeing it, and even today are telling this beautiful Christmas story to their own children.

Las Bodas de la Tía Cucaracha

The following story, told to me in Spanish by José Hernández, interests me especially because it is a distinctly Mexican version of "Ratoncito Pérez." La cucaracha, that pestiferous cockroach which grows to nearly the size of a mouse in South Texas and in Mexico, has always been looked upon with humor and almost fondness by the Mexicans. They regard him as something between a pet and a necessary evil, which they accept with the stoic resignation of the Indian. It is not surprising that they would substitute the cockroach for the ant in the old folktale. Espinosa gives three versions of the story (Numbers 271-73), and Thompson classifies it as Type 333. (B285)

Tía Cucaracha was busily sweeping her house one day, singing while she worked but somewhat sad because she was not yet married. As she passed her broom in a far corner of the room, she heard a noise. Looking down, she beheld to her great surprise a shining silver coin.

"How wonderful!" thought Tía Cucaracha. "Now I can buy some beautiful clothes and some powder for my face and catch a husband!"

After she had returned from her shopping tour, she powdered her face, put on her fine clothes, and sat in the window which faced the street.

It was not long before Tío Perro came along. Noticing Tía Cucaracha sitting there in the window looking so attractive, he paused to talk.

"How beautiful you look!" he exclaimed. "Will you marry me?"

"How is your behavior?" questioned Tía Cucaracha.

"Well, at night I bark, 'Guau, guau, guau!'" answered the dog.

"Then I can't marry you. You would make too much noise and keep me awake," she answered.

Next, there passed by *la Paloma*, who stopped to rest on the window sill and talk to the beautiful Tía Cucaracha.

"My! how *chula* you look!" exclaimed the dove. "Will you marry me?"

"No," replied Tía Cucaracha. "You fly around everywhere and someone will soon shoot you. I would soon be left a widow."

Finally, a rat came along the street.

"Tía Cucaracha, how lovely you are! I had never really noticed before. Will you marry me?" he asked.

"What is your behavior?" she demanded.

"Well, I go around at night saying, 'Eeeee!' and in the daytime I usually sleep."

"That is fine," she said, smiling. "I will marry you."

The *bodas* were celebrated with music and feasting, and the couple went to live in the house of Tía Cucaracha. The first Sunday after the wedding, as Tía Cucaracha was *muy católica*, she arose early to go to mass. Waking up the rat, she said, "Watch the *arroz con leche* which I have put on to cook. When I return, we will have our breakfast."

Tío Ratón agreed, but turned over and went back to sleep. Some minutes later, he awoke suddenly, remembering the *arroz*, and ran quickly to the stove, where the mixture was boiling.

Pobrecito de él! He lost his balance and fell head first in the pot. There Tía Cucaracha found him, *patas arriba* and quite dead, when she returned.

All the animals came to the funeral, and each expressed his regret for the misfortune Tía Cucaracha had suffered. The dog even said he would not bark at night for a while in deference to the departed.

Tía Cucaracha was very sad for a time, but it was not long before she could be seen sitting in the window again, dressed in her fine clothes and looking for another husband.

The Corn Was Disappearing

The tall tale, especially the traveler's tall tale, dates back much farther than Baron Munchausen's Narratives and is a beloved possession of folk in all lands. Don Epitacio, a veritable Don Cacahuate (proverbial Mexican teller of tall tales and jokes), is typical of those artistic liars whose tales have never lacked for an appreciative and delighted audience.

"The Corn Was Disappearing" and the one which follows this were written in English for me by Poque Valverde, one of my students, whose grandfather was a personal friend of Don Epitacio Palos and can vouch for the authenticity of the tales. "One day," said Poque, "I went to my grandfather's house and found him full of spirit and happiness. It was his eighty-fourth birthday, and he was celebrating it by telling old tales. He sat down and started. 'Today I remember when Don Epitacio came

to our house and, after asking for a cup of coffee, told us many good stories of wonderful and strange adventures that he had a few years back.' Then my grandfather related to us some of the best of these stories." I have rewritten them, preserving as far as possible the style and vocabulary of the original.

A journey to another world, the principal theme in "The Corn Was Disappearing," is a very old motif which is found in various forms in all parts of the world.

"The rope from the sky is also found everywhere and in a number of contexts."[9] (F51, K2371.1)

Don Epitacio Palos had a small farm near the city of Mier, Tamaulipas, Mexico, on which he raised corn. In one part of his field he had extra big stalks of which he was very proud. One day he went to the field and found that some of the large corn was missing.

"Ay de mí!" he wailed. Who could be the thieves that were stealing his prize ears? He searched in vain for tracks and signs the bad ones could have left. After thinking about his problem for some minutes, he decided that the best thing to do was to sit up all night and watch for them. He went home, ate some *frijoles* and fresh *tortillas* which his wife had prepared, and started again for the cornfield, taking with him a soft pillow. He concealed himself behind some bushes near the fence and made himself comfortable on his pillow. He waited a long time; then, being very tired and not accustomed to staying awake so late, he fell asleep. The next morning he again found some of his choicest corn missing.

He became very angry with himself, and that night when he came to watch, he did not bring his pillow. "Hm," he said, "this thief is good; he does not make noise." He watched, and around one o'clock in the morning, he saw a rope dropping down from the sky. At first he was terrified at this strange occurrence, but he sat very still to see what else would happen. In a few minutes he saw two angels sliding cautiously down the rope. They had with them two big sacks, which they quickly filled with corn, taking care to choose the very finest ears. Don Epitacio was so furious he could hardly keep from shouting at them; but he decided that if he was to stop this heavenly stealing, he would have to control his temper and consider the best method to follow. The two angels soon started back up the rope. Don Epitacio grabbed hold of the rope and reached Heaven along with the angels. They turned back to close the door and were astonished to see a man there. One of them ran quickly to tell the Lord about it and was told to bring the man to the Lord's office. When Don Epitacio reached the office, he bowed and sat down.

"Well, Epitacio," said the Lord, "what brings you here?"

"My Lord," he answered, "I just came to tell you that your people have been stealing my corn. They have already finished with one *milpa* and are beginning on another one."

"Oh, Epitacio, I am extremely sorry!" exclaimed the Lord. "I thought the matter had been explained to you. As you may know, now and then we run out of corn up here; and as there are so many here who cannot survive without it, we have to get some from the earth. I looked over all the cornfields and selected yours as the best. Now, however, we are beginning to have enough of our own, and this will be the last time that we have to trouble you."

Bowing again to the Lord, Don Epitacio went again through the door and began to slide down the rope. Not being accustomed to descending such a distance in this manner, however, he slid down so fast that he was unable to stop when he reached the ground and went right on through the earth, coming out on the other side at the house of his sister who lived in China.

Don Epitacio's Trip to the Sun

In the sun-snaring myth of the Wyandots, a strong child climbed a tree and reached the land above the sky, where he set snares for game. He snared the sun instead. Thereafter there was no day until the sun was released by a mouse.[10] *In one of* Baron Munchausen's Narratives *there is a story of a man who tied his horse to what he thought (at the height of a blizzard) was a post, but discovered the next morning—sun shining, snow all gone—the horse tethered to the church steeple.*[11] *The story which follows combines both motifs. Poque Valverde is the informant. (H1250, F17, E168)*

Don Epitacio started out early one Sunday morning to find where the sun rose. His wife, as was the custom, baked some corn bread, stuffed a hen, and boiled some eggs for his lunch. He placed the food in a canvas sack, mounted his horse, and left. Each night he would unsaddle his horse and eat a little of the food, which he wanted to make last the whole trip. He traveled for a long time, and it seemed that he never would reach his goal. One night he thought that it might be better to continue traveling even after dark, but the moon did not shine early that night, and the darkness was so dense that he could not see where he was going. Finally, he came to a place where something seemed to hold him back. It was something like a wall, and he thought it might be the wall around China.

He ran his hands along the wall and found something that felt like a hole. Into this he stuffed his large sombrero. Then he hung his saddle on a small hook which was near the hole and hitched his horse to another hook not far away. He looked for his lunch, but remembered that he had left his bag hanging on a tree where he had spent the previous night. Weary from his long ride, he lay down and was soon asleep. He slept for a long time; and when he awoke, it was still dark. This seemed strange, as by the light of the moon, which was still shining, he could see that his watch showed eight o'clock.

When Señor Palos saw how late it was and that the sun had not come out, he said, "I must have gone past the sun and did not know it." He looked up to see the moon, and what do you suppose he saw? His horse and saddle were way up in the sky hanging on the two horns of the new moon. He looked for his hat and finally found the hole where he had placed it. As he pulled it out, the sun, which had been penned up inside the hole, came rushing out. This made him very happy, for now he knew that he had accomplished what he had set out to do.

He had a long *riata* there with him, and he threw a *lazo* to the moon. His aim was good, as always, and he soon pulled the moon down, untied his horse and saddle, and started back on his way.

He came to the tree where he had left his bag of lunch and was amazed to find that the hen had hatched the eggs, and now there were many stuffed chickens all over the tree. He took them all home with him and showed them to his family. They and all their friends had baked chicken for months.

The King's Horns

> *Several marvelous legends, told of Ancient Greek Gods or heroes, have lived on and are met today in unexpected quarters. Such for instance is the group of legends around King Midas: the person with the ass's ears (F511.2.2); the magic reed which grows from the hole where the king has whispered his secret and which spreads his secret to the rest of the world (D1316.5); the king's barber who discovers the ears and who lets the world know. (N465).*[12]
>
> *The following story, which combines several of these themes, was written in English for me by Homer Espino, one of my students, who says he got it from his grandmother. It is one of the many stories built around the old saying, "The walls have ears."*

In Spain there once lived a vain king who was noted over the province for his chivalry and honor. He usually wore clothes designed especially for him by his tailor, who made it his business to see that the king's clothes were in the very latest style. The king also had his private cook, barber, and coachman. Besides these, there were the members of his royal court who admired him and yielded to his every whim.

There came a time when his court noticed that there was something worrying him which seemed to take his mind from everything else. Each one sought to find the cause of this and do what he could to restore the king to his former merry mood. The first to learn of the trouble of the king, however, was his barber, whom he took into his confidence under penalty of death, should he disclose his intimate secret. This secret was his recent discovery of two horns on his head, which were slowly becoming more and more noticeable.

After some time, the barber felt that he could keep the secret no longer; many times he started to tell his wife, but the thought would come into his mind about the promised punishment if the news got out—and it surely would if his wife ever became aware of his itching secret.

At last he decided he could bear it no longer, feeling that if he could only shout out his secret, relief would come. Traveling to a near-by lonely place and making sure no one was around, he dug a deep hole. He then let himself down into it with a rope. Once down, he shouted, "The king has horns!" again and again until he felt exhausted, but relieved.

Several years later the rumor arose that the king had horns. After some investigation, it was discovered that the words which had been shouted some years back by the barber were inscribed on the leaves of a strange tree growing in an isolated spot.

Even though the barber had never told anyone his secret, the words he shouted in the hole seemed to have taken root and now appeared on the leaves of the tree.

Death up a Tree

The idea of death sticking to a tree can be traced back to antiquity where it is found in both Greek and Hebrew originals. The story ... appeared in literary form in Italian as early as 1525 and became the subject of a very popular French chapbook, 'Histoire nouvelle et divertissante du bonhomme misere, par le sieur de la Riviere' (Rouen, 1719). This was often reprinted and has been the basis of many literary treatments. The most striking part of the story, Death on the Tree, was recently used as the central motif of the cinema production 'On Borrowed Time.'

> *The story has had considerable popularity as an oral tale, whether or not the tradition may eventually go back to a written form. It is known literally all over Europe and as far east as the Caucasus and Palestine. It is found in Iceland, Scotland, Spain, and Italy, but its greatest popularity is in central and northern Europe—Germany, Lithuania, Estonia, and Finland. At least twenty-five versions are found in Russia.[13]*

José Hernández, who told the story to me in Spanish, got it from his mother. He said that he had never seen the cinema production nor read the story anywhere, but that it was known by all the gente. From this, it appears that the present version is from oral tradition. Thompson classifies the story as Type 330A. Espinosa records a similar story in No. 171.

There was once a man named Pepe, who owned a very beautiful tree on which grew grapes as large as oranges. Many people from far and near came to see the tree and taste of its fruit. But Pepe always had difficulty in collecting for what they ate. The *gente* would climb up the tree, eat of the unusual fruit, descend, and go on their way, disregarding Pepe's request for a few *centavos* for their treat.

In desperation, he appealed to the gods for help and was granted the magic power to keep a person up in the tree until he was given permission to come down. In this way Pepe was able to collect his fee from everyone. His income was sufficient to supply him and his family with all they needed, and he lived in peace for many years.

When Pepe was getting to be an old man, with deep creases in his face, browned by many suns, and his hair white as the tip of the gull's wing, he had a strange visitor.

"I have come for you, Pepe," he said. "Your time is drawing near."

It was *La Muerte*.

Now Pepe was not yet ready to die. He enjoyed sitting out there day after day under his tree, watching the birds and talking with the *gente* who came from such far places to taste the wonderful fruit. Besides, who would guard the tree, if he were taken and there was no one else who had the magic power the gods had given him? Thinking quickly, he asked Death if he would not enjoy some of the fruit before they started out on their long journey.

"It looks very delicious," Death replied, "and though I am in a hurry as I have other calls to make, I will try it."

Pepe wondered if his power would work on Death as it did on people, and was delighted to find that it did. Death, after eating his fill, could not descend.

"This is wonderful," thought Pepe. Now everyone was protected from Death. There would be no one who would have to die.

Weeks passed and people began to wonder why there were no deaths. Some, very old and tired of living, had been patiently awaiting the call of Death; and when they heard, as the news began to leak out, about the predicament of Death, they sent messages to Pepe to release him. Each day when Pepe sat under the tree, Death would beg him to give him permission to descend. Finally Death made a promise to Pepe. "I will not take you if you will only let me down!"

Pepe readily agreed, and Death went on about his work.

As years passed, Pepe himself grew tired of life. He had a great weariness upon him, and he was frequently in much pain. He was now ready to go on to that other land with Death. He sent message after message, but Death was so far behind in his work because of the time he had lost up in the tree, that it was a year before he could answer Pepe's plea. Pepe had to suffer and wait; it was payment for the trick he had played on Death.

1. J. Frank Dobie, ed., *Tone the Bell Easy* ("Publications of the Texas Folklore Society," X [1932]), p. 5.
2. Dobie, *Folklore of the Southwest*. Reprinted from *Chronicles of Oklahoma*, II (September, 1924), 274.
3. Aureliano Espinosa, *Cuentos Populares Españoles* (Palo Alto, California: Stanford University, 1926), III, 12.

4. Stith Thompson, *Motif-Index of Folk-Literature* (Bloomington: Indiana University, 1932-36).

5. Type numbers indicated in the headnotes refer to Stith Thompson, *The Folktale* (New York: Dryden Press, 1946), and story numbers to Aureliano Espinosa, *Cuentos Populares Españoles.*

6. Thompson, *The Folktale*, p. 76.

7. *Ibid.*, p. 77.

8. George M. Foster, "Mexican and Central American Folklore," *Standard Dictionary of Folklore, Mythology, and Legend* (New York: Funk & Wagnalls, 1950), p. 715.

9. Thompson, *The Folktale*, p. 225.

10. "Ascent to Upper World," *Standard Dictionary of Folklore, Mythology, and Legend*, p. 80.

11. "Munchausen," *Standard Dictionary of Folklore, Mythology, and Legend*, p. 761.

12. Thompson, *The Folktale*, p. 265.

13. *Ibid.*, p. 46.

Folklore of the German-Wends in Texas

GEORGE R. NIELSON

ON THE MORNING of December 16, 1854, the immigration authorities at Galveston went out to meet the *Ben Nevis*, an English sailship, which had arrived in the harbor. On board they examined the papers and the physical condition of the five hundred Wends who had come to settle in Texas. Seventy-three had died since the band had left their homes in Germany; but since none on board were ill, the authorities permitted the settlers to land.[1]

Although these Wends came from Prussia and Saxony, they were not Germans, but descendants of the Veneti of ancient times and the Polab Slavs of the Middle Ages. They called themselves Serbes or Serben, but to avoid confusion with the Serbs of the Balkan region, anthropologists named them Serbo-Lusatians or Wends.

These once numerous people had become more restricted in area until they were surrounded by Germanic tribes, and as far back as 1346 the Germanization of the Wends had begun. The Wendish culture was not related to that of the Germans. Their language resembled that of the Czechs, Poles, and Russians, and their dress, folklore, and literature were more Slavic than German. In 1815, however, the Congress of Vienna divided Lusatia, giving Upper Lusatia to Saxony and Lower Lusatia to Prussia. That was the beginning date of an organized and ruthless program launched by the Prussian government to make the Wends German.[2]

The most isolated part of the Lusatias, and thus the part that resisted Germanization longest, was the Spreewald, in Upper Lusatia, where the Spree River divides into hundreds of small streams, brooks, and marshes. Here the houses were built on islands, and flatboats furnished transportation during the warm months. The signboards gave the distances from one place to another not in kilometers, but in the time required for the pushing of the boat. In winter, when the canals froze, travel was by sled or skates. The occupation of the Wends here, as well as of those living outside the Spreewald, was mostly agriculture. They grew primarily vegetables and fruits, and in addition cared for domesticated animals and captured the eels which crowded the streams in the spawning season.

The folklore of the Serbo-Lusatians was among the richest in Europe, possibly as a result of their late conversion to Christianity. It was basically the same as that of other groups in Europe, but it was more varied. Included in their beliefs were remnants of the preceding centuries such as animism—the belief that all objects possess a natural life or soul—and the worship of early pagan deities, the personifications of forces of nature. Two of these gods were *Belbog* and *Cernobog*, the white and black gods standing for Life and Death, Light and Darkness, or the Good and Evil Spirits. As Christianity was slowly accepted by these people, this dualistic conception of good and evil was carried on, and the names were changed to God and Devil. The poetic temperament of the Slavic people molded their interpretation of life and nature into stories possessing great charm. These people also expressed themselves so freely in songs that the Wends had one song for every 150 people. The Poles were second in this respect, having one song for every 1,000 inhabitants.[3]

The only trait that the Wends and Germans held in common was religion. They were either Lutheran or Roman Catholic. Most of the Wends were Lutheran, but they were not united with the German Lutherans, because the writings of the church had been translated into Wendish and the services were conducted in that language. However, when a parish needed a pastor, and there was a possibility that a portion of the congregation would accept a German clergyman, the government would immediately send a German-speaking pastor. By 1848 there were only thirty-six Wendish preachers left.

The Germans also discriminated against the Wends in economic activity. The Wends had little capital for investment, and any attempt on their part to improve their lot was opposed by the Germans. The majority had to labor with their hands, only a few being able to break through restrictions to become professional men.[4]

In 1840 the 140,000 people speaking Wendish were dissatisfied and unhappy; and when the king, the "Pope in Berlin," forced the union of the Lutheran and Reformed churches, emigration increased and approximately 580 Wends under the leadership of Pastor John Kilian left their homes for Texas.[5]

After landing in Galveston, they quickly took a boat to Houston, thus avoiding contact with the yellow fever epidemic in the Island City. From Houston they crossed the fertile prairie until they came to the Post Oaks near Rabb's Creek in what was then Bastrop County. For fifty cents an acre they got some of the worst land in Texas, whereas for fifty cents more they could have had the fertile prairie or bottom lands. They realized as much, but nearly all were completely without money. They had had little in Germany and after the trip they had even less. If they settled on the prairie, in addition to paying the higher price for land, they would have to buy wood for their houses, fences, and furnishings, whereas in the Post Oaks they could cut their own timber.[6]

Under these conditions it is not difficult to see why the Wends kept little European folklore. Much of their folklore had been associated with trees, animals, and land; so when they saw mesquite, scrub oak, and oleanders instead of birches, chestnuts, and alders, and coyotes, skunks, possums, armadillos, scorpions, and tarantulas instead of the few wolves, rodents, and deer of Europe, the stories must have lost their meaning. And how could one possibly imagine that spirits and fairies would exist in the same woods with the wild Indians? Any costumes that were brought over were soon ruined by living under primitive conditions, and if there was money, it would be spent for land and not on new clothes.

As a result, the folklore which developed in Europe was almost completely lost in this new environment, with the exception of those customs which were practical and necessary, such as cures, planting and harvesting ways, and those practices associated with the church. This loss can probably be illustrated by an incident related by my grandmother. Once when her father was telling the children some stories, the mother interrupted the story-telling because she wanted the children to amount to something. By that she meant that she wanted them to work or learn something that would yield financial returns.[7]

Ironically, the Wends did not escape from German influence. There were Germans in Texas when the Wends landed in Galveston, and in 1860 a large migration of Germans brought many to the vicinity of Bastrop County. In this instance the church was the unifying factor for the two groups and fraternization and intermarrying resulted. The question of language was the only real problem, but the pastor and the people were bilingual, knowing both Wendish and German. Services were conducted in both German and Wendish until the 1920's, when German became the only language used in public worship.[8] Folklore, as a result, is also a combination of the two cultures, and it is impossible to separate the German from the Wendish folklore.

The most common and rich category of German-Wendish folklore is that of the folk cures. My first memories of these cures go back to my childhood when I stepped on a nail. In the hot summers of central Texas going barefooted was taken for granted, and along with the pleasure went the occasional injuries from grass burrs, mesquite thorns, and goatheads. A wound from a rusty nail, however, was a different matter, and in modern times the injured person would be punished further with tetanus shots. In the days when doctors were far away, and the transportation was slow, the remedies had to be applied at home. In this case the treatment was painless and effective. A piece of bacon rind was placed on the wound, and then the foot was set in a shallow pan containing turpentine. The combination of the two caused a drawing effect on the wound, and the strong odor of the turpentine had the desired psychological effect. This remedy was said to be good not only for wounds, but also for curing boils and chest colds. For curing the chest colds, strips of fatty bacon were sewn on a woolen cloth, saturated with turpentine, and then applied to the chest of the patient. The uncomfortable person had to sleep all night with the sticky, gooey, and evil-smelling poultice, but in the morning the cold was broken.

Our skins suffered not only from the sharp spines of the thorns, but also from the sharp stingers of the yellow jackets and bees, and the painful bites of the big red ants. These were unavoidable. Sometimes we asked for it by standing on the anthill while holding our breath, or by knocking down the yellow jackets' nest from underneath the eaves with fishing poles, but at other times we were innocently playing or picking cotton. If we were near my uncle, we would go to him for aid, and he would remove part of his chewing tobacco cud and place it on the bite. If we were closer to the house, we would run in to Mother who would then place a teaspoon of baking soda on the wound and pour on a little vinegar. It fizzed, and the cooling relief was felt immediately.

Not all the remedies were from materials in the home; occasionally the adults ordered some from Germany or bought them in town. One such medicine, called *Blitz Öl* (Lightning Oil), was, in my grandfather's opinion, the final word in pharmaceutics. If any of the children hurt themselves, he would administer the medicine, even though it was hated and feared because its burn was worse than the pain of the original wound. One day, however, as Grandfather was splitting wood, the ax slipped and grazed his knee. Quickly he went onto the back porch, for this was his first opportunity to apply the medicine on himself. When he did so, the burning was as fierce as lightning and he gave the bottle a good heave into the pasture. Needless to say, the children were not sorry to see it go.[9]

If this medicine was not effective, there were others that were. The efficacy of one of them was proved by an injury suffered by my Great-grandfather Schneider. He was binding oats, and it took a great deal of skill to drive the four horses as well as operate the machine. In an attempt to obtain additional leverage, he wrapped the lines controlling the horses around his thumb; but on this occasion the trailing lines got caught in the big bull-wheel, and the thumb was wrenched off. All that held it was a bit of skin on one side. He went home, doused the thumb with *Heil Öl* (Heal Oil), and wrapped it snugly with cloth. The thumb healed, and he regained its complete use.[10]

A very popular cure was the *Lebenswecker* (Life Awakener), which was used to cure sore muscles, stiff joints, strokes, mastoids, and nearly everything else. It was a contraption the main part of which was a handle with a head the size of a fifty-cent piece made up of hundreds of little needles. The instrument was placed against the ailing part and the handle was drawn back and then released, causing the many small needles to prick the outer layer of the skin. No blood was drawn, but the areas would be red from irritation. Then a little *Lebenswecker Öl* was applied with a feather. The patient was forbidden to get his hands wet for the next three days.[11]

The *Lebenswecker Öl* was also used internally, but with great care. A girl, by the name of Alma Leitco, was taken to the Hamilton hospital with a severe case of locked bowels. Drs. Beecher, Chandler, and Cleveland tried everything but finally had to give the case up as hopeless. When Oswald Melde heard of it, he got some of the oil from Great-grandmother, went to Hamilton, and asked for permission to use the oil. The doctors said that since they had given up twelve hours earlier, they would consent. The father hesitated, but then gave his permission. Several years before, he had had a constipated mule and had tried the *Lebenswecker Öl*. A few minutes after the application, the mule had gotten up, jumped, and run, but then dropped dead. The only reason Mr. Leitco now gave permission was that he had prayed for help only fifteen minutes before, and he believed that Oswald Melde was the answer to the prayer. Nevertheless, Mr. Leitco went home. Three drops of the oil were mixed with the yolk of an egg and administered orally. Several hours later the girl passed a tapeworm thirty feet long, and when the father returned she was on her way to recovery.[12]

Some of the cures that interested me, but were not used by my immediate family, were the numerous teas. The older women in the community placed great faith in them. For general health, tea made from linden, rose, or camellia leaves was good. As a specific remedy *Schreck Tee* (Fright Tea) was among the most popular. Anyone who was startled or shocked could get sure relief from a drink of this tea. About three heads of dried *Schreck Kräuter* (Fright Herb) were boiled for about thirty minutes in two cups of water. The patient drank the brew and went to bed, enjoying complete relaxation. The part of the plant that was boiled resembled the blooms of a thistle. It was not purchased, but usually grown in the corner of the garden, and after it was dried, stored in a fruit jar.[13] Some people say that for added effect, the patient should take part of the object that startled him and boil it along with the tea. If it was a dog, he should take one of the hairs, place it in a tablespoon, roast it, and add it to the tea.[14]

Few of the cures are as unpleasant as the cure for bed-wetting. The ingredients are several newly born mice without hair. These are chopped up (without being cleaned), fried, and fed to the child. To keep the child ignorant of what he was eating, the cook would chop up steak in a similar way and give it to the others.[15]

Unpleasant in odor was the preventive measure used especially during epidemics. Asafetida was carried either in a bag around the neck or in the pocket. It was used to ward off the germs. Because it was an evil-smelling resin, the nickname for it was *Teufel's Dreck*.[16]

Present in several of the cures is the element of mysticism. It is most difficult to find a complete recitation of one of the curing verses. Most seem to mention the name of Jesus and the number three. Here is one used to cure bleeding:

In meines Jesu Garten	In my Jesus' garden
Stehen drei bäumelein	There are three trees
Eins heist . . .	One is called . . .
Das zweite heist . . .	The second is called . . .
Das dritte heist . . .	The third is called . . .
Blut halt stille.	Blood stop.

The bleeding would stop almost immediately, but this help should only be used in extreme cases, because while this verse would stop the bleeding, the healing of the wound would be slow.[17]

Since there was also a verse to promote healing of the wound, possibly these two should have been used together. The only line known is: "Est stehn drei blumen auf Christi grab . . ."[18] ("There are three flowers on Christ's grave . . ."). Many of the mystical cures of the Wends centered around Mutter Spielert, who lived in Giddings. Great powers were attributed to her, including the ability to cure erysipelas, a common Wendish disease.[19]

The cure for warts requires a person to hold a silk thread over the wart and tie a knot in it. The thread is then buried next to the house where there is moisture. When the thread rots, the wart will be gone.

The remedy for side-ache caused by walking is even simpler. To cure the side-ache, the person should stop, pick up a rock, spit on it, and replace it.[20]

When you ask the *Grossmutter* (Grandmother) if the cures are any good, she will smile and say, "Sie leben noch" ("They are still living").

Home cures were also used on animals. There was usually a man or woman in the community who had power over the worms in animals. This was a helpful person, for young calves often get worms at the navel before the navel dries. In most cases the owner merely went to the person and described the calf. When he returned home the calf would be walking around the lot bleeding at the place where the worms were. The owner then applied some salve on the wound so the flies could not get to it. If the wound was at the navel, it would be necessary to pull some of the skin together with a string.[21]

In curing a sick horse, the healer drew blood from the horse, fastened cotton on a stick, and daubed the blood with the cotton. Then he placed this cotton in the hole of a tree.[22]

To prevent their stock from being stolen, the Wends called upon a Mr. Drosche for help. He made the sign of the cross on the ground in the middle of the lot and as he mumbled something he would make signs on the animals and on the ground around them. After this treatment the horses would throw the thieves or refuse to be driven by them. Another way to prevent the stock from being stolen was to nail horseshoes to the ground and drive the cattle over them.[23]

The immigrants had to have some kind of variety in their life of hard work, and that variety was supplied by the church. Sunday service or any function of the church was time for worship—and everything else. The customs observed at marriages and funerals shed a great deal of light on the life of the people.

In the years immediately after the migration the marriage customs were almost identical with those used in Europe. Wedding celebrations usually lasted three days. Announcements and personal invitations were issued weeks in advance. The wedding party assembled at the bride's home, and before they left for church, they would sing a hymn and say the Lord's Prayer. The bride was dressed in a very tight-fitting black gown, which symbolized the sufferings of the new life ahead of her. (In the 1890's gray was substituted for black, and after 1900 white was accepted.) Flowers were used generously on the carriages, the horses, the church, and the attendants. There were usually ten bridesmaids and ten groomsmen. After they had taken their places at the altar, the congregation sang a hymn, and the pastor preached a short sermon. The vows were then exchanged and the groomsmen laid money on the altar for the pastor and the organist.

After the ceremony, everyone rushed to the bride's home for the celebration. Usually some children had the road roped off, and the groom had to bribe the children with small change so they would lower the rope. When the party and guests arrived at the house, the pastor and cantor led the people in hymns and a prayer, and the eating began. Since there were few tables, the wedding party ate at the first table, and then the rest of the people ate in shifts late into the night. The bride and groom remained at the table until midnight. During the course of the evening someone would pull off one of the bride's shoes, which would then be passed around and the guests would contribute for another shoe. Beer and whiskey, bourbon for the men and *Kümmel* for the women, helped make the celebration lively.[24]

If the parents wanted to be sure that the daughter and son-in-law would never go hungry they would get a barrel (196 pounds) or four sacks of flour, and use it all for the wedding celebration. Every kind of pastry was baked; any not eaten was given to the guests as they departed.[25]

Good fortune was also indicated by drizzle or fine rain falling on the bride's hair as she entered the house. Another saying favored marriages in cold weather:

> Heirat in Januar wenn's eisig und kalt
> Erlangs du Reichtum wenn auch nicht balt.
>
> (Marry in January when it's icy and cold
> Eventually you will become rich if not quite soon.)

Bad fortune, however, was indicated if the string of pearls the bride was wearing should break, for she would cry one night for every pearl on the string.[26]

At the present time the weddings held among the people in the rural communities have changed somewhat. The celebration now lasts only one day, but the relatives who have moved out of the community return for a few days before the wedding. The weddings continue to be held in the church, but with much smaller parties. After the ceremony, the guests follow the wedding party to the bride's house—in automobiles. After greeting the parents of the bride and all the friends the guests gradually work their way to the woodshed where the beer is dispensed. Soon the coverings are removed from the tables and barbecue and all the accompanying dishes are served. Later in the evening, with the beer still flowing, dominoes, 42, and *Schafskopf* (sheepshead) are played. Occasionally the Hungry Five, consisting of a trumpet, baritone, clarinet, trombone, and snare drum, play some old German songs, such as *"Gerade aus das Wirtshaus."* When the players get thirsty, they play *"Bier Her"* and the bartender answers immediately with five schooners. Most of the guests leave between twelve and three in the morning, but some celebrate much later.

Sometime after midnight the newly married couple will steal away and go to their home, or to some other home in the area. About half an hour later the young men will follow with plowshares, hammers, and any kind of metal that will produce vibrations. The charivariers approach the house quietly and suddenly begin the *Katzenmusik* (cat's music). Sometimes they are invited in, but in most cases they give up and go back for more beer.

Many different customs are connected with death. In Europe one custom is to cover the mirror with a cloth and scatter the clothes of the deceased person over the floor and leave them for four weeks.[27]

Some of the people still cover the mirror when one of the family dies. Others have been known to keep the doors to the room where the person died closed for a period of one year and then get a neighbor to open it.[28]

The death of a person is signaled by the tolling of the church bell. It is rung for a minute, and after a brief pause, rung for another minute, followed by another pause, and then rung for a third minute. This practice symbolizes the Trinity. Then the age of the person is counted out with the bell strokes. The people in the community know who is ill, and from the number of bell strokes can usually guess who has died. The burial takes place several days later, in the afternoon. The school children sing, and after the sermon the body is viewed. The procession to the *Kirchhof* (cemetery) is led by the pastor and teacher, who are followed by the pallbearers. At the grave another hymn is sung, led by the cantor.

There are other folk stories or customs which are without a doubt related to some in Europe. Great-grandfather Schneider was a blacksmith, but he learned his trade in Germany. Usually the *Meister* or teacher would take several boys and teach them the trade as they worked without pay. One Sunday when the *Meister* was at church the boys looked around the shop and in some of the cupboards which the teacher kept closed. In one they found a book, supposedly the Seventh Book of Moses, which they began reading. Soon a crow flew in through the window and lighted on a beam. The boys continued reading, and another crow flew in. More crows came until there were crows outside as well as inside the shop. When the boys noticed this, they became frightened and replaced the book. At the same time the teacher came out of the church and saw the crows. He went to the shop, took the book, and began reading it backward. As he did so the crows flew away in the same order in which they had come, and when he reached the first word all were gone.[29]

In Europe the folk place great confidence in the water dipped from a spring or stream on Easter morning. This idea also exists among the American Wends. One woman I knew would rise before sun-up on Easter morning, draw some water from the well, and make a small trail of water around the house. This would keep out insects the rest of the year. Another belief is that water dipped on Easter morning is healthful and that even though kept for some time it continues to taste good.

Other stories are definitely of American origin. Many of the Wends and Germans also came to America to avoid the draft. When they came to Texas they were faced with the draft for the Confederate Army. They did not want to fight, and if they did they would rather fight against slavery and thus eliminate the competition of slaves in agriculture. Many stories are told of how the young men evaded the draft. Most of them hid out when they heard that strangers were in the community. If work had to be done they wore dresses and sunbonnets in the fields. My Great-grandfather Moerbe was caught one day and was about to be drafted when they noticed his bowlegs. People say he was so bowlegged that a pony keg could have been placed between his knees. He could not be taken into the army, but when the officials discovered that he was a tailor, he was encouraged to go to San Antonio to sew uniforms.[30]

A final major category of folklore is of dubious parentage. Many of the beliefs regarding planting and agricultural activity are also found among the English-speaking people, but since these sayings are widely accepted by the German-Wends, they should be included.

It is generally believed that the moon has a powerful influence on the earth, for no one questions the moon's control of the tides. It is logical, therefore, that its power would be felt in other areas than the tides. If both plants and humans, as the scientists tell us, consist of a large percentage of water, why should not the moon dictate to plants and man the courses they must take?

People who are close to nature are strongly conscious of this influence. If, for example, the corn is planted on the decrease of the moon, the ears will be large, but if it is planted on the increase of the moon, the stalk will be large. It is also true that if calves are branded on the increase of the moon, the brand will grow, whereas if they are branded on the decrease of the moon the brands will either keep the same size or diminish in size. Farmers and ranchers also know that if trees are killed on the decrease of the moon they will not send up shoots as they would if they were chopped down on the increase of the moon. This influence is even true of hair. If hair is cut on the decrease of the moon, it will grow more slowly, and it will not be necessary to return to the barber so soon.[31]

The signs of the zodiac also regulate farm activity. Animals should be castrated under Pisces, but never under Cancer. Potatoes should be planted on February 22 and cucumbers on Maundy Thursday.[32] If the cucumbers continue to grow too much foliage and not enough cucumbers, a shoe should be buried among the plants.[33] Crops planted under Cancer will be injured by insects. Any pest, such as Johnson grass, is best killed under the sign of Cancer.[34]

Finally, there are some folk-sayings of various kinds:

"If you walk backward while talking you will push your mother and father to hell."

"Do not burn old clothes, bury them."

"Do not move a broom along."

"Do not move or marry on Friday."

"If a bird flies into the church or the house, it is bad luck."

"If the procession bearing the corpse from the church to the graveyard is stopped, someone will die from the same house as the deceased."

"Do not eat a lunch wearing your hat, even outside, or the devil will laugh."

"After you eat, an angel waits for the prayer of thanks to take it to heaven."[35]

1. Anne Blasig, *The Wends of Texas* (San Antonio: Naylor Co., 1954), pp. 27-29.
2. George C. Engerrand, *The So-Called Wends of Germany and Their Colonies in Texas and Australia* (University of Texas Bulletin, No. 3417; Austin: University of Texas, 1934), pp. 11, 22.
3. *Ibid.*, pp. 14-17, 47-58.
4. *Ibid.*, pp. 29-31.
5. Blasig, *op. cit.*, pp. 17, 18.
6. *Ibid.*, pp. 29, 30.
7. Interview with Mrs. E. F. Moerbe, Pottsville, Texas, November 2, 1958.
8. Blasig, *op. cit.*, p. 82.
9. Interview with Mrs. Esther Gromatzky, Pottsville, Texas, November 2, 1958.
10. Interview with Martin Moerbe, Taylor, Texas, November 16, 1958.
11. *Ibid.*
12. Interview with Mrs. Eleanore Schneider, Austin, Texas, December 10, 1958; interview with Oswald Melde, Aleman, Texas, January 11, 1959.
13. Interview with Arthur Moebus, Serbin, Texas, October 18, 1958; interview with Mrs. Mitschke, Serbin, Texas, October 18, 1958.
14. Interview with Robert Malke, Serbin, Texas, October 18, 1958.
15. Interview with Oswald Melde.
16. Letter from Mrs. Wm. H. Nielsen, Vernon, Texas, December 2, 1958.
17. Interview with Oswald Melde. Mr. Melde did not know the names of the trees, but believed that no other names could be substituted.
18. Interview with Martin Moerbe.
19. Interview with Oswald Melde.
20. *Ibid.*
21. Interview with Arthur Moebus.

22. Blasig, *op. cit.*, p. 59.
23. Interview with Oswald Melde.
24. Blasig, *op. cit.*, pp. 54-56.
25. Interview with Oswald Melde.
26. *Ibid.*
27. Engerrand, *op. cit.*, pp. 49-51.
28. Interview with Oswald Melde.
29. *Ibid.*
30. *Ibid.*
31. Interview with Arthur Moebus; interview with Robert Malke.
32. Interview with Otto Schneider, Austin, Texas, September 3, 1958.
33. Interview with Mrs. Arthur Melde, Aleman, Texas, January 11, 1959.
34. Interview with Otto Schneider.
35. Interview with Oswald Melde.

Tales the German Texans Tell

CAROLYN MANKIN

BECAUSE Texas as a society is so young, in many ways it has not developed its own distinctive characteristics; rather the characteristics of each old society which has contributed to the life and growth of the new land are yet distinguishable. This is true of the folktales told in Texas, a large number of which were brought from the citizens' old homelands and still retain the settings and styles of the older countries. Germany is one of the many countries which have contributed folktales to the culture of Texas.

The folktales in this paper were secured by means of direct interviews with four German-speaking citizens of Dallas. Not only do these tales reflect the cultural influence of Germany, but each one also reflects the sub-culture or part of Germany from which it came.

Tales from the Berlin Area

Willie F. Mueller, a stocky, middle-aged German who was born and reared in the Berlin area, came to the United States in the mid-1920's at the age of twenty-four. Many tales he had learned as a schoolboy. He pointed out that the tales from Berlin were much more sophisticated than those from other parts of Germany. The citizens of Berlin were not so superstitious as were the farmers and miners in rural areas. Many of the city's tales were meant to convey a lesson. Two tales of this type are "The White Sparrow" and "The Journeyman and the Clock." Since the citizens of Berlin were noted in Germany for their quick wit, many anecdotes and jests such as "The Hackman and the Stranger" and "The Cobbler and the Apprentice" were told for enjoyment. Also prevalent were tales of such culture heroes as Frederick the Great. King Frederick was supposedly very progressive; he educated his subjects and moved among them incognito. His lack of religious beliefs was also a subject for tales.

THE WHITE SPARROW

Once there was a farmer who was good, but he was very lazy and did not prosper. One day he was telling a friend his troubles. The friend, being very diplomatic, did not wish to offend the farmer by advising him. He asked the farmer if he had ever seen a white sparrow. The farmer thought, and then said that he had not.

"Would you like to see one?" asked the friend.

"Yes," said the farmer, "that would be a sight to see."

"Then," said the friend, "you must arise very early in the morning, for that is the only time when one may be seen."

So the farmer arose early the next morning to see the white sparrow. When he went out, he saw the milkmaid taking a pail of milk down a path away from the farm and a farmhand giving away a sack of grain. The farmer never saw a white sparrow, but he became more prosperous.

THE JOURNEYMAN AND THE CLOCK

A journeyman, traveling through the land, entered a village. In the village he passed a bakery. He went into the bakery and looked at all the breads and wished he had some, but he had no money. Then he happened to notice a clock in the bakery. He watched the pendulum as it passed back and forth, back and forth. It gave him an idea.

"How old is that clock?" the journeyman asked the baker.

It was over a hundred years old, he was told.

"For a hundred years that clock has swung back and forth, back and forth, and I bet you couldn't do it for thirty minutes."

"I bet you I could if I had to," the baker replied.

"All right, I bet you."

So the two made a wager and the baker faced the clock and began to swing his arm back and forth. The journeyman filled his knapsack with bread and left the store and the village while the baker continued to swing his arm back and forth, back and forth.

After a time, the baker's wife came in and looked at her husband.

"You fool," she said, "what are you doing? Stop that!"

But the baker continued to swing his arm until the half-hour was up and the journeyman was well down the road enjoying the bread.

THE HACKMAN AND THE STRANGER

A stranger came to Berlin and hired a hackman to show him the sights of the city. The hackman began to point out the city's various buildings.

"That building is over a hundred years old," he said.

"How long did it take to build it?" asked the stranger.

"Ten years," said the hack driver.

"In my country, they could build it in two!" retorted the stranger.

"There is a famous building," said the hackman.

"How long did it take to build it?"

"Twenty years."

"In my country, we could do it in four!"

As the two passed through the city, the conversation continued in this manner. Each time the stranger said that the building could be made faster in his own country. Then they came to the largest building in the city.

"How long did it take you to build that?" demanded the stranger.

The hack driver looked at it in disbelief and scratched his head.

"I don't know," he said, "but it wasn't here yesterday."

THE COBBLER AND THE APPRENTICE

There was a cobbler who had two hired helpers and an apprentice. When the cobbler died, his wife told the helpers and the apprentice to take turns during the night sitting up with the corpse. The two hired men sat up first, and then came the time for the apprentice to sit up.

"To make good use of time, you can do some work while you're sitting here," the cobbler's wife told the apprentice, and she left him working on a pair of shoes.

The apprentice grew bored with the silence and began to whistle.

Out of the darkness came a voice: "When one is sitting up with the dead, one does not whistle."

Without protesting, the apprentice fell silent, but after a while he became bored again. He began to hum.

"When one is sitting up with the dead, one does not hum," said the voice from the darkness.

Again the apprentice fell silent, but when he became bored again, he began to sing.

"When one is sitting up with the dead, one does not sing."

The apprentice jumped up from his bench, ran to the coffin, and slapped the corpse on the face.

"When one is dead, one does not speak!"

TALES OF FREDERICK THE GREAT

During the reign of Frederick the Great, he received a letter from a priest who wanted a horse so he could ride to visit his churches. Frederick answered that the Bible says, "Go ye into all the world and teach all nations." Nothing is said about riding.

Frederick the Great often went about the land disguised as

a peasant or wanderer. One day he saw a boy who was not in school. The boy had already secretly recognized him. When Frederick asked, "Why are you not in school?" the boy answered, "You want to be emperor and don't know that there is no school on Saturday."

Tales from the Erzgebirge Area

The Erzgebirge (Ore Mountains) is a mining region in the state of Saxony. The mountain range forms a natural boundary between East Germany and Czechoslovakia. The people of this area, who are mostly miners, tend to be very superstitious. Ella Kraus Wolfe was born in the small village of Soza in the Erzgebirge area. A member of a mining family, she received much of her entertainment in the form of folktales told in the evenings in front of the fire. She related with a tone of belief in her voice a tale about a murder solved by a red rooster.

On the other hand, Hanna Teubner Becker, who was born and reared in the same village, did not hear many such tales during her childhood. She was born into a family of teachers who looked down on folktales as silly superstitions. However, one of her favorite high-school teachers was interested in the folklore of the miners, and from Professor Sieber's collection she learned some of the tales of her homeland.

MURDER SOLVED BY A RED ROOSTER

There was a beautiful girl in Soza who was loved by a young man, but refused to marry him. Every day she had to walk through a woods to catch a train in order to go to school. One day she did not return home. There was a search, and her body was found in the woods where she had been murdered. The murder was not solved immediately.

On the day of the funeral, the procession passed through the village. As it went by the home of the girl's suitor, a red rooster flew out of his yard and perched upon the coffin. Then the people of the village knew that the young man had committed the murder. Soon the young man became very sick with a fever. He sent for the priest and confessed his crime. Not long afterward he died.

TALES OF THE MINES

In front of the shaft or behind the smelter lurk ghostlike animals. The Hüttenmops of Olbernhau, who once was an official of a mine, after death was required to go from hut to hut and from mine to mine haunting because of his unfaithfulness. And in the form of an ugly dog, he would spring upon the backs of the miners.

At the Donat Spat mine, near Freiburg, lived Hans, a poor miner who complained often and loudly about his poverty and his many cares. One day, as he was working and complaining in the mine, a rock suddenly opened and the mountain spirit stepped from this stone doorway. He promised help if the miner would daily bring him a penny loaf of bread and a penny candle. But no one should be told about this. From this hour on, Hans had good fortune and lived happily and comfortably. However, he became drunk at a miners' celebration and revealed the source of his money. The next day he was pulled up dead in the miners' bucket. Around his corpse burned the penny candles he had brought as an offering to the mountain spirit.

The owner of the "Trust in God" mine promised the miner who first discovered a vein of silver half of the yield. When one single miner, who despite all failures persevered and finally did discover ore, joyfully brought the owner to the shaft to show him the find, the miser killed the faithful miner. Thereupon the mountain spirit, becoming enraged, concealed his treasures again and turned the heart of the mine owner into a boulder in the Schwarzwasser River.

Tales of the Lost Nigger Mine

GAYLE L. COE

SINCE I WAS raised in the Big Bend country, where the "Lost Nigger Mine" is supposedly located, my interest in the mine was newly aroused when I read J. Frank Dobie's account in *Coronado's Children*. To find out whether people in the region were still interested in the mine, I talked with a number of them. Following are a few of the things I was told.

The Lost Nigger is also referred to as the Reagan Mine, and Dr. D. B. McCall of San Saba believes that the Nigger Mine and the Lost Apache Mine are one and the same.

According to Mrs. Beulah Van Deman of Marathon, the Nigger Mine was found around 1896 or 1897. The Reagan brothers, John, Jim, Lee, and Frank, had been ranching on the Devil's River. When a drought hit that area, the brothers moved their cattle down to the Big Bend at the mouth of a canyon which later came to be known as Reagan Canyon.

When the Reagans moved, they took with them a young Seminole Negro boy about eighteen or nineteen years old. He had come to them several months before the move, looking for work. He was from an Indian reservation near Santa Rosa, Mexico. His name was Bill Kelley.

Soon after moving to the Big Bend, the Reagans sent Kelley across the river to look for some strayed horses. After some time Kelley returned, but without the horses. Instead of horses, he had brought with him a large chunk of gold ore. The Reagans ignored Kelley's claim that he had found a gold mine and sent him across the river to look for horses again. Once more Kelley returned with gold ore and no horses.

Soon after that, Kelley was sent to Sanderson to get supplies for the ranch. He took a sample of his gold with him to show to his friend, Lock Campbell, a conductor on the Texas and New Orleans Railroad.

Kelley returned to the ranch, and Campbell sent the ore off to have it assayed. After several weeks, Campbell received the reports from the assay office. The gold samples assayed at approximately $75,000 a ton.

Campbell quickly rode to the Reagan ranch to tell Kelley the good news. When he got there, Kelley was gone. He had again been sent to look for horses, but some Mexicans had told him that the Reagan brothers were out looking for him and were plenty mad. On hearing this news, Kelley had gone to the Stillwell ranch up the river. John Stillwell took Kelley with him on a cattle drive to Mexico City, and Kelley did not return.

C. M. Hunter of Alpine tells almost the same story, except he says that the mine was found in 1894, and the gold assayed at $80,000 a ton. He also has added to the story. Mr. Hunter told me the tale of the Reagan brothers' hunting for the mine after Kelley had disappeared. According to Hunter, the Reagans spared neither time nor money in the search.

When they had expended all their prospecting knowledge, the Reagans brought in a mining engineer from California, paying him $10.00 a day and all expenses for six months, to hunt for the mine. When the time came to pay the engineer, Jim Reagan had to sell eighty of his fine fat steers to pay the bill. At this same time, Campbell and others were hunting for the mine.

During the first year of the search, all activities were centered on the north side of the Rio Grande. When experts who knew something of gold-bearing formations were brought in, the search was extended into Mexico around the El Picotero country which is located some twenty miles inside the border.

After a long and fruitless search, all those involved in looking for the mine decided to pool their resources for one big drive. D. C. Bourland, one of the prospectors, suggested that first of all they try to find Bill Kelley. Bourland, having heard that Kelley had some relatives in Austin, went to that city, where he found one of Kelley's relatives living on a small but prosperous farm just outside the city limits. The relative refused to tell Bourland where Kelley was, but said that some prospectors from Colorado who were looking for the mine had a map that was given to them by Kelley.

Bourland immediately returned to the Big Bend to find the men from Colorado. Upon finding them, he made a deal with them. Bourland was to furnish burros to carry all the equipment, and, for this, he would get a share of the profits when the mine was found.

A time and place were designated for a meeting between Bourland and the prospectors, but the men from Colorado never showed up. Up to this point, some $4,500 had been spent on the search without one speck of gold being found.

My grandmother, Mrs. W. W. Crawford of Marathon, told me a story of the Nigger Mine that was told to her by her father. Some years prior to the coming of the Reagan brothers, an old prospector by the name of Corbitt moved to what is now the Reagan Canyon area. Corbitt had brought with him many samples of gold ore from Alaska and Panama and had stored them in a cabin built on the exact spot where the Reagans' cow camp was later located.

Corbitt, being afflicted with consumption, had come to the Big Bend because he thought the dry desert air would help him. But it did not. After a short time, he died. No one would bother the cabin or its contents for fear of contracting the disease that had killed Corbitt. People just let the cabin stand and rot.

One night a terrible windstorm came up, wrecking the

cabin and strewing its contents over the hillside. The greater portion of the wreckage was gathered up by two neighboring ranchmen, Jim Wilson and J. E. Davenport.

One day Wilson and Davenport, being practical jokers, conceived the idea of playing a joke on the newly arrived ranchmen, the Reagan brothers, and their Seminole Negro hired hand, Bill Kelley. They took Corbitt's gold ore, broke it into small pieces, and hid the pieces in good places. Then they steered Kelley to the gold. The plan worked far better than they had expected, for Bill Kelley immediately took the gold ore in to show the Reagan brothers.

From this point on the story is about the same as those previously related. One peculiar or ironic twist to the story is that one of the men who played the joke did such a fine job of selling that he sold himself and in later years spent thousands of dollars looking for his own lost gold mine.

Hallie Stillwell, widow of the late Roy Stillwell, of Marathon and Alpine, told me a story that her husband had told her about the Nigger Mine. According to the late Mr. Stillwell, Bill Kelley found the gold, not in a mine but on a well-known trail that for many years had been used by Indians to bring gold from Mexico to the United States. Undoubtedly some of the ore had been dropped on the trail, where Kelly found it.

Mr. Stillwell was sure that the gold was found not on the Texas side of the Rio Grande, but around El Picotero, about twenty miles from the river. He said that when he could have gone into Mexico to look for the mine, the political situation was very bad. It was no place for a white man to be.

Mrs. Stillwell's story about the Indians is somewhat related to the story of Dr. D. B. McCall, of San Saba, who has been searching for the mine for over thirty years.

In a letter I received from Dr. McCall on April 29, 1960, he told me of his first knowledge of the mine. He calls the mine the Lost Apache Mine, but says it is the same thing as the Lost Nigger Mine.

In his letter, Dr. McCall said that in October of 1924, a Mexican-looking man came into his office on South Alamo Street in San Antonio. At the time, McCall was thirty-five years old; the visitor, as he later learned, was sixty-seven.

The man spoke English fairly well and told McCall he was deaf. He wanted McCall to treat him as a charity patient as he had no money, relatives, or friends. He told McCall his name was Solito Gonzales. McCall treated him, and in about a month his hearing had improved. Solito disappeared, and McCall did not hear from him again until January, 1925.

Solito had returned to pay Dr. McCall for his help. He pointed to a crudely-hammered-out gold ring on his finger and told McCall he knew where plenty of gold was and would show him.

McCall was doubtful at first, but after hearing Solito's story agreed to go with him. Solito told McCall that as a young boy he had been captured by Apaches near Fort Stockton and taken to a camp on the Maravillas Creek in the Big Bend. There he was raised by the Apaches.

After being with the Apaches for about nine years, Solito was taken to the Apache "gold place" by Chief Old Wolf. Old Wolf told Solito that when he was sixty years old and needed help, he might find a white man to trust. When he found this white man, he was to tell him of the gold.

According to McCall, he was the man. But before McCall could start his digging, Solito became very ill with food poisoning and had to be taken back to San Antonio. There he died.

McCall has gone to the Big Bend every year since, but has not again located the gold. He has leased the mineral rights on the spot shown to him by Solito. Dr. McCall told me that if I was interested, he would let me go prospecting with him next year.

McCall also says, "If I owned all the gold in the Rocky Mountains, I'd still want to get in and develop this mine. It's the only real frontier spot left in Texas. Some things seem to be meant for certain individuals. I may be the individual for whom this gold is meant. It sure was not meant for some other men who have tried for it. I am going to keep after it until I die or dig it out."

Mrs. Zola Dorris of Alpine told me a story different from those previously related. She says that instead of a mine, the Nigger Mine was a storage of bullion left by the Spanish conquistadores.

The Negro is said to have brought in a block of the bullion which assayed at $90,000 a ton. Some Mexicans learned about it and planned to surround his camp, capture him, and force him to disclose the whereabouts of his find.

Somehow the Negro must have found out about the Mexicans' plans. He caved off the bluff under which the gold was hidden and fled some sixty miles down the river to his mother's place. The Negro was never heard of again.

Another interesting tale of the Nigger Mine is that anyone who seriously searches for the mine comes to a tragic end. My grandmother told me of Will Stillwell, brother of Roy, who searched for the mine and was shot by Mexicans across the river while he was serving as a Texas Ranger at Terlingua. Also, Mrs. Van Deman says that had not her brother, Allen Burnam, been searching for the mine he would never have died of asthma.

Most of the old-timers around Marathon and Alpine to whom I have talked or from whom I have received letters have offered to help me find the mine. They firmly believe it exists, in one form or another.

One of the most sincere offers I received came from L. S. (Lee) Dickson of Marathon, who was a close friend of Lee Reagan's. In a letter, he said, "The Reagans never found the Negro or the mine so it is still over thar and if you want to hunt for it I will go with you and put you on the trail, as Lee told it to me."

Mrs. Van Deman gave me directions on how to find the

area of the mine. She got her information from a letter she received from Frank Reagan in 1941. The letter said:

Go down the river until you get opposite Cafisical Mountain. You will recognize the mountain for it is round topped and stands out by itself and bluffs all around it. It is on the Mexican side of the river.

Where we were camped was on the east side of this but on down the river about a mile and a half, where the river makes a bend. We built a mesquite corral, some of these poles may still be in evidence. This is about all I can tell you about getting to the location.

In the preceding tales it was mentioned several times that Bill Kelley disappeared and was never heard of again. But W. E. Young, deputy sheriff at Marathon, told me a different tale. He said that while he was in the Texas Ranger Service under Captain Andrews, John Payne, or Mariscal, told him this story: Bill Kelley was a cousin to John Payne (now deceased). They had a woman relative in Musquiz, Coahuila, Mexico, who was coming to visit John, and she could tell them where Bill Kelley was living in Oklahoma. Before time for the woman to come, there was a flood which cut off all travel, and they never saw her. This goes to show, according to Mr. Young, that Bill Kelley might still have been living in the 1920's.

Who knows? There may really be a Lost Nigger Mine, and some day someone may find it! Anyone for prospecting?

Family Stories and Sayings

KIM S. GARRETT

EVERY FAMILY that recognizes itself as a unit has its own taboos, legends, and traditions. It even has its own language which is built on shared experiences and expresses common values and goals. The members of such a family are fortunate because they have that deep-rooted security that can come only from a sense of unity and continuity. Family lore, like other folklore, not only mirrors the group's habits, motivations, and aspirations, but also acts as a cement that welds individual members of the group together in time as well as in space.

All of my mother's people—the Stevensons, Polleys, Baylors, Cones, and Burrows—have lived in Wilson County since the early 1850's. They came from well-established homes in New York, Georgia, Tennessee, Kentucky, and Virginia, and were all fairly well educated, but I doubt whether they had a thousand dollars in cash among them. The Stevensons, Polleys, and Baylors constitute what my grandmother calls "the tribe," and it is from them that the following stories come.

My mother, grandmother, and great-grandmother were all born in Wilson County and grew up among their kin. When the cousins come to see us the talk never slacks up, because at the first suggestion of a lull someone always starts it full blast again with a "do-you-remember." Much of the conversation would be unintelligible to an outsider because of the many family sayings and references, most of which are based on people known intimately by the family or have grown out of incidents in which members of the family have participated. Some, of course, have been handed down from generation to generation with no known family origin and are probably universally recognized.

One of the latter which I heard often when I was younger is the family name for a whining child, "Ransy Sniffle." Mother would say to me, just as her grandmother had said to her mother, and her mother had said to her, "Ransy, what are you doing here? What did you do with my Kim? Go away, Ransy Sniffle, I want my own sweet child back." Ransy Sniffle has been the unwelcome guest of at least four generations, and not too long ago I heard my mother ask Ransy what she had done with my daughter.

"Watch out now"—Grandfather Baylor would have said, "mind out"—"or I will pull off my shoes, pin back my ears, and jump down your throat." My grandmother says that her grandfather made this playful threat to her, just as my mother has often made it to me and my friends. While it sounded like a joke, we knew that it also carried a warning.

The true family sayings that follow all have well-remembered origins. Most of them are in current use and are familiar to me. My grandmother has heard and used all of them.

For nearly a hundred years "Strodie's pig" has been a specter hovering over any Stevenson-Baylor child who is inclined to overeat. "Remember Strodie's pig!" is always fair warning that third helpings are out. Back in the sixties Sister Rhoda had a pet pig that died from overeating or "busted from too much buttermilk."

Every pouting child in the family has been asked if some one had "turned his rooster pattridge out." Orrin Stevenson, my great-great-uncle, was a broody child given to long periods of sulking. He set great store by a pet quail he had trapped and tamed. Someone accidentally let the bird loose and for weeks little Orrin sulked and dragged his lip. The only response anyone could get out of him was a muttered, "Somebody turned my rooster pattridge out."

"Thank God for guts and gristle!" is the tribe's battle cry when a particularly hard and dirty job has to be done. One of Great-grandmother Stevenson's relatives was very genteel and determined to make little ladies and gentlemen out of her three whimpering, puny children. She assumed a great air of superiority and constantly reminded everyone that her children were sensitive and delicate because they were all brains and nerves. Finally, my Great-grandmother Stevenson, who was raising five robust, self-reliant hellions, could take it no longer. She spoke for the rest of the family when she retorted, "Your children probably are all brains and nerves, but thank God mine are all guts and gristle."

"The very same thing, Gustie" is the cryptic Baylor way of saying, "Don't be a stupid sheep." The story goes that one of my three-times-great aunts, who was a chameleon at heart, was Grandmother Baylor's shadow and echo. "I do the very same thing, Gustie." "I think the very same thing, Gustie." "I want the very same thing, Gustie." Sick of the constant refrain, Grandmother vowed she would put a stop to it. She set a trap before all the family one night at supper. In a discussion about the best way to broil a quail she said she always spit in the frying pan to test it for the proper temperature. Aunty automatically replied, "I do the very same thing, Gustie," and never lived it down.

The next two stories have to do, not with family, but with what my uncle Kim called "shirt-tail kin"—the Murphys, who were distantly related by marriage. Both the sayings originated sometime in the sixties and are still in use. They were favorites of my Great-grandfather Stevenson, who had no patience with stupidity in any form. He dismissed anyone guilty of it with one scornful phrase, "Oh, he was kicked by the Murphy mule." It seems that none of the Murphy boys were too bright but one of them just didn't have *any* sense. His brothers always excused his actions by reminding people that he had been kicked by a mule in his youth. Another member of the same family, Jesse, was one of those big talkers whose tongue was hung in the middle and wagged at both ends. He could and did expatiate at length on any subject, and was fond of handing down solemn opinions with an air of finality. His contemporaries paid little attention to him, however, because they knew that both his talk and his opinions were based on nothing more substantial than his own ridiculous suppositions. When my grandfather found any of his family guilty of what he called "running off at the mouth" he would silence them with, "That sounds like a Jesse Murphy supposition to me."

"Weather to bring the stock into the parlor" was one of my Grandfather Stevenson's sayings. Though I never heard the reference as a child, I enjoyed the story behind it. The saying dates from the storm of '86 when all "the tribe" sought shelter in Grandfather's stone house in Sutherland Springs. The family at that time included Telegraph, Uncle Alley's big white horse. Uncle Alley was badly crippled (a fact that Telegraph seemed to understand) and looked on his horse as a beloved companion as well as safe transportation. Telegraph was stabled on the porch at first, but as the storm grew worse, Uncle Alley grew more restless. No one thought it too strange when he asked that Telegraph be brought into the house. The parlor was the only room not crowded with kin, so Telegraph spent the rest of the night surrounded by family daguerreotypes and fancy antimacassars.

Two family references which are used with resignation have to do with long-dead ancestors. When my sister and I are obviously avoiding work, my mother shakes her head sadly and says, "A true Baylor." The story behind her remark goes back almost two hundred years to a hot day in Virginia. The eldest Baylor, John Walker, who was then an old man, rode out into the heat to attend to some plantation business. His sons, reclining on the shady veranda with their juleps and palmetto fans, remonstrated with him, saying he would kill himself working so hard on such a hot day. The old gentleman replied that if he should die while tending to his business, he wanted his gravestone inscribed as follows: "Here lies the only Baylor who has ever died from overwork."

The other ancestor is James Britton Bailey. Whenever a member of the family indulges in a little fancy hell-raising or plain cussedness, someone will inevitably comment with a shrug, "That's just Old Brit coming out." Brit was my four-times-great grandfather and his capacity for drinking and fighting was prodigious. Contemporary stories of his carousing and boisterous horseplay grew with each telling. He and his family were well established on the Brazos when Austin introduced his colony in 1819. No one knows his origin or even his real name. He is suspected of being everything from a member of Lafitte's pirate crew to the victim of political shenanigans back East.

We know that Captain Bailey was a better-educated man than most of his contemporaries, but few facts about him can be documented. There are a few letters among the Austin Papers attesting to his honesty and acumen on the one hand and to his horse-stealing tendencies on the other. There are records of his commission as captain of militia from Viesca, of his participation in the Battle of Velasco, and of his will. This document includes the usual preamble and bequests, but differs in the final request. As unconventional in death as he was in life, Brit was buried as he directed—standing erect and facing the west. Storytellers could not resist adding a picturesque phrase, "with his gun at his side and his jug at his feet."

It was inevitable that Grandfather and the great Austin would have their run-ins. Austin naturally disapproved of everything about Brit and ordered him off his land and out of the colony. Brit claimed prior rights and won title to his land. Still in rebellion, however, he showed his defiance by building his home on the highest point of his land and painting it bright red, so that it dominated the landscape for miles around.

Another story about Brit and Austin concerns the rumor that Brit had served a term in the penitentiary back in Kentucky. When confronted with the story by Austin, Grandfather freely admitted that he had served a term in the Kentucky penitentiary. He then begged Austin with tears in his voice and the devil in his eye to please try to put a stop to the other rumor that he had also served two terms in the Kentucky legislature.

The story about Grandfather Brit that I like best is one told to my mother over thirty years ago by one of the Polley uncles (grandsons of James Britton Bailey). She forgets which one.

Come Saturday night Brit and his black boy Jim rode into town as was their custom. Nobody had told Brit that there was a big preaching going on that night, so they found Brazoria almost as quiet as their own prairie. Even Brit could mind his manners, so he took the road back home with Jim following after. He couldn't bear to go to the house, though, and stopped at the big oak back of the corral. Sitting down among the huge roots, he ordered Jim to fetch his jug. He took a swig and settled back with the jug cradled in his arms. Jim lounged close by. There the two sat for a spell. Ten o'clock on a Saturday night, a jug still half full, and only the bullfrogs and whippoorwills to keep him company. A Saturday night shot to hell! It was not to be borne. With an inspired yell Brit turned to his boy Jim. "Set a light to the crib," he ordered, "I'm going to have some fun if I have to pay for it myself!" The bullfrogs were silent and the whippoorwills hushed as the flames crackled and roared into the sky. Not until the flames had died to a glow and the jug diminished to the dregs did Brit and his black boy call it a night. Grandfather had had himself a time!

Another one of my favorite stories has nothing to do with the family, but is the basis for one of my mother's admonitions, "Be sure you are inviting the man, not the clothes." The story was told to her back in 1932 by an eighty-eight-year-old native of Wilson County, Bruno Villarreal. It was told to Mr. Villarreal by his father, who had heard it from one of the men who had been there. Here is the story as mother wrote it at the time.

It seems that Don Rocque Garre was a very rich and eccentric man who owned and accompanied a cart train that promoted brisk trade between Mexico and her Texas provinces. He drove eighteen mules to a cart and did a flourishing business.

Once the train encamped close to the Francisco Flores rancho.[1] A big fiesta was in progress and Don Francisco, being a hospitable gentleman, went over to the camp to invite Don Rocque. Since he did not know Don Rocque personally, he was at a loss as to whom to address. However, on looking around he saw two men standing by one of the carts; one young, small, and dapper, dressed in the finest fashion; the other, huge and black-bearded, dressed in rough buckskin with a battered hat on his unkempt hair and a vicious-looking bull whip in his hand.

Without hesitation Don Francisco walked straight to the younger man and, with many sonorous compliments and fine phrases, invited him to the fiesta. In some confusion the young man admitted that he was only the mule captain and introduced his companion as Don Rocque. With profuse apologies Don Francisco turned to Don Rocque and again offered his hospitality. At first Don Rocque refused, saying that his mule skinner was the one to go since he was the one who was invited, but finally he promised to come.

That evening the fiesta was in full swing and only Don

Rocque's arrival was awaited so that the cockfighting and dancing could be abandoned for the feast of *cabrito* and other fine meats sizzling over coals. With a clatter of hoofs Don Rocque rode up the lane at a full gallop. In one motion he pulled to a full stop and dismounted with a flourish, like the *caballero* he was. Dressed in the softest doeskin breeches and satin shirt with scarlet sash about his waist, he was truly a fine sight. His sombrero was heavy with silver and a hundred-dollar watch[2] dangled from a heavy gold chain.

Being the guest of honor, he was seated next to Don Francisco where all could see him. The savory meats were brought to him and then the *dulces*. He took generous portions of everything offered but did not at once begin to eat. To everyone's amazement he rubbed the food over his clothes, filled his pockets, and even put a cut of beef in his hat!

Don Francisco remonstrated. "But Don Rocque," he said, "you are ruining your beautiful clothes. And your fine sombrero! Look, the juice is dripping through!"

"Bueno! That is good," Don Rocque replied in high good humor. "Since it was really the fine clothes that were invited to the fiesta, it is only right that they should be served first."

This story of Don Rocque, while the basis for a family maxim, is not restricted to the family or even to Wilson County.[3] One counterpart is found in Turkish folklore, where the Hodja assumes the role of Don Rocque.

It would be very difficult to find close analogues for or to classify the maxims that originated in our family. These sayings have been inherited along with the blue eyes, blond hair, and the grandfather clock. These stories are not *Sagen* or tales of extraordinary happenings. Neither are they merely humorous anecdotes. For the most part the stories and the morals extracted from them are simply vehicles used by the family to pass on its ideals and modes of conduct. The tribe reveals itself as clannish, sharp-tongued, and tough—independent in thought and action—people who stood on their own feet and

FAMILY STORIES AND SAYINGS 281

looked at themselves and the world with a broad tolerance and a twinkle of humor. There was nothing "lost" or "beat" about them.

Such family lore is a growing, living thing. My parents, my sister, and I make cryptic references to incidents and people just as did the grandparents about whom I have been writing. I wonder if our children and grandchildren will know what these references mean. I hope so, for it is by such tenuous yet strong threads that generations are knit together.

1. This is the family for which the town of Floresville was named—the ranch house is still in use.

2. Mr. Villarreal, even though his English was poor, used this very American description of affluence.

3. Following is another story told by Mr. Villarreal about Don Francisco Flores which might prove of interest but has nothing to do with family lore. This story and the one related above were published in the *San Antonio Express* in April, 1936.

The Flores family, besides cultivating the rich valley lands, owned thousands of cattle. Once another ranchman living at some distance from Challopines took up some cattle and claimed them as his own. They were branded, but not with a brand recognized by anyone in the country. However, when Don Francisco saw them he said they were his, marked with his brands. The Flores brand, like all the old Spanish brands, was an elaborate interlacing of hooks and curves.

A serious dispute arose which finally got into the courts. At the trial Don Francisco, when asked to prove his contention, stood up before the court and demanded, "Who am I?"

"Francisco Flores," replied the puzzled judge.

Francisco dropped to the floor and stretched out. Looking up at the judge he demanded, "Who am I?"

"Francisco Flores," came the surprised answer for the second time.

Then throwing his feet into the air and all but standing on his head, he demanded for the third time, "Who am I?"

"Francisco Flores," came the inevitable reply.

"All right," the old man said, jumping to his feet, "I am Francisco Flores whether I stand, lie on my back, or stand on my head. It is the same with my brand. The brand on those cows is put on upside down, but it is still the brand of Francisco Flores."

The cows were adjudged his without further ado.

The Origin of the Word *Gringo*

ROBERT H. FUSON

A WORD that conveys many shades of meaning throughout the Spanish-speaking world, *gringo* is always used to mean either a "strange language" or a "stranger." It may or may not carry derogatory overtones. Its origin is well known and well documented, yet folk etymologists continue to clog popular publications with myths concerning this origin.[1] Probably the most persistent "school" is the one which maintains that *gringo* was a by-product of the United States-Mexican War (1846-48). They would have it that United States soldiers (though some say sailors) sang a marching song that began, "*Green grow* the lilacs" (or rushes, or some other botanical phenomenon). Usually, Robert Burns is credited with the authorship of the "Green grow" original. From this the Mexicans supposedly concocted *gringo* and applied the label to all English-speaking Americans. This explanation of the origin of the word *gringo* is pleasing, plausible, logical, and wholly erroneous.

Any good dictionary of the Spanish language will inform the reader that *gringo* is derived from the Spanish word *griego*, or Greek. In Spain, long before the Mexican War, anyone speaking an unfamiliar tongue was speaking *griego*, or unintelligible gibberish. English-speakers say, "It's Greek to me," and all Western Indo-European languages carry a similar expression. Even outside the Indo-European family, most peoples appear to associate all strange tongues with the one language with which they are best acquainted. In Thailand, for example, the speaker of an unfamiliar idiom is called a *farangsed,* or Frenchman.

The Spaniard has probably connected *griego* with gibberish since the Greek colonization of Iberia's Mediterranean coast over two millennia ago. Through normal Castilian reduction *griego* became *grigo,* and *grigo* evolved into the present-day *gringo.* Later, after the eighth-century Moorish invasion of Iberia, the Spaniards began to say, "Está en arábico," a term still used to mean, "It's Greek to me." *Arábico* and *griego (gringo)* meant the same to the Spaniard: *any* incomprehensible language. Similarly, *habla una barbaridad* (he or she talks like a barbarian, or with barbarity) is an expression now slanted at anyone who talks constantly, especially about nothing in particular. It was first used, however, to refer to the meaningless talk of the "barbarians" (Moors). A person speaking gibberish, usually rapidly and with no discernible pauses between words, speaks *like* a Moor, but is not necessarily speaking Arabic.

There is extant excellent evidence to prove that *gringo* was used in Spain during the eighteenth century.[2] After that time references are prolix.[3] *Gringo* does not seem to have evolved from *grigo* and *griego* prior to the eighteenth century. Cervantes uses *griego* in *Don Quixote* when referring to an unfamiliar language, as do Alarcón, Góngora, and Maestro Correas in their writings.[4]

Folk etymologists not only ignore these proofs concerning the origin of *gringo,* but seem to delight in attaching a derogatory meaning to the term. It may indicate ill-will or displeasure on the part of the speaker at a given time and place, but it may be used just as frequently as an affectionate name. In Spain today *gringo* refers primarily to an incomprehensible language, even if that language be one of the Romance branch (with the exceptions of Catalán, Gallego, and Portuguese). In America it is employed, usually, as a reference to a person speaking an unfamiliar tongue, not to the tongue itself.

English-speaking Americans are called *gringos* throughout Spanish-speaking America. But in Argentina, Italians and Germans are also *gringos*. Germans are *gringos* in other areas, especially in Guatemala, where the English share the same tag. The English are normally called *gringos* in Peru and Chile, and in Venezuela anyone is a *gringo* who speaks poor Spanish or none at all. Rural Panamanians use the term as a sincere and friendly greeting, especially to Anglo-Americans. Aspiring politicians in Spanish America often use the word with contempt, as do many Spanish-speaking peoples living near United States military establishments in the area. *Gringo* is still used in Guam and the Philippines, where the degree of cordiality varies with the occasion.

The widespread distribution of the word *griego* (before the eighteenth century) and *gringo* (after that century) occurred simultaneously with the general diffusion of Spanish culture during the same span of time. No mystery surrounds the word or its origin. It is hoped that the folk etymologists will now turn their collective attention to some other term and accept *gringo* for what it really is.

1. The most recent excursion into folk etymology that the author is aware of was published by Dr. Hermann Deutsch in the *New Orleans States-Item* for January 28, 1959. The most recent mention of the origin of the word *gringo* known to the writer appears in John P. Bloom, "Johnny Gringo at the Pass of the North," *Password,* IV (October, 1959), 134. Bloom states that the origin of the word is obscure.

2. P. Estéban de Terreros y Pando, *Diccionario Castellano,* II, 240, col. 1 (Madrid, 1787). "*Gringos* llaman en Málaga a los estranjeros, que tienen cierta especie de acento, que los priva de una locución fácil y natural Castellana, y en Madrid dan el mismo nombre con particularidad a los irlandeses."

3. A lengthy bibliography is given in Juan Corominas, *Diccionario Crítico Etimológico de la Lengua Castellana* (Bern, 1954), II, 783-85.

4. *Ibid.*

On *Gringo, Greaser,* and Other Neighborly Names

AMÉRICO PAREDES

IN A RECENT ISSUE of *Western Folklore* Archer Taylor notes that a quotation from Andy Adams' *The Log of a Cowboy* (Boston, 1903) makes it appear that *gringo* was not used by those who spoke Spanish in referring to visitors from the United States. "The fact," Dr. Taylor adds, "is curious, but is not explained." The quotation from Adams is as follows: "I at once proclaimed Fox Quarternight, whose years and experience outranked mine, the *gringo* corporal for the day, at which the vaqueros smiled, but I noticed they never used the word."[1]

The question raised by Dr. Taylor is of special interest to me because I come from the Brownsville-Matamoros area, where the incident narrated by Adams is supposed to have happened. Also, I have been interested for some time in the origins and the precise connotations of words like *gringo, greaser,* and other less well-known epithets that have been used in neighborly interchange along the Texas-Mexican border.

In spite of what Andy Adams says, it seems pretty certain that by the 1880's the word *gringo* was used by Rio Grande Mexicans referring to the *norteamericano.* It is hard to say, however, how strong the connotations of *gringo* were at the time. They may have been no stronger than those of *yankee.*

Adams was either misinformed about the usage of *gringo* or ambiguous in his own use of "never" in "I noticed they never used the word." What he may have meant was that the Mexican vaqueros never used the word during the time they worked with the Americans in crossing the herd. The smiles of the vaqueros when Adams called Fox Quarternight a *gringo* would be embarrassed smiles, such as one might expect among a group of Americans if a Mexican they were entertaining referred to himself as a *greaser*.

I have noticed on my own campus, where we have many students from other countries, that some of our local students feel our visitors should not be called *foreign* students. Not even the most insensitive would call them "you foreigners." Like *foreigner*—and perhaps some racial or cultural labels such as *yankee* and *limey*—*gringo* is a word whose connotations may vary from the contemptuous through the merely patronizing to the actually affectionate, depending on the intent and the tone of the voice of the speaker. Americans who have lived in Mexico know this, and they often refer to themselves as *gringos*, to the puzzlement of some Mexicans, who are not quite sure what attitude each individual American will take toward the word. Andy Adams' vaqueros apparently found themselves in the same predicament when he told them that Quarternight would be his *gringo* corporal.

Folk etymology has developed quite a line of descent for *gringo*,[2] but Spanish dictionaries define it as "foreigner," especially an Englishman. In Spanish America, according to Larousse, it has been applied to all non-Spanish-speaking strangers. To speak in *gringo* is to talk gibberish. That is to say, *gringo* among the Spanish-speaking peoples has until recently meant "stranger" or "barbarian" in the ancient Greek sense of the word. It has come to mean "American" during the past century because the *gringo* from the United States was the one who made himself most conspicuous, especially in Mexico.

The fact that the word originally was meant to denote the American's strange manners and unintelligible speech, not to express hostility toward him, may explain why *gringo* is so rare in Mexican folklore of the 1840's and 1850's. The anti-American *décimas* composed during the American occupation of Mexico City use *yanqui* instead of *gringo*. Mexican girls who took up with American soldiers are bitterly criticized; but they are said to be *ayankadas* rather than *agringadas*.³ It must have been several decades before *gringo* came to mean "American" rather than "foreigner," used as a term of reproach. By the time of the Revolution (1910-1930) *gringo* appears in Greater Mexican folksongs such as "La Persecución de Villa" ("The Pursuit of Villa") as an insulting epithet.

The folklore of the Rio Grande border presents a more difficult problem for two main reasons: the relative objectivity of the border-conflict *corrido*, with little emphasis on name-calling, and the dominance of the *decía* (said he) line, in which *americano* fits the required syllable count while *gringo* does not. *Corridos* about Cortina (1850's), about the Kansas Trail (1860's), and about José Mosqueda (1890's) all use *americanos* in the line "Decián los americanos" rather than *gringos*.

"Los Sediciosos" (1915) uses both: *gringo* in the mouth of a character and *americano* in that of the narrator himself.

Decía Gregorio Fuentes en su chico caballazo "Échenme ese gringo grande pa' llevármelo de brazo."	Then said Gregorio Fuentes On his great big horse, "Let me take on that big gringo, So we can amble arm in arm."
Contesta el americano con su sombrero en las manos, "Yo sí me voy con ustedes; son muy buenos mexicanos."	The American answers, Holding his hat in his hands, "I *will* go with you; You are very good Mexicans."

If one is to believe John C. Duval's *Bigfoot Wallace*, Mexicans in the Lower Rio Grande were calling Americans *gringos* back in 1842. On the march from Mier to Matamoros after being captured with his companions of the Mier Expedition, Wallace (or Duval) reports:

In some places the inhabitants, and especially the women, seemed to compassionate the miserable conditions of the "Gringos," as they called us, and gave us water to drink, and sometimes more substantial refreshments. In others, we were hooted at by the mob, that was sure to collect around us whenever we stopped for a few moments, who would call us by all sorts of hard names, and pelt us with stones and clods of earth, and stale eggs.[4]

Even if we suppose that Duval has put words into Wallace's mouth, he could have done it no later than 1871, the date of publication of his book, and he would have drawn from his earlier experiences in Texas and Northern Mexico. But another interesting thing about this passage is that Border Mexicans in 1842 called the Texans *gringos* when they felt sorry for them. "All sorts of hard names" were applied to the Texans when they were pelted with stones and eggs. Perhaps *gringo* also came into use on these occasions. *Heretic* and *Lutheran* were probably among the epithets too. But one can only wonder what other names were thrown with the stones. Other twentieth-century terms for American, such as *gabacho, bolillo, güero,* and *chicas-patas,* obviously date from much later times.[5]

But the earlier, and still current, form of *chicas-patas—patón*—was probably one of the dirty names used in 1842, along with *heretic* and *Lutheran.* Wallace later appropriated the name because, of all the big-footed Americans, he was the one with the biggest feet. Duval has Wallace learnedly and accurately explain the reason for the name *patón.* "The Mexicans are generally a small people compared with the Americans, and their feet are still smaller in proportion; consequently they were much astonished at the size of mine, and from that time forward, and as long as I remained in the City, I was known among them as 'Big-Foot.' "[6]

"Bigfoot," however, does not carry the same connotations as *patón.* Because of the attractive alliteration, perhaps, *gringo* has always been coupled with *greaser* in the minds of most Americans.[7] But the nearest equivalent to *greaser* in the Mexican idiom is *patón.* Like *greaser,* it refers to some imputed physical characteristic of the enemy. *Pata* is the word used for an animal's foot; there is also the understood addition that the beastly American's big feet carry an unbearable stink, as ample as the feet themselves.

So this is how Mexicans and Americans saw each other about a century ago. On one side we have a dirty, oily rascal who couldn't be trusted; on the other a big-pawed, evil-smelling Abominable Blond-Man, who in kindlier moments might be thought of as a *gringo*, a gibberish-talking outlander. But you didn't call him that to his face. Some people just don't like to be called foreigners.

1. Archer Taylor, "Gringo," *Western Folklore*, XIX (January, 1960), 58.
2. The latest folk etymology that has come to my attention—and a very recent one it must be—concerns the Mexican who comes to the United States and is caught in downtown traffic. The lights say, "Red stop; green go." So he calls Americans *gringos* because they go on green.
3. Vicente T. Mendoza has published a number of *décimas* about the American occupation in *La Décima en México* (Buenos Aires, 1947) and *Glosas y Décimas de México* (Mexico, 1957).
4. John C. Duval, *Bigfoot Wallace* (Philadelphia, 1871; facsimile edition issued by the Steck Company, Austin, 1947), p. 174.
5. *Gabacho*, from *gave* (mountain torrent in the Pyrenees), was applied to Frenchmen by the Spaniards. It is used as an insulting term in Mexico in the *décimas* composed against Maximilian's French troops. In Texas at least, it has been transferred to the American.

Bolillo is a small knob, also a small loaf of French bread. Current newspaper etymology is that *bolillo* was applied to Americans because they are as white as French bread. It is more probable that *bolillo* was first applied to the French invaders, who ate the *bolillos* made of bread.

Güero is merely "blond or fair one." It is much used especially in Texas in reference to Americans. But in the 1860's it was used in Mexico in reference to the French.

Chicas-patas originally was a zoot-suiter word for American, a variation on *patón*. The ironic use of *chico* to mean "huge" instead of "little" is common in Mexican speech. "Huge-footed" instead of merely "big-footed" as in *patón*.
6. Duval, *op. cit.*, pp. 221-22.
7. The history of *greaser* is as clouded as that of *gringo*. The first printed use of the word mentioned in standard reference works such as the *NED* and the *Dictionary of American English* is from the *Spirit of the Times*, July 11, 1846. The word here is used in reference to Mexicans.

H. L. Mencken, however, notes that *greaser,* or more politely *lubricator,* was also applied to Italians in California. He also notes that *grease-ball* is applied in the United States to "any foreigner of dark complexion," though principally to Greeks. (*The American Language,* Supplement One, New York, 1948, pp. 609-10.) It would be some sort of irony of history if both *gringo* and *greaser* could be traced to the Greeks.

The reason for *greaser* is evident—the fact that people of darker complexions have oilier skins than do the Nordics. It would seem that like *gringo* it was a term of general application, later narrowed down to one particular people, the Mexicans. *Greaser* also has its folk etymologies. The one mentioned by Mencken *(ibid.),* the Mexican who greased carts for Americans, was probably never taken seriously by anyone. Luther Giddings in *Sketches of the Campaign in Northern Mexico* (New York, 1853, p. 59) gives another etymology in a more serious vein. He describes the brush vaquero of the Lower Rio Grande, with his "jerkins and pants of leather" and adds, "To Rancheros, who wear this economical apparel,—so suitable to their occupation in the thorny chaparral—the Texans have given the expressive name of Greasers" because their leather clothes "shining from grease and long usage" suggested it.

Contributors

JOHN Q. ANDERSON, student of the Southwest, author of many articles, and editor of an important Civil War diary, spent his boyhood in the Texas Panhandle. He now teaches English at Texas Agricultural and Mechanical College.

MODY C. BOATRIGHT is secretary and editor of the Texas Folklore Society. He has published two books on frontier humor and one on the folklore of the oil industry. At the University of Texas he teaches graduate courses in American thought and southwestern literature.

ELEANOR MITCHELL BOND is a graduate student and teaching fellow at Texas Technological College.

HALDEEN BRADDY is both a medievalist and a folklorist. A member of the English staff at Texas Western College in El Paso, he has had excellent opportunity to study the folklore and folkways of the upper Rio Grande Valley. He is author of *Cock of the Walk*, a life of Pancho Villa.

ROBERT H. BYINGTON, who wrote a dissertation under the supervision of MacEdward Leach at the University of Pennsylvania, now teaches at the Martin Branch of the University of Tennessee. His paper was read at the 1959 meeting of the American Folklore Society in Mexico City.

GAYLE L. COE is from Marathon, Texas. She is a senior at the University of Texas, majoring in English.

J. FRANK DOBIE, more than anyone else, has made the nation conscious of the traditions and literature of the Southwest. For twenty years he edited the annuals of the Texas Folklore Society. His books are numerous and well known wherever English is spoken. A master storyteller, he may now be heard on a record, *The Ghost Bull of the Mavericks and Other Tales*, brought out by Domino Records in Austin.

ROBERT FUSON teaches geography at the New Orleans Branch of Louisiana State University.

KIM S. GARRETT is a student of mathematics at the University of Texas. His present article is based on a paper written for a course in the folktale under Américo Paredes.

HUMBERTO GARZA is a student in Pan American College at Edinburg, Texas. His paper, written under the direction of Professor Meade Harwell, won first prize in the 1960 TFS student contest.

EDWIN W. GASTON teaches English at the Stephen F. Austin State College and collects folklore in East Texas.

WILLIAM HENRY HARDIN grew up in Coryell and Bell counties in Texas. After graduating from high school in McGregor, he joined the regular army. Now a retired officer, he lives in Austin and is a graduate student at the University of Texas.

STANLEY W. HARRIS is a graduate of Texas Technological College. He is now teaching at Monahans, Texas.

GEORGE D. HENDRICKS teaches at North Texas State University. He has written *The Bad Man of the West* and is a frequent contributor to periodicals devoted to folklore.

MIRIAM HIESTER teaches English at the Brooke Hospital Center in San Antonio.

RICHARD C. KING is an assistant professor of journalism at the University of Texas who likes to delve in local newspaper files in search of folklore.

MAC EDWARD LEACH, professor of English at the University of Pennsylvania and internationally noted ballad scholar, is secretary of the American Folklore Society.

JAMES WARD LEE teaches English at North Texas State University at Denton.

JOSEPH T. MC CULLEN, JR., is a native of North Carolina. He now teaches English at Texas Technological College. His field of specialization is Shakespeare and the Renaissance.

CAROLYN MANKIN is a graduate student in English at the University of Texas.

VICENTE T. MENDOZA, one of the founders of the Mexican Folklore Society, has published fundamental studies of the Mexican *décima* and the Mexican *corrido*. *El Romance Español y el Corrido Mexicano*, published in 1939, established him as an authority on Mexican folk music. He is at present a member of the Institute of Esthetic Investigations of the University of Mexico and is at work on an anthology of Mexican folksong.

A. L. MILES is a native of Coryell County, born there in 1885. Long connected with the cottonseed oil business in various parts of Texas, he now lives at Gatesville, where he manages his own stock farm, works with the Soil Conservation Agency, writes for soil conservation magazines, and as a hobby collects folklore.

GEORGE NIELSON was a graduate student at the University of Texas when he wrote on the folklore of the German-Wends in Texas. He now teaches at Concordia Teachers College at River Forest, Illinois.

HERMES NYE sings folksongs (he has recorded several albums for Folkways Records) and practices law in Dallas.

AMÉRICO PAREDES grew up in Brownsville, where for a while he was a reporter for the *Herald*. In 1958 he published a book on the hero of a South Texas *corrido*, Gregorio Cortez—"*With His Pistol in His Hand.*" At the University of Texas he teaches the ballad, the folktale, and the literature of the Southwest.

ALVA RAY STEPHENS is a graduate student in history at the University of Texas.

TUCKER SUTHERLAND was a student at Texas A. and M. College when he wrote "Ghost Stories from a Texas Ghost Town." He now works on the Robstown *Record*.

GRACE PLEASANT WELLBORN was born in Wise County, Texas. She teaches English at Texas Technological College.

Index

Agriculture, beliefs relating to, 257
Alamo, defense of, 59

Badger fight, 112-14
Bailey, James Britton, 277-79
Ballads: Arkansas variants of Texas ballads, 212-17; doubtful value as socio-historical evidence, 31-35; plea for an intrinsic study of ballads as works of art, 35-45
Bear stories, 8, 10, 11, 12-13, 14
Bedbugs, 5, 6
Bedichek, Roy, 6, 28
Burges, Will, 28
Burton, Wes, 19-20

Canción, Mexican: beginnings, 47-49; classification, 53-54; culmination, 51-52; decline and passing, 52-53; development, 49-51
Cantú, Saturnino, 16-17
Cattle, beliefs relating to, 257
Central Texas Wolf and Fox Hunters Association, 197-201
Chapultepec, defense of, 60
Charms, 183-84
Coal mining in Texas, 107-8
Cock fighting, 98-106
Cole, Bill, 20-24
Cooking without recipe, 184
Coronado's Children, 12, 18-19, 23
Corridos, in relation to history, 62-68
Cortez, Gregorio, 26
Cortez, Santos, 3-5
Coryell County Fox and Coon Hunters Association, 197-98, 201
Cowboy: split by barbed wire, 176; stories about Georgie Sennitt, 166-72; *see also* Hero, frontier
Coyotes, hunting, 196-97, 202-4
Customs; *see* Folk customs

Dead woman returns to life, 175-76
Diction: of lawyers, 92-97; of lumbering, 181-82
Dobie, Bertha McKee, 5, 6
Dobie, J. Frank: 215, 226; as a story hunter, 3-29
Dobie, Jim, 3
Dow, Lorenzo, 185, 186, 190-93

Evans, Dub, 13

Family saga, 273-81
Flores, Don Francisco, stories about, 279-80, 281 n.3
Folk cures, of the German-Wends, 247-52
Folk customs: in old Thurber, 107-14; of the German-Wends, 244-59
Folk sayings, of the German-Wends, 257-58
Folklore and history, 56-68
Folksay of lawyers, 92-97
Folksongs, Texas: Arkansas variants of, 212-17
Folktales: German, 260-65; Texas-Mexican, 226-43
Fox hunting; *see* Hunting
Frederick the Great, tales of, 263-64
From Hell to Breakfast, 17

Gay, Leeper, 19
Gentleman Killer; *see* Motifs
German tales in Texas, 260-65
German-Wends, folklore of, 244-59
Ghost Lore, 5
Ghost stories, 116-22
Ghost towns: Cold Springs, 123-31; San Patricio, 115-22; Seattle, 123; Thurber, 107-14
Gold, buried, 119
Greaser, meaning and use, 288-89, 289-90 n.7
Gringo: origin of the word, 282-84; meaning and use, 285-88

Haley, Evetts, 29
Hamer, Captain Frank, 28
Hardin, Jack, 124
Hero, frontier, 140-55; *see also* Motifs
Horse race, 169-70
Hound dogs: field trials, 201-2; hunting with, 194-204; inability to strike the trail of a coyote with sucking pups, 202-4
Hunting, with hound dogs, 194-204

Immigrants: German, 260-65; German-Wends, 244-59; Irish, 115; Italians, 110-12; Poles, 108-10
Insall, Clarence, 13
Irish immigrants, 115
Irish Lad, The; *see* Georgie Sennitt
Ismael, a storyteller, 9-10
Italian immigrants, customs of, 110-12

Kennon, Bob, 12
Kilian, Pastor John, 246
Kittens, change religion when eyes open, 127-28

INDEX

Language of sawmill, 181-82
Lawyers' argot, 92-97
Legends of Texas, 5, 18
Lie, a kind of story, 15-16, 17
Ligon, Stokley, 13
Lobo story, 12
Lomax, John A., 4, 28
Looking back, superstition against, 69-75
Lost Adams Diggings, 13-14
Lost Nigger Mine, 266-72
Lost San Saba Mine, 19
Lumbering, tales about, 178-84

Medicine, in sawmill settlement, 182-83
Mines, tales of, from Germany, 262-65
Motifs: in history, 61; five primary motifs of the Gentleman Killer—Cain, 143-46; Hamlet, 150-51; Ishmael, 146-49; patrician, 151-54; renunciation, 149-50; A162, 231; B285, 234; B700, 228; D658.1, 229; D1235, 228; D1316.5, 239; D1622.3, 232; D2661.1.2, 228; E168, 238; F17, 238; F51, 236; F511.2.2, 239; G211.1, 229; H1250, 238; K2371.1, 236; N465, 239; V236, 231; V412, 232
Mule, balking, 175
Mustangs, The, 26, 27

Negro, wanting to join church of whites, 126-27

Oil promotion; *see* Trickster
Owls, as witches or wizards, 218-25
Oxen, story about, 26

Paisano, 176-77
Panther stories, 3
Pardner in the Wind, 27
Pepper, too much, 128
Polish immigrants, customs of, 108-10
Potter, Andrew Jackson, 185-90
Prayer meetings, 132-39
Preachers, frontier: Andrew Jackson Potter, 185-90; Lorenzo Dow, 190-93; stories about, 124-28

Rain, praying for, 135-36
Remington, Frederic, 9
Revival meetings, 124-25, 139
Rigby, John, 27

Rogers, Will, 169
Russell, Charles M., 11, 12

Sandburg, Carl, 28
School children, stories about, 128-29
Sennitt, Georgie, 166-72
Shrewish woman, 175-76
Smith, Henry Nash, 5
Smith, Railroad, 24-26
Snow, Bob, 16-17
Snyder, Marcus, 10, 11
Square dancing, 168-69
Starr, Belle, 156-65
Storytellers, 3-29
Straw, Nat, 12-14
Superstition; see Looking back
Surprise story, 176-77
Syfert, Dr., 27

Tall tales: cowboy split in two, 176; lumbering, 178-80
Thorp, Jack, 27
Three councils, 173-75
Thurber, in Erath County, 107-14
Tongues of the Monte, 4
Trailing men with hounds, 200-201
Trick, played on farmer, 130-31
Trickster, oil promoter as, 76-91
Types of the folktale: Type 592, 228; Type 333, 234; Type 330A, 241

Villa, Francisco, 60, 66

Warts: German-Wend cure for, 251-52; removed by magic, 205-11
Webb, Walter P., 28
Wends; see German-Wends
Whiskey, for fainting, 125-26
Willis, Sid, 11
Witchcraft: crows, 255-56; owl-bewitchment, 218-25
Wolves, hunting, 196-97
Work songs, 180-81

Yellow Tail, Chief, 10-11
Yelvington, Henry, 5

www.ingramcontent.com/pod-product-compliance
Lightning Source LLC
Chambersburg PA
CBHW030307080526
44584CB00012B/468